THE GATE OF

Also by Margaret Barker and published by SPCK:

The Older Testament
The Survival of Themes from the
Ancient Royal Cult in Sectarian Judaism
and Early Christianity

The Lost Prophet
The Book of Enoch
and its influence on Christianity

Margaret Barker

THE GATE OF HEAVEN

The History and Symbolism
of the
Temple in Jerusalem

First published in Great Britain 1991
SPCK
Holy Trinity Church
Marylebone Road
London NW1 4DU

© Margaret Barker 1991

All rights reserved. No part of this book may be reproduced or transmitted in any form or by any means, electronic or mechanical, including photocopying, recording, or by any information storage and retrieval system, without permission in writing from the publisher.

The Scripture quotations in this publication are from the Revised Standard Version of the Bible, copyrighted 1946, 1952, © 1971, 1973 by the Division of Christian Education of the National Council of the Churches of Christ in the USA, and are used by permission.

For George Bebawi

British Library Cataloguing in Publication Data

Barker, Margaret *1944*—
The gate of heaven. The history and symbolism of the Temple of Jerusalem.
1. Israel. Jerusalem. Temples. Temple of Jerusalem, history
I. Title
956.9442

ISBN 0-281-04510-0

Typeset by Pioneer Associates, Perthshire
Printed in Great Britain by
The Longdunn Press, Bristol

I was glad when they said to me, 'Let us go to the house of the Lord!'
Our feet have been standing within your gates, O Jerusalem!

PSALM 122.1–2

CONTENTS

Acknowledgements   ix

Introduction   1

1 **The House of the Lord**   5

A Brief History — Ancient Temples in Israel — King David — The Rock — Constructing the Temple — The Temple and its Courts — The Temple Interior — The Furnishings of the Temple Court — Sacrifices — The Passover — The Day of Atonement — The Music of the Temple — The End of the Temple

2 **The Garden**   57

Time and Place — The Great Sea — The Temple as Eden — The Place of Judgement — The King in Eden — The Source of Life — The Eternal Covenant — The Gift of Rain — The Rivers of Paradise — The Tree of Life — Odes and Hymns

3 **The Veil**   104

Between Heaven and Earth — The History of the Veil — The Symbolism of the Veil — The High Priest — Philo's Logos — Some Gnostic Texts — The Early Christian Writings — Beyond the Veil

CONTENTS

4 The Throne   133

The Presence of the Lord — The Ark — The
Cherubim — The Enthronement — The Great
Light — Visions of the Throne — Visions of the Throne
in the Apocalypses — The Mystics' Visions of the
Throne — The Fiery Angels

5 'But Israel had no Mythology'   178

Bibliography   182

Index of Names and Subjects   187

Index of Primary Sources   191

ACKNOWLEDGEMENTS

I am grateful, as ever, to those who make my writing possible. I should like to thank the staff at the University Library, Nottingham, where I do the greater part of my work, and the friends who help in so many ways: Dr Ernst Bammel and Robert Murray SJ for hospitality and the loan of materials from their own shelves, Dr Sebastian Brock for allowing me to use some of his translations of St Ephrem, and Dr George Bebawi from whom I have learnt so much about the Coptic Church. It is to him that I should like to dedicate this book.

Margaret Barker
Whitsun, 1990

INTRODUCTION

For over a thousand years there was a temple of the Lord in Jerusalem which dominated both the city and its people. Even after the Roman destruction in AD 70, it continued to influence the thought and literature of the Jews. Christianity was born a few years before the destruction, and the first Jewish Christians, who wrote most of the New Testament, were steeped in its ways. The Fourth Gospel, the Letter to the Hebrews and Revelation were all directly inspired by the world of the temple.

But what was this world? It is extraordinarily difficult to reconstruct the theology, the reasoning, the mythology, whatever it was which gave meaning to that place of worship. There is a reasonable amount of contemporary evidence for what it looked like and what happened to it at various times. Instructions survive about the sacrifices and rituals, about the rights, duties and revenues of the priests, about the work of building and rebuilding and so forth, but there is very little about the meaning of this whole gigantic system of worship which was the heart of pre-Christian Judaism. Everything written about the *meaning* of the temple has to be derived from second and third hand and we have to sift the surviving literature, both biblical and non-biblical, for anything which might be an allusion or a memory. There are enormous problems for anyone attempting to write about the temple and I am only too well aware of them. There are few certainties and many possibilities.

I shall begin with a brief account of the externals of the temple: the structure itself, how it was built and rebuilt, how it was furnished, how the services were conducted. Some of this material would be found in any standard treatment of the temple but some would not and I thought it important that an account of the temple should precede any reconstructions of the myths it expressed. This section is in no way comprehensive but intended simply as a frame of reference to link features of the myths to the actual buildings. The temple was a place where the Lord appeared, a garden sanctuary, the place of the divine throne, the great bronze sea, the foundation rock and the altars. Sacrifice is mentioned in the broadest outline simply because any account of the temple which omitted this significant feature would be distorted. I make no attempt to interpret any of the sacrifices, except those of the Day of Atonement, since this has been done in countless books already. Nor have I dealt with the manifold complications of the lesser orders of the priesthood since these, too, have been amply covered elsewhere.

My main concern is with aspects of the temple mythology which are less well known and I shall reconstruct them largely from extra-biblical texts, also less well known, to show the extent to which a wide range of themes and imagery had their common root in the temple. First, there will be evidence for the temple as a place of creation and renewal; these themes centre upon the garden of Eden, which the temple was built to represent. Second, there will be evidence for the temple as a place of mediation and atonement, themes associated with the veil of the temple which symbolized the boundary between the material and spiritual worlds. Third, there will be evidence for the temple as the place where some could pass beyond the veil and experience the vision of God, seeing into the essence of all things past, present and future. These were the visions of the divine throne which are best known from the Revelation of St John. In each case I shall give one or two examples to show how these ideas passed first into early Christian thought and then into the imagery of many well-known hymns. One of the most extraordinary aspects of temple mythology is that, for all the remoteness of its origins, it proves to be very familiar.

A small work such as this cannot be comprehensive; indeed, any detailed study of the temple would require several large volumes, and this is not the purpose I had in mind when writing. I hope only that this book might serve as an introduction to an important subject by revealing the roots of much Christian imagery. I have worked directly from ancient texts which deal with the temple and all passages are quoted in full since I know how difficult it can be to find copies of some of them.

Since my concern is with Jewish and Christian accounts of the temple, the great majority of the texts used are of Jewish or Christian origin. There is a whole aspect of temple study which seeks to set the ancient temple in the broader context of the ancient Near East as a whole, but this is a very speculative business and one which can lead to foreign ideas being used as the *basis* for studying the temple, rather than as an interesting sidelight upon it. I have tried to avoid this danger of imposing ideas known to be foreign upon texts known to be Jewish or Christian.

All the biblical quotations are from the RSV, a version which has kept much of the temple terminology. One of the problems with many modern translations of the Bible is that these terms have been modernized or even written out in the interest of simplification. Thus the temple setting has been obscured in many cases and the reader cut off from the theological context of the original. The meaning in such cases, far from being made clear, has been lost.

CHAPTER ONE

THE HOUSE OF THE LORD

A Brief History

There have been three temples of the Lord in Jerusalem; the first was built by Solomon in the middle of the tenth century BC (1 Kings 5—8; 2 Chron. 3—4) and destroyed by the Babylonians in 585 BC (2 Kings 25.8—17); the second was built by the exiles when they returned from Babylon (Ezra 3.8—13) and dedicated in 515 BC (Ezra 6.16—18). The 'third' was the temple enlarged and largely rebuilt by Herod the Great in 20 BC. Throughout its long history the temple was the scene of violence and conflict because temples were as much a statement of political status as they were evidence of piety; the power of the nation's god and king was reflected in the splendour of his cult and in the success of his people. Conversely, the defeat of a people was a sign that the god had been disgraced and his sanctuary desecrated.

The first temple was a part of the palace complex built by Solomon and for four centuries the kings in Jerusalem were central to its cult. The wickedness of the kings was blamed for its downfall (2 Kings 24.3—4), or so one of the histories tells us. Such sweeping judgements on the kings have coloured most of the surviving evidence for the first temple and this has almost certainly distorted the descriptions not only of the worship of the temple but even of the building itself and its furnishings, since no part of the ancient temple was theologically neutral. Everything — buildings, furnishings, liturgies, sacrifices, vestments, calendar — everything was integrated, but what it expressed we can only guess.

Two kings of Judah reformed and purified the temple, but in each case the motives were political. Hezekiah (715–687) 'did what was right in the eyes of the Lord' and removed signs of pagan worship: the high places, the pillars and the Asherah, the symbol of a goddess. He also destroyed a bronze serpent 'for until those days the people of Israel had burned incense to it' (2 Kings 18.4). We are not told that the serpent was in the temple but this is usually assumed. His reformation was not simply an act of piety even though that is how it is depicted. It was the king's way of asserting his independence from the Assyrians (2 Kings 18.7). The presence of foreign cult objects was, in the ancient world, a way of acknowledging an overlord, and the purification of the temple was an act of rebellion. (A longer and much more elaborate account of the reform, not above suspicion of having been exaggerated in order to emphasize the glory and purity of the temple, is found in 2 Chron. 29—30). This reform took place in the time of Isaiah who had promised that the Lord would defend his city: 'For I will defend this city to save it, for my own sake and for the sake of my servant David' (Isa. 37.35; cf. Isa. 10.13—19; 14.24—7). Sennacherib, the king of Assyria, invaded Judah and began to devastate the rebel kingdom. Hezekiah's resolve wavered, a huge quantity of gold and silver was paid from the temple treasury and gold was even stripped from its doors. The Assyrian army reached the very walls of Jerusalem and then 'the angel of the Lord went forth and slew a hundred and eighty five thousand in the camp of the Assyrians' (2 Kings 19.35). The enemy returned home, and the people of Jerusalem were content to believe that the presence of the temple had saved them and would continue to do so. Jeremiah 7 is a later response to this overconfidence in the temple. The presence of the temple and its cult, said the prophet, was no substitute for real devotion to the Lord.

The other reformer was Josiah (640–609) who succeeded his assassinated father and inherited the cosmopolitan prosperity of his grandfather Manasseh. During Manasseh's fifty-five years as king (687–642) he had permitted many things in his kingdom which were regarded as pagan (2 Kings 21.1—9). His grandson, influenced, we are told, by the rediscovery of an ancient lawbook (possibly a part of Deuteronomy; 2 Kings 22.8—13), set about implementing the requirements of that law. His most far-reaching reform was the abolition of all places of sacrifice outside Jerusalem, in accordance with Deut. 12.5—7. The cult was centralized and therefore made easier to control. This must have increased enormously the power and influence of the Jerusalem temple, but it angered the priests of the rural shrines. Everything associated with foreign worship was destroyed, including the priests and temple personnel (2 Kings 23). Horses dedicated to the sun and rooftop altars were removed from the temple itself, and the whole process culminated in a great Passover feast the like of which had not been seen 'since the days of the judges who judged Israel' (2 Kings 23.22). Such a loyal servant of the Lord should have prospered, but Josiah died fighting Pharaoh Neco at Megiddo (2 Kings 23.29). The fate of Josiah prompted much soul-searching; why had so great and zealous a reformer of the temple been cut down at the hand of a foreigner?

The sages who promulgated the teachings of Deuteronomy, with its very puritanical ways, had a very clear view of what Israel's religion had been and should be. It is quite likely that their heirs, the so-called Deuteronomists, were responsible for the suppression of many of Israel's myths and the royal ideology associated with them. Since they wrote one of the two surviving accounts of the monarchy and the temple (1 and 2 Samuel and 1 and 2 Kings, the *Deuteronomic History*) we have always to bear their reforming zeal in mind when reading these texts. They did not flatter the kings and they were reticent about certain aspects of the temple, as we shall see. Their view has come to be accepted as *the* view of what happened, and what they chose not to record is thought never to have existed. But there are other sources which give a significantly different view of Solomon's temple and its cult, and it is to these that we must turn if we are to call up the ancient kings. The prophets and the psalms are full of colourful imagery which may once have been more than mere imagery. Many later texts are thought to be bizarre growths upon the purity of the old religion when in fact they are memories of the older ways as they really had been. Many of the 'innovations' of Christian belief were in fact ancient ways which had taken on a new significance with the life and death of Jesus. The Deuteronomists were fervent monotheists, which has led us to believe that all the Old Testament describes a strictly monotheistic religion. They also said that God could not be seen, only heard. There were, however, ancient traditions which said otherwise in each case; there was, as we shall see, a belief in *a second divine being who could have human form* and this became the basis of Christianity.

It was fundamental to the teaching of the Deuteronomists that purity of worship was rewarded by the Lord with a long life of prosperity in the promised land (Deut. 8). When Jerusalem was attacked and defeated by the Babylonians in 597 BC, the questions became even more urgent. It was decided that the destruction of the city and the temple was a punishment from the Lord for the sins of Manasseh (2 Kings 24.3—4), whose wickedness had been so great that even the good deeds of Josiah could not remove the guilt. The Babylonian army returned in 586; the temple was destroyed and all its treasures were taken to Babylon as spoils of war. Many of the people went into exile.

In 538 BC Cyrus ordered that the exiled Jews be allowed to return from Babylon, taking with them the temple vessels which Nebuchadnezzar had taken to Babylon and placed in the temple there (Ezra 1.7—11). Their first act was to rebuild the altar of burnt offering and to celebrate the autumn Feast of Tabernacles (Ezra 3.2—6). In the following year they began rebuilding the temple, but were frustrated by local opposition (Ezra 4.1—5). Eventually their right to build was confirmed and the king ordered that the cost of rebuilding be met from the royal revenues (Ezra 6.1—12). The temple was finally completed in 515 BC (Ezra 6.16—18). No description of this temple survives in the Old Testament even though there are lists of priests, levites and temple servants who returned (Ezra 2.36—54), and records of the provisions made for sacrifices (Ezra 7.11—20); Neh. 10.32—9). It is not until the beginning of the second century BC that there is any record of the temple's appearance. Aristeas, a visitor to Palestine from Egypt, left a tourist's account of its marvels:

> When we arrived in the land of the Jews we saw the city situated in the middle of the whole of Judaea on the top of a mountain of considerable altitude. On the summit the temple had been built with all its splendour. It was surrounded by three walls more than seventy cubits high . . . The temple faces east and its back is towards the west. The whole of the floor is paved with stones, and slopes down to the appointed places, that water may be conveyed to wash away the blood from the sacrifices, for many thousands of beasts are sacrificed there on the feast days. And there is an inexhaustible supply of water, because an abundant natural spring gushes up from

within the temple area. There are moreover wonderful and indescribable cisterns underground, as they pointed out to me, at a distance of five furlongs all around the site of the temple, and each of them has countless pipes so that the different streams converge together ... They led me more than four furlongs outside the city and bade me peer down toward a certain spot and listen to the noise that was made by the meeting of the waters, so that the great size of the reservoirs became manifest to me as has already been pointed out.
(Letter of Aristeas 83, 88—91)

The temple was pillaged by the Syrians shortly after this; Heliodorus, the agent of Antiochus Epiphanes was sent to take the treasure, but as he attempted to enter the treasury he was struck down by a heavenly horseman; 'For there appeared to them a magnificently caparisoned horse, with a rider of frightening mien, and it rushed furiously at Heliodorus and struck at him with his front hooves' (2 Macc. 3.25). The unfortunate agent was lucky to escape with his life, and the treasure was safe for a while. Then in 169 BC the king himself visited the temple, entered the sanctuary and took away all the temple treasures. He even stripped the gold from the front of the temple (1 Macc. 1.20—4). Two years later he ordered the temple to be desecrated and made into a temple of Olympian Zeus (2 Macc. 6.1—6). Offerings in the sanctuary ceased, and a pagan altar was erected on the altar of burnt offerings in the temple court (1 Macc. 1.54). In 164 BC Judas Maccabeus recaptured the temple and it was reconsecrated (1 Macc. 4.36—59).

Pompey besieged Jerusalem in 63 BC and after three months he took the temple on the Day of Atonement. The priests carried on with the rites even as the Romans burst in:

> Just as if the city had been wrapt in profound peace, the daily sacrifices, the expiations and all the ceremonies of worship were scrupulously performed to the honour of God. At the very hour when the temple was taken, when they were being massacred about the altar, they never desisted from the religious rites for the day. (Josephus, *Jewish War*, 1.148)

The victors then entered the holy of holies: 'And not light was the sin committed against the sanctuary, which before that time had never been entered or seen. For Pompey and not a few of his men went into it and saw what it was unlawful for any but the high priests to see' (Josephus, *Antiquities*, XIV. 71—2). Pompey did not take anything from the temple, and the following day he ordered that the temple be cleansed and the sacrificial rites resumed.

Herod the Great began enlarging and rebuilding the temple in 20 BC; Josephus described it thus:

> He prepared a thousand waggons to carry the stones, selected ten thousand of the most skilled workmen, purchased priestly robes for a thousand priests and trained some as masons, others as carpenters and began the construction only after all these preparations had been made by him. After removing the old foundations he laid down others and upon these he erected the temple which was a hundred cubits in length . . . and twenty more in height, but in the course of time this dropped as the foundations subsided . . . the temple was built of hard white stones each of which was about twenty-five cubits in length, eight in height and twelve in width.
>
> . . . the entrance doors, which with their lintels were equal in height to the temple itself, he adorned with multicoloured hangings with purple colours and with inwoven designs of pillars. Above these, under the cornice, spread a golden vine with grape clusters hanging from it a marvel of size and artistry to all who saw with what costliness of material it had been constructed. And he surrounded the temple with very large porticoes, all of which he made in proportion to the temple, and he surpassed his predecessors in spending money so that it was thought that no one else had adorned the temple so splendidly. The temple itself was built by the priests in a year and six months and all the people were filled with joy and offered thanks to God . . . And it is said that during the time when the temple was being built, no rain fell during the day but only at night, so that there was no interruption of the work. (*Antiquities*, XV. 390—1; 394—6; 421; 425)

In addition to these descriptions of the temple, there are two passages in Exodus (chapters 25—31 and 36—40) which describe the desert tabernacle. This elaborate tent was the shrine used by the Israelites in their desert wanderings. The furnishings were, in general, a miniature version of the furnishings of the temple

THE HOUSE OF THE LORD

adapted so as to be portable and the descriptions can therefore be used to supplement those of the temple.

Finally, there is the largest and most controversial of all the Dead Sea Scrolls, the Temple Scroll. This text was written to be a sixth book of Moses, forming a logical sequel to Deuteronomy and describing how the temple was to be built once Israel had reached the promised land.

Despite this wealth of information, it is very difficult to know exactly what any of these buildings was like, and, more important, exactly what went on in them. This is because none of the descriptions is an entirely objective account. The temple was a cause of controversy from the very start. Nathan the prophet was dubious about having a temple at all (2 Sam. 7). The Third Isaiah questioned the value of any temple (Isa. 66.1). The writer of 1 Enoch thought that the cult of the second temple was impure: 'And they began again to build as before . . . and they began to place bread on a table before the tower, but all the bread on it was polluted and not pure' (1 Enoch 89.73). The returned exiles were also called 'an apostate generation' (1 Enoch 90.9). It is hardly surprising that most of the surviving descriptions reflect the controversies in which the writer was involved. Thus, as we shall see, the account of Solomon's temple in 1 Kings, though the most detailed, has several interesting silences which lead one to suppose that the author has left some things unsaid. The account in 2 Chronicles includes significant detail not in the 1 Kings account. The account in Ezekiel is in the form of a vision of the restored temple, and raises the question: 'Was Ezekiel describing something he knew, or something he envisaged for the future?' Was it an actual or an ideal temple? The descriptions of the desert tabernacle in Exodus are clearly meant to show that the temple in Jerusalem was modelled on the earlier desert shrine, but it is generally agreed that the desert tabernacle was an idealized retrojection of the later temple, designed perhaps to legitimate the temple by rooting it in Israel's most ancient past. This in itself suggests that there was a need to justify the form of the temple. If we could date the material in Exodus, we should be able to know which temple the 'tabernacle' was describing. If it was the first temple, it could be valuable additional information to supplement the account in 1 Kings, and help formulate some questions about this account; if it was the second temple, some equally interesting questions arise. The Temple Scroll, in giving instructions for building a temple different from any other known temple, implies that the existing temple, because it was incorrectly constructed, was not capable of fulfilling its sacred role.

Constant controversy indicates that the temple was important; the details of those controversies show what the temple meant to those involved in the disputes. Thus we see that the actual shape of the temple was vital; each aspect of the building and its decoration was significant. Ezekiel's vision (Ezek. 40—48) and the Temple Scroll give detailed specifications for the buildings. The purity of the priesthood was vital; Zechariah had a vision of the Lord purifying the high priest for his new duties in the restored temple (Zech. 3.1—10). Genealogies were recorded to ensure that the family line was pure (Neh. 12.1—26). Negligent priests were condemned (Mal. 2.1—9). Those who tolerated the new Greek ways in the second century BC were cursed: '... there was such an extreme of Hellenisation and increase in the adoption of foreign ways because of the surpassing wickedness of Jason who was ungodly and no High Priest' (2 Macc. 4.13). The villain of the Dead Sea Scrolls was the 'Wicked Priest', the 'Spouter of Lies' who 'became proud, and he forsook God and betrayed the precepts for the sake of riches ... and he lived in the ways of abominations amidst every unclean defilement' (*Commentary on Habakkuk*, QpHab VIII). The calendar which determined the dates of the great festivals was important; a festival performed on the wrong day was not valid, a ritual not effective. A substantial section of the Book of Enoch describes how the angel Uriel revealed the true ordering of the heavens to the Seer. Those who had introduced a new calendar had acted contrary to the divine order in creation. The seasons would go astray and the crops would not grow: 'And in the days of the sinners the years shall be shortened and the moon shall alter her order and not appear at her time' (1 Enoch 80.2, 4). The Book of Jubilees, a rewriting of Genesis in the second century BC, warned of a time when Israel would commit a great sin: 'And they will go astray as to new moons and sabbaths and festivals and jubilees and ordinances' (Jub. 1.14).

The *Damascus Rule* from Qumran also emphasized the need for the correct calendar: 'But with the remnant which held fast to the commandments of God he made his covenant with Israel for ever, revealing to them the hidden things in which all Israel had gone astray. He unfolded before them his holy sabbaths and his glorious feasts, the testimonies of his righteousness and the ways of his truth' (CD III). The details of all these controversies are lost; we can only guess at the significance of the architecture, the place of the calendar and the role of the priests.

The temple generated strong feelings for many centuries. From the time of the restoration in the sixth century BC to the time of St John's Revelation, the temple in Jerusalem was called a harlot by those who had reason to quarrel with the priesthood of the day. The Third Isaiah condemned those who could accept Persian money for the rebuilding of the temple whilst excluding some of the indigenous worshippers of the Lord because they had become technically unclean: 'Upon a high and lofty mountain you have set your bed, and thither you went up to offer sacrifice . . . for, deserting me, you have uncovered your bed, you have gone up to it, you have made it wide' (Isa. 57.7—8).

Similarly the first Christians knew a temple which had become a market place and where the priests had been puppets of the Romans, had crucified Jesus and caused the death of many of his followers: 'Come I will show you the judgement of the great harlot who is seated upon many waters . . . drunk with the blood of the saints and with the blood of the martyrs of Jesus' (Rev. 17.1, 6).

Despite such invective, the temple was central to the hopes of even its fiercest critics. This power of the temple must have been rooted in its remotest past, in the time before it became the subject of such bitter controversy. What gripped the minds and hearts of all sides in these disputes was not the actual temple in Jerusalem, but the ideal, the memory of a temple which was central to the heritage of Israel. It is this ideal, this vision at the heart of the ancient cult which has been lost. How such a thing could have happened is, in itself, an important question. The shadows of the temple fall across the writings of the prophets and the psalms, and from these we have to guess the beliefs which inspired its rituals and the heavenly world which it represented. The writings of the visionaries and the later mystics are also set in this world of the ancient temple. To reconstruct this world we must cast our net wider than just those writings which describe the temple; we must look also at those which are set within it, those in which the golden cherubim on the walls of

14 THE GATE OF HEAVEN

Solomon's temple become the living creatures of the heavenly sanctuary and the olivewood cherubim overlaid with gold become the chariot throne of God.

Ancient Temples in Israel

Solomon's was not the first Israelite temple to be built, or even the first temple to be built in Jerusalem. The stories in the books of Judges and Samuel are full of references to older temples. Some are mentioned by name as temples, others are assumed to have existed because events happened there 'before the Lord'. The temple at Shiloh, where the young Samuel was brought up, is the best known. Eli was the priest there, and Elkanah and his family went up to the temple every year to offer their annual sacrifice (1 Sam. 1.21). In that temple there was a lamp of God and the ark (1 Sam. 3.3). From earliest times the temple was the place where the Lord appeared (1 Sam. 3.21). Other stories remember that there was a tent of meeting at Shiloh (Josh. 18.1; 19.51), and an altar (Josh. 22.29). The ark was lost to the Philistines (1 Sam. 4.17—22) and never returned to Shiloh (Ps. 78.60—1). There were also temples at Dan and Bethel; Jeroboam set up the golden calves there (1 Kings 12.28—9). Bethel was a royal sanctuary (Amos 7.13) but was condemned alongside Gilgal and Beersheba as a place of corrupt worship (Amos 3.3; 4.4). Saul had been made king 'before the Lord in Gilgal' (1 Sam. 11.15) and Agag king of the Amalekites had met his end there 'hewed . . . before the Lord in Gilgal' (1 Sam. 15.33). Hosea condemned the place (Hos. 4.15; 9.15; 12.11). At Mizpah Samuel wrote a book of the rights and duties of kingship and deposited it 'before the Lord' (1 Sam. 10.17, 25). There was a temple at Nob whose priest gave David the bread of the Presence to eat (1 Sam. 21.6). Goliath's sword was kept there 'behind the ephod' (1 Sam. 21.9).

In these early stories we glimpse several features which were to appear in the later temple in Jerusalem: there was the ark, the lamp of God, the bread of the Presence, the altar of burnt offering and the ephod. There were also images; golden calves were set up in Dan and Bethel (1 Kings 12.28), and the shrine at Dan had a graven image which had been brought by the settlers, along with an ephod, teraphim and a molten image (Judg. 17.14). Such images should not occasion too much surprise;

there were cherubim in the temple at Jerusalem and bronze oxen in the temple court there. The prohibition of images must have been a later development than the building of temples. Those who prohibited images also denied that the Lord could be seen; the temple was a place of prayer but not of vision.

King David

When David conquered Jerusalem, he conquered a Jebusite city which would have had its own established cult and temple. Of this nothing is known for certain, although it is widely thought that the mysterious Melchizedek figure who appears in the Abraham stories (Gen. 14.18—20) is a memory of the cult of the Canaanite high god El Elyon in Jerusalem. The Old Testament never condemned El Elyon when Baal and all the other Canaanite gods were denounced, which suggests that the high God, in some form, retained a place in the new cult of his ancient city.

The ark was brought to Jerusalem to establish its status as the capital city (2 Sam. 6). David went with a great procession of his people and the sacred object was brought with singing and dancing towards Jerusalem. A strange happening accompanied its progress; Uzzah touched the ark when he thought it was about to fall from the cart and he died. The procession was abandoned. Three months later David made a second attempt to bring the ark to Jerusalem; he offered sacrifices every few yards along the way, and eventually, amidst great festivity, it was set in the tent which had been prepared for it in the city. More sacrifices were offered, all the people feasted, and it is here that the story of Solomon's temple begins.

David recognized that a tent was not a suitable place for such a holy object, especially as he was himself by that time living in a 'house of cedar' (2 Sam. 7.2). He wanted to build a more permanent home for the ark, but met with opposition from Nathan the prophet. The prophets had always been opposed to the idea of kings in Israel; they were a threat to their power. Samuel had warned the people against them (1 Sam. 8.10—22), and had only anointed Saul with great reluctance. Samuel wanted to retain his own position as leader, and friction soon developed between him and the king. When Samuel was seven days late in coming to officiate at a ceremony, Saul presumed to offer a sacrifice himself, and thus took over one of the prophet's privileges. Samuel warned Saul that such disobedience would cost him his kingdom (1 Sam. 13.14). When Saul disobeyed Samuel a second time and refused to sacrifice all the booty of the Amalekite wars, including Agag their king, Samuel deprived Saul of his kingdom: 'The Lord has torn the kingdom of Israel from you this day' (1 Sam. 15.28). He then went on and anointed David, perhaps hoping to find in him a ruler who would not resist the prophets and their established power. The issues were clear; the Lord was the true king of Israel (1 Sam. 8.1—7); the prophets were his spokesmen and the affairs of the cult such as sacrifice were not to be ceded to anyone. A few years later, this same David was planning to build a temple. The prophet Nathan would have seen this as the first step towards asserting royal power in religious affairs, and thus he resisted it. There had been temples before; but there had not been a royal temple. Nathan did not say that a temple could not be built; he told David that the time was not right. His son would build a house for the ark. David was told that, as a man who had shed blood, he was not fit to build a holy place (1 Chron. 28.3).

The plan of the proposed temple was, however, 'revealed' to David. He passed on to Solomon his son a detailed specification of all that had to be done, and the Chronicler records that this was 'made clear by the writing from the hand of the Lord concerning it, all the work to be done according to the plan' (1 Chron. 28.19). How this heavenly plan was revealed is not known, but there was an exactly similar tradition about the plan for the desert tabernacle. Moses had to make it in accordance with the plan he had been shown on the mountain (Exod. 25.40). These two curious pieces of information are very important for understanding the temple. First, the tabernacle and the temple were consciously related in every detail. Both had been revealed by the Lord, both were built according to a heavenly plan. The Wisdom of Solomon, probably written in the first century AD, makes that king say: 'Thou hast given command to build a temple on thy holy mountain, and an altar in the city of thy habitation, a copy of the holy tent which thou didst prepare from the beginning' (Wisd. 9.8). Second, we see that the earthly sanctuary, whether it was the tent or the temple, was thought to reflect a heavenly pattern. Later tradition understood this to mean that the earthly sanctuary was a copy of the heavenly reality; the Epistle to the Hebrews mentions it: 'They serve a copy and shadow of the heavenly sanctuary; for when Moses was about to erect the tent he was instructed by God, saying, "See that you make everything according to the pattern which was shown you on the mountain"' (Heb. 8.5). It was not only the structure that corresponded; one of the keys to any understanding of the temple cult is the realization that the rituals and the personnel were also thought to be the visible manifestation of the heavenly reality. The priests were the angels, the high priest was the representative of the Lord. Third, no matter how closely archaeologists may be able to relate the style and practices of the temple to those of the surrounding people, Israel herself remembered that the temple in all its detail was part of the divine plan, revealed, along with the commandments, on Sinai. This accounts for the later emphasis upon building everything exactly as prescribed.

The temple was built where the Lord appeared to David. An appearance of the Lord was the prerequisite for any holy place; Genesis is full of such stories. The Lord appeared to one of the patriarchs, an altar was built there, and it became a holy place. Thus Abraham built an altar by the oak of Moreh, where the Lord had appeared to him (Gen. 12.6–7); Isaac built one in Beersheba (Gen. 26.24–5); Jacob set up a pillar at Bethel (Gen. 28.18). David saw the angel of the Lord threatening destruction upon Jerusalem, because he had disobeyed the Lord and conducted a census of his people. The punishment was a plague which killed thousands and was threatening the capital itself. David had a vision of the destroying angel of the Lord, with his sword stretched over the city. He was standing by the threshing floor of Ornan the Jebusite (1 Chron. 21.15); the version of the story in 2 Sam. 24.16 calls him Araunah the Jebusite. David and his elders repented in sackcloth, the plague was averted, and the angel told David to build an altar on the threshing floor. David said: 'Here shall be the house of the Lord God and here the altar of burnt offering for Israel' (1 Chron. 22.1). Thus was the site chosen, but note well the circumstances. The Lord had appeared threatening judgement, and that judgement had been averted. The Lord and his judgement were to be a prominent feature of the future temple cult.

The Rock

The great rock of the threshing floor became an important part of the temple; today it is marked by the Dome of the Rock. Beneath the rock is a cave, and there is evidence of an old channel running to the north of it. Opinion is divided as to whether it became the basis of the great altar in the temple courtyard or was incorporated into the Holy of Holies. Had it been the basis for the great altar, which the story in 2 Chronicles suggests, it would have stood to the east of the temple itself and this creates problems. The temple hill slopes down sharply to the west of the holy rock, which would have meant building an artificial platform for the rest of the temple. It would, however, explain the channel as the means whereby the blood and water from the sacrifices were carried away. Many scholars now opt for the other possibility and think that the great rock became the foundation of the Holy of Holies at the western end of the temple, especially as the floor of that part of the building seems to have been considerably higher than elsewhere. A Christian pilgrimage in Jerusalem in AD 333 saw a stone at the temple site which was revered by the Jews as a sacred object: 'Two statues of Hadrian stand there, and, not far from them, a pierced stone which the Jews come and anoint every year. They mourn and rend their garments and then depart' (*The Pilgrim of Bordeaux*, in J. Wilkinson, *Egeria's Travels*).

The later crusaders were less scrupulous about sacred objects in Jerusalem; they cut altar stones from the rock to take home to Europe.

If the facts about the sacred rock are less than clear, its significance is not. Later tradition called it the *'eben sh'tiyyah*, the foundation stone. Remembered as the foundation of the sanctuary, it was the rock on which the high priest sprinkled blood on the Day of Atonement in the time of the second temple, when the ark and the cherub throne were no longer in the temple. Remembered as the rock on which the altar stood, it was the place from which all the waters of the earth had to be controlled. The waters under the earth were all gathered beneath the temple, they believed, and it was necessary to ensure that sufficient was released to ensure fertility, but not so much as to overwhelm the world with a flood. King David had played a

THE HOUSE OF THE LORD 19

prominent role in controlling these underground waters; the Babylonian Talmud records one such legend:

> Rabbi Johannan said . . . When David dug the Pits . . . the Deep arose and threatened to submerge the world. 'Is there anyone', enquired David, 'who knows whether it is permitted to inscribe the Name upon a sherd and cast it into the Deep that its waves should subside?' . . . Ahitophel said, 'It is permitted'. David inscribed the Name upon a sherd, cast it into the Deep and it subsided sixteen thousand cubits. When he saw that it had subsided to such a great extent, he said, 'The nearer it is to the earth the better the earth can be kept watered', and he uttered the fifteen Songs of Ascents and the Deep reascended fifteen thousand cubits and remained at one thousand cubits (b. *Sukkah* 53b).

Stories such as these are recorded in the Talmuds and attributed to rabbis of the third century AD, but they are much older than that. This association of the temple with the control of water and the forces of chaos goes back to earliest times. The psalmist could write: 'The Lord sits enthroned over the flood; the Lord site enthroned as king forever' (Ps. 29.10). Thus it came about that this rock was the beginning of the creation, the fixed point from which the land was formed. (Several of these stories are told in b. *Yoma* 54a). The waters of Noah's flood welled up from this point. It became the site of many of the great events in Israel's history: dust was scraped from its stone to create Adam; Adam, Cain and Abel offered their sacrifices there; Abraham and Melchizedek met; Abraham came there to offer Isaac as a sacrifice; and Jacob slept there when he saw the ladder which reached up to heaven. The temple was built on a crucial spot; it was the bastion against ever threatening chaos. Evil and disorder, as we shall see, were represented by the subterranean waters of the great deep, waters which had to be driven back before the creation could be established and God's people live in safety. The temple blocked these forces of evil and prevented their eruption.

From time to time in the Old Testament there are hints of a creation story older than those in Genesis. The Lord had defeated the primeval deeps, depicted as a sea monster but representing all the forces of evil and chaos that threaten life, and thus he had founded the earth.

> Thou dost rule the raging of the sea;
>   When its waves rise thou stillest them.
> Thou didst crush Rahab like a carcase,
>   thou didst scatter thy enemies with thy mighty arm.
> The heavens are thine, the earth also is thine;
>   the world and all that is in it,
>   thou hast founded them. (Ps. 89.9—11)

The king, as the Lord's agent, his 'son', continued to hold these forces in check and thus to provide security for his people.

> I will set his hand on the sea
>   and his right hand on the rivers.
> He shall cry to me, 'Thou art my Father,
>   my God, and the Rock of my salvation.'
> And I will make him the first-born,
>   the highest of the kings of the earth. (Ps. 89.25—7)

Presumably there had been rituals whereby the creation was sustained and renewed; this is yet another area where there is insufficient evidence to say anything with certainty but it is possible that these were an element of the new year festival. There are so many passages in the Old Testament, which, for all our ingenuity, are still opaque. Some of them may contain relics of, or allusions to, these older ways. It is hard to search for a needle in a haystack, and even harder when one has never actually seen a needle!

Constructing the Temple

Building the temple was an enormous and costly business. The Chronicler says that David had made provision for some of the materials; he had accumulated silver and gold, bronze, onyx, precious stones and marble. The leaders of the people were also invited to contribute (1 Chron. 29.2—9). The writer of 1 Kings says only that Solomon had to buy cedar and cypress wood from Hiram king of Tyre, and that this was purchased with a crippling quantity of wheat and oil (1 Kings 5.10—11, cf. 2 Chron. 2.15). The servants of Hiram felled the trees and then transported them as rafts down the coast to Joppa, whence Solomon's men took them to Jerusalem (2 Chron. 2.16). In the hill country there were 'eighty thousand hewers of stone' (1 Kings 5.15) who 'quarried out great costly stones in order to lay the foundation of the house with dressed stones' (1 Kings 5.17). All the stones for the building were prepared and shaped at the quarry; no cutting or preparation was done on the sacred site (1 Kings 6.7). The master craftsman was Huram-abi, sent from Tyre by Hiram, a man skilled in 'gold, silver, bronze, iron, stone and wood, and in purple, blue and crimson fabrics and fine linen' (2 Chron. 2.13). The bronze for the temple was cast in clay beds by the Jordan, between Succoth and Zarethan (1 Kings 7.46). Solomon built a fleet of ships to sail the Red Sea and bring back gold from Ophir. Here, too, he was dependent upon the expertise of his Phoenician friends, because we read that 'Hiram sent with the fleet his servants, seamen who were familiar with the sea, together with the servants of Solomon' (1 Kings 9.27).

A comparison of these two accounts of the building begins to show the particular concern of the two writers. The writer of 1 Kings did not favour the monarchy, and records all the details of the terrible price Israel had to pay for the temple. The work was done by forced labour; thirty thousand Israelites were sent to Lebanon for one month in three, in addition to the eighty thousand serving in the quarries. At the end of twenty years of such building, buying timber and gold from Tyre, Solomon had to pay his debt by giving to Hiram twenty cities in Galilee (1 Kings 9.10—11). After his death, the people rebelled against such a harsh imposition, and asked his son Rehoboam to lighten the burden. When he would not grant their request, the people of the northern tribes refused to acknowledge him as king, and the kingdom was divided into two. The new ruler of the northern kingdom was Jeroboam, newly returned from exile in Egypt. He had been a leader of one of the forced labour gangs and had received support from the prophet Ahijah for his move against Solomon. The power of the prophets had asserted itself yet again, and it is surely not coincidence that Ahijah came from Shiloh, the place of the former temple! (1 Kings 11.26—12.20).

The Chronicler paints another different picture. The building work, he says, was done by aliens (2 Chron. 2.17—18; 8.7—10), and there is no mention of the cities ceded in payment. These tendencies must be borne in mind when reading the rest of their accounts. The Chronicler saw the temple as something glorious; he dwells at length on its splendour and the details of its music. The writer of Kings, influenced as he was by the reforming

22 THE GATE OF HEAVEN

ideals of the Deuteronomists, saw it differently. There is good reason to believe that some aspects of the temple and its worship were simply not recorded by him. It is an effective form of censorship which has made reconstruction so difficult.

The Temple and its Courts

The temple was a rectangular building, twenty cubits wide and seventy long. It was divided into three parts; the porch or vestibule (the *ulam*), which was ten cubits long; then the temple or palace (the *hekal*) which was forty cubits long; and finally the holy of holies (the *debir*) which was twenty cubits long. The *hekal* and *debir* formed 'the house' which was thirty cubits high (1 Kings 6.2), but the *debir* was a perfect cube, twenty cubits high (1 Kings 6.20). This raises a problem: was the ceiling of the house lower at the far end, or was the *debir* raised up above the floor level of the *hekal*? The latter seems more likely, especially if it had been built over the great rock. The Greek version of the Old Testament says that the house was only twenty-five cubits high, which would have meant that the raised floor of the *debir* would have been only five cubits (i.e. just over two metres) higher than the rest. On three sides of the house there were three storeys of store chambers, each chamber being five cubits high (1 Kings 6.5, 8—10). This threefold division was the common pattern for temples in the ancient Near East and several examples have been found.

The walls of the courtyards were built of dressed stones and timber (1 Kings 7.12), and it is possible that the temple itself was constructed in the same way. Other temples of the time were built with a foundation of dressed stones on top of which there was a structure of timber and brick. The walls of the second temple were built in the same way (Ezra 6.4) with three courses of stones and one of timber.

The 'house' was surrounded by a courtyard (the inner court, 1 Kings 6.36) and beyond that was the great court which enclosed both the temple and the palace. These courtyards were to be altered and extended over the years. In the time of Jehoshaphat (873–849) there was a new court (2 Chron. 20.5) and by the time of Manasseh (687–642) there were two courts in the house of the Lord (2 Kings 21.5). One generation later Baruch, Jeremiah's scribe, read the words of the prophet in the chamber of Gemariah

THE HOUSE OF THE LORD

which was 'in the upper court, at the entry of the new gate of the Lord's house' (Jer. 36.10). These courtyards represented areas of increasing sanctity as one approached the holy place. Since the temple was built upon a hill, the more sacred areas were raised above the less sacred, and the temple itself was right at the top. Ezekiel's vision of the temple, which may or may not have been a memory of the one he had known in Jerusalem before the Babylonians destroyed the city, had an outer court five hundred cubits square (Ezek. 42.15—20), to separate the holy from the common, and within this an inner court one hundred cubits square (Ezek. 40.47), immediately to the east of the temple itself. The great altar stood in this inner court. Only the priests, apparently, were allowed into this area; the 'prince' had to watch proceedings from the eastern gate, as did the common people (Ezek. 46.1—3). In the middle of the second century BC Alcimus the high priest ordered this wall of the inner court to be removed, and he was punished with a terrible death (1 Macc. 9.54—6). Around the walls of the outer courtyard in Ezekiel's temple there were thirty chambers (Ezek. 40.17), and at the four corners there were small courtyards (Ezek. 46.21—4). These were the areas for cooking and eating such of the sacrificial offerings as the laity were permitted to consume. The priests had similar rooms in the inner courtyard (Ezek. 42.13—14), at the western end. Their bathrooms and lavatories were underground, heated by fires.

> ... he would go out and along the passage that leads below the temple building, where lamps were burning here and there ... There was a fire there and a privy, and this was its seemly use: if he found it locked he knew that someone was there; if open he knew no one was there. He went down and immersed himself, came up and dried himself, and warmed himself by the fire. (Mishnah, *Tamid* 1.1)

He then had to leave the temple as he was considered unclean until sunset. There was also a special area for slaughtering the sacrificial animals (Ezek. 40.38—43). Ezekiel describes the tables, the slabs, the washing arrangements and all the utensils set out by the north gate of the outer court.

In Herod's temple the outer courtyard was about 240 metres square and open to either Jew or Gentile. In the north-west corner was the Antonia which housed the garrison. Soldiers could be sent down to the temple quickly should there be any trouble, as there was when Paul was arrested (Acts 21.31—4).

> Proceeding across this towards the second court of the temple, one found it was surrounded by a stone balustrade three cubits high and of exquisite workmanship; in this at regular intervals stood slabs giving a warning, some in Greek, others in Latin characters, of the law of purification, to wit that no foreigner was permitted to enter the holy place, for so the second enclosure of the temple was called. (Josephus, *War* V. 193—4)

One of these slabs has been discovered. It reads, in Greek, 'No foreigner is to enter within the balustrade and embankment around the sanctuary. Whoever is caught will have himself to blame for his death which follows.' Paul was accused of bringing a Greek into this sacred area, and that is why he was arrested (Acts 21.28). The vivid description in Acts 21.27—40 of the near riot which ensued shows the rigour with which this law was enforced even by the Romans. Within the holy area itself there was first the court of women, so called because it was as far as women were allowed to pass, and this led to two courts, the court of Israel and the court of the priests, which were in reality one. The court of Israel was a narrow strip at the entrance to the priests' court, separated from it by a low balustrade and two steps. Above this stood the temple and the altar of burnt offering.

The Temple Scroll, the pattern for the ideal temple, has yet another system of courtyards. The outer courtyard was 1600 cubits square (about half a mile!) and corresponded in function to the court of women. The ideal temple had no place for Gentiles. There were three gates in each side of the outer wall, and each one bore the name of one of the twelve tribes. The most ancient calendars of Israel were also probably based upon this system of temple gates, especially those in the eastern wall which corresponded to the position of the sunrise on the longest and the shortest day. One such ancient calendar survives, in a much mutilated form, in the Ethiopic Book of Enoch, and there each of the calendar gates was guarded by an angel, who presided over the turning of the year at its longest and shortest day, and at the equinoxes. It is interesting, therefore, to see that just such an arrangement was known to St John. When he had his vision of the heavenly city, 'foursquare, the length the same as its breadth' (Rev. 21.16), he saw that it had 'a great high wall with twelve gates, and at the gates twelve angels, and on the gates the names of the twelve tribes of the sons of Israel were inscribed' (Rev. 21.12). Within the great court was the middle court, 480 cubits square, which was for ritually pure men, and within this there was the court of the priests, 280 cubits square and the most sacred of all. In both ideal and actual temples, then, there was a pattern of concentric areas of holiness and, because the temple site was a hill, the holier the place the higher it was situated. The Mishnah extends this to the whole land of Israel:

> There are ten degrees of holiness. The Land of Israel is holier than any other land . . .
> The walled cities [of the Land of Israel] are still more holy, in that they must send forth the lepers from their midst; moreover they may carry a corpse therein wheresoever they will, but once it is gone forth [from the city], they may not bring it back.
> Within the wall of Jerusalem is still more holy, for there [only] they may eat the Lesser Holy Things and the Second Tithe.
> The Temple Mount is still more holy, for no man or woman that has a flux, no menstruant, and no woman after childbirth may enter therein.
> The Rampart is still more holy, for no gentiles and none that have contracted uncleanness from a corpse may enter therein.
> The court of women is still more holy, for none that had immersed himself the selfsame day [because of uncleanness] may enter therein, yet none would thereby become liable to a Sin offering.
> The Court of the Israelites is still more holy, for none whose atonement is incomplete may enter therein, and they would thereby become liable to a Sin offering.
> The Court of the Priests is still more holy, for Israelites may not enter therein save only when they must perform the laying on of hands, slaughtering and waving.
> Between the porch and the altar is still more holy, for none that has a blemish or whose hair is unloosed may enter there.
> The sanctuary is still more holy, for none may enter therein with hands and feet unwashed.
> The Holy of Holies is still more holy, for none may enter therein save only the High Priest on the Day of Atonement at the time of the [Temple] service (Mishnah, *Kelim* 1.6—9).

This list of what made unclean explains many of the gospel incidents: the lepers, the woman with the flow of blood, the priest and the levite who dared not touch a man who looked dead and left him for the Samaritan.

The Temple Interior

Concentric areas of holiness can also be seen in the descriptions of the desert tabernacle. The more holy the area, the more elaborate the curtain which formed it and the more costly its fittings. The outer tent was made of goats' hair with bronze clasps (Exod. 26.7, 11). Next came the screen for the door of the tent, made of coloured wools and linen, *roqem* work. *Roqem* means variegated, perhaps woven or embroidered. Then there were the tabernacle curtains, made of linen and wool, *hoseb* work. *Hoseb* means cunning work and is thought to indicate a more intricate form of brocaded or embroidered fabric since the curtains depicted cherubim (Exod. 26.1). Last of all, and holiest of all, there was the veil which hung before the ark and separated the 'holy place from the most holy place' (Exod. 26.31—3). This veil was made of wool and linen, also *hoseb* work, and also depicting cherubim. The wool and linen curtains had clasps not of bronze but of gold (Exod. 26.6). Wool and linen was a significant mixture; it was considered to be a holy fabric, and forbidden for ordinary use (Lev. 19.19; Deut. 22.11). Similarly a 'mixed' crop might become 'holy' and therefore forfeit to the sanctuary (Deut. 22.9).

The interior of the *hekal* in Solomon's temple was panelled with cedar wood, and the floor was made of cypress (1 Kings 6.15). The walls of the *debir* were overlaid with gold (1 Kings 6.20). All the walls of both the inner and the outer rooms were decorated 'with carved figures of cherubim and palm trees and open flowers' (1 Kings 6.29). These corresponded to the cherubim of the tabernacle curtains, but the tabernacle had no trees and flowers, no garden motifs. The doors of the inner sanctuary were made of olivewood, and they too were carved with cherubim, palm trees and flowers, all overlaid with gold. The Chronicler's account differs in several details. He says that the *hekal* was lined with cypress wood and that it was all overlaid with gold and precious stones. On the walls were cherubim (2 Chron. 3.5—7). Ezekiel's details are different again; he describes the carved likenesses of cherubim and palm trees alternately round the walls. The cherubim had two faces; one was the face of a man and the other of a lion (Ezek. 41.18—19). The temple interior was a garden representing the heavenly garden on the mountain of God, the original Garden of Eden. Ezekiel described it in his oracle against Tyre (Ezek. 28); the jewelled trees were those of the temple, and the judgement of the proud prince must have had its counterpart in temple rituals.

In the inner sanctuary there were two cherubim, carved from olivewood and overlaid with gold. The cherubim known elsewhere in the ancient Near East were monstrous figures with the body of a winged animal and the head of a human being. The cherubim of the *debir* were ten cubits high and had a wingspan of ten cubits also. They stood with their wingtips touching and thus they spanned the width of the *debir* (1 Kings 6.23—8). When the temple was consecrated the ark was brought into the *debir* and placed under the wings of the cherubim (1 Kings 8.6). That is all the writer of 1 Kings tells us about the *debir*; he has omitted some significant details, and one wonders why. The Chronicler, for example, says that David had told Solomon of his plans for a 'golden *chariot* of the cherubim that spread their wings' (1 Chron. 28.18); in other words, the cherubim formed a chariot throne exactly as is depicted in several Canaanite carvings of the period. This was the throne of the Lord of which Hezekiah spoke: 'O Lord of Hosts, God of Israel, who art enthroned above the cherubim' (Isa. 37.16). 1 Kings says nothing about this chariot throne. One wonders why; it must have been a part of the cult, the place of the presence of Yahweh. Later texts, as we shall see, had vivid descriptions of this throne at the centre of the heavenly world. The account in 1 Kings also omits to mention the great curtain. In front of the *debir*, says the Chronicler, was a curtain, 'the veil of blue and purple and crimson fabrics and fine linen', with cherubim worked upon it (2 Chron. 3.14). Later writers said that it represented the material world and thus came between the worshipper and the presence of God. Both the throne and the curtain seem to have expressed important aspects of the theology of the royal cult, and yet the dominant strand of the Old Testament omits both. One possible explanation for this silence is that the tradition represented by 1 Kings, that of the Deuteronomists, did not agree with those aspects of the temple represented by the veil and throne. The role of the Deuteronomists in transmitting the accounts of Israel's history may be one of the reasons why so little is known of the ancient cult.

The *hekal* was furnished with a gold altar of incense, a gold table for the bread of the Presence, and ten gold lampstands (1 Kings 7.48−9), or, according to the Chronicler, with a gold altar, ten tables for the bread of the Presence and ten lampstands (2 Chron. 4.7, 8, 19). A third account of the contents of the *hekal* is found in the account of the desert tabernacle, which represented the ideal on which the temple was based. Bezalel made the ark of acacia wood overlaid with gold, the mercy seat of pure gold, the cherubim of hammered gold, the table for the bread and the altar of incense of acacia wood covered with gold, and one lamp, the great seven-branched *menorah*, of pure gold (Exod. 37.17−24). The furnishings of the house, therefore, were made of gold. The furnishings of the courtyards were made of bronze. The altar of burnt offering was overlaid with bronze and its utensils were made of bronze. The laver was also of bronze (Exod. 38.8). This distinction between gold and bronze was also true of the temple; everything used inside the house was of gold whilst everything used in the courtyard was of bronze.

The golden altar of incense stood in the centre of the western end of the *hekal*, in front of the *debir*. It had horns at each corner, and the high priest had to burn a special incense upon it every morning and every evening. This was made of frankincense and three sweet spices (stacte, onycha and galbanum) beaten together with salt. Such incense was to be used only in the temple; anyone who used it elsewhere was 'cut off from his people' (Exod. 30.34−8). Offerings outside the *hekal* were accommpanied by frankincense alone (Lev. 2.1; 6.15). Philo interpreted the four spices as symbols of the four elements: 'Now these four, of which the incense is composed, are, I hold, a symbol of the elements out of which the whole world was brought to completion' (*Who is the Heir?*, 197). The Book of Jubilees, written in the second century BC, said that Abraham had offered seven spices in his incense: 'frankincense and galbanum, and stacte and nard and myrrh and spice and costum . . . crushed, mixed together in equal parts and pure' (Jub. 16.24). Later sources say that there were thirteen spices in the incense: 'the altar of incense, by the thirteen fragrant spices from sea and from land, both desert and inhabited, with which it was replenished, signifies that all things are of God and for God' (Josephus, *War*, V.218).

The bread of the Presence was twelve loaves set out each sabbath in two rows of six on the golden table. The table was placed on the north side of the *hekal*. There were also two tables in the temple porch for the bread: 'On the table of marble they laid the bread when it was brought in, and on that of gold [they laid it] when it was brought out, since what is holy must be raised in honour and not brought down' (Mishnah, *Shekalim* 6.4). The bread was prepared outside the temple, but baked within the precincts according to one tradition, but another said that it had to be wholly prepared in the temple (Mishnah, *Menaḥoth* 11.3). The bread was treated as a grain offering, sprinkled with pure frankincense and later eaten by the priests 'in a holy place' (Lev. 24.5—9).

On the south side of the *hekal* was the great lamp, made of solid gold, which had to be fuelled with pure olive oil (Exod. 27.20). It was made like a seven-branched tree, decorated with almonds and flowers (Exod. 25.31—7). At the top of each branch was a lamp; it was these seven lamps which Zechariah saw in his vision and recognized as the eyes of Yahweh (Zech. 4.10). The sevenfold lamp will prove to be important evidence for understanding the temple cult; the Lord was not singular but plural. In the older cult the manifold Lord was present in the temple, whereas in the 'reformed' worship the Lord was One (Deut. 6.4), and only his Name was in the temple (Deut. 12.11).

The Furnishings of the Temple Court

The courtyard was furnished with bronzes. Two bronze pillars stood in front of the entrance. They were eighteen cubits high and had bronze capitals a further five cubits high. They were decorated with pomegranates and 'lily-work', nets of chequer-work and wreaths of chain-work (1 Kings 7.15—22). Their purpose is not known, and, as with so much in the temple, if there is no evidence in the ancient sources, scholars have to resort to guesswork. Some have suggested that the pillars represented sacred trees, fertility symbols. There are stylized trees standing on either side of the entrance on several models of shrines which have been unearthed. Another possibility is that they were fire altars, or that they represented the pillar of fire and the pillar of cloud which led the Israelites in the desert. Yet another idea is that they symbolized the strength of the deity; this would certainly account for their names: Jachin, 'Yahweh will establish'; and Boaz, 'in strength'.

To the south-east of the temple there was the bronze 'sea'. This was an enormous bronze basin of water, ten cubits in diameter, i.e. half as wide as the temple itself. It was supported on twelve bronze oxen, in four groups of three, and it was for the priests to wash in (1 Kings 7.23−6; 2 Chron. 4.1−6). There were ten smaller lavers, each four cubits across, which stood five on each side of the courtyard to the north and south (1 Kings 7.38). They were used to wash the offerings (1 Kings 7.38; 2 Chron. 4.6). In later interpretation, as we shall see, the whole of this courtyard represented the sea; the entire temple complex 'was' the creation, with the temple as the created and ordered firmament in the midst of a hostile sea. This bronze sea was probably the concrete representation of the sea which features in so many of Israel's myths.

In front of the temple was the bronze altar, the altar of burnt offerings. This is not described in the account of the temple in 1 Kings, but it is mentioned in the account of the dedication. The bronze altar was too small to cope with all the offerings made on that day (1 Kings 8.64). It was, apparently, movable, and may have been a grid of the type used by the Phoenicians. In the time of King Ahaz it was replaced by one of a different type. The king had seen an altar in Damascus and ordered Uriah the priest to have a similar one installed at Jerusalem. The original bronze altar was moved to the north of the courtyard and kept for the king's personal use (2 Kings 16.10−16). The Chronicler says that Solomon built an altar twenty cubits square and ten high (2 Chron. 4.1); this would hardly have been movable, and has led to the suggestion that the Chronicler gave to the original bronze altar the dimensions of the larger one which existed in his own time. Ezekiel gives a very detailed account of the altar in his temple (Ezek. 43.13−17), but again, we cannot know whether this was his ideal, or based upon the one he had known in the first temple. His altar had three levels: the first level was two cubits high, 'the bosom of the earth' ('the base on the ground' in the English versions); the second was four cubits and the third was four cubits. This top section was to be twelve cubits square

THE HOUSE OF THE LORD

and was called 'the mountain of God' ('the altar hearth' in the English versions). At each corner it had a 'horn' one cubit high, and there were steps up to the top on the eastern side, i.e. the side furthest from the temple. Ezekiel does not give exact dimensions for the base of this altar, but it seems to have been about sixteen to eighteen cubits square.

There are two descriptions of the great altar in the second temple, both written about 200 BC. The Letter of Aristeas, which describes his visit to Jerusalem, says that the altar was

> in keeping with the place itself and with the burnt offerings which were consumed by fire upon it, and the approach to it was on a similar scale. There was a gradual slope up to it, conveniently arranged for the purpose of decency, and the ministering priests were robed in linen garments down to their ankles. The temple faces east and its back is toward the west. The whole of the floor is paved with stones and slopes down to the appointed places, that the water may be conveyed to wash away the blood from the sacrifices, for many thousands of beasts are sacrificed there on feast days . . . (Letter of Aristeas 87—8).

The other account is a quotation from Pseudo-Hecataeus in Josephus (*Against Apion* I.198). He says that the altar was twenty cubits square and ten high, built of unhewn stones i.e. in accordance with the law of Moses: 'If you make me an altar of stone, you shall not build it of hewn stones; for if you wield your tool upon it you profane it' (Exod. 20.25).

When Antiochus Epiphanes began his persecution of the Jews, he desecrated the temple in 169 BC. All the golden vessels were looted (1 Macc. 1.20—4), and a pagan altar was built on the great altar. (1 Macc. 1.54, 59). This pagan altar was the 'desolating sacrilege' mentioned in Daniel (1 Macc. 1.54; Dan. 9.27; 11.31; 12.11). When Judas regained Jerusalem and purified the temple (the events now remembered at the feast of Chanukkah each December), the defiled stones were removed.

> They deliberated what to do about the altar of burnt offering, which had been profaned. And they thought it best to tear it down lest it bring reproach upon them, for the gentiles had defiled it. So they tore down the altar and stored the stones in a convenient place until there should come a prophet to tell

them what to do with them. Then they took unhewn stones, as the Law directs, and built a new altar like the former one. (1 Macc. 4.42—7)

Josephus has left us a description of the altar in Herod's temple:

> In front of [the temple] stood the altar, fifteen cubits high and with a breadth and length extending alike to fifty cubits, in shape a square with horn-like projections at the corners, and approached from the south by a gently sloping proclivity. No iron was used in its construction, nor did iron ever touch it. (*War*, V. 225)

The Mishnah has different measurements; the altar was thirty-two cubits square at its base (about fifteen metres), and rose in three stepped stages leaving for the altar fire an area twenty-four cubits square (Mishnah, *Middoth* 3.1). A red line was drawn horizontally all around the middle of the altar; the blood of the offerings had to be sprinkled either above or below this line:

> [The blood of] a bird that is a Sin offering is sprinkled below [the red line] and [the blood of] a beast that is a Sin offering is sprinkled above. [The blood of] a bird that is a Whole offering is sprinkled above [the red line] and [the blood of] a beast that is a whole offering is sprinkled below. (Mishnah, *Kinnim* 1.1)

At the south-west corner of the altar were two holes into which the blood drained away into a channel '. . . and flowed away into the brook Kidron. And it was sold to the gardeners as manure' (Mishnah, *Yoma* 5.6). At the same corner of the altar was a slab which gave access to the pit below the altar into which the wine from the libations flowed. 'Once every seventy years the young priests would go down there and gather up the congealed wine which looked like circles of pressed figs and they burned it in a state of sanctity' (Tosefta, *Sukkah* 3.15). What the great altar represented is not known; it must, however, be significant that it was called the mountain of God, that there was a great pit underneath and that it was regularly covered with blood, i.e. life.

Sacrifices

The great altar was the place of sacrifice. Sacrifice was the central act of Israel's cult, and yet it is almost impossible to understand what was intended by it. There are several reasons for this; one is that the whole idea of blood sacrifice is so alien to modern ways of thinking; another is that the prescriptions for sacrifice in the Old Testament are not at all clear, and may come from several different periods. Leviticus 1−7 is thought to be the rules for sacrifice in the period of the second temple, and these will serve to show something of the complexity of the system. There are five main types of sacrifice described in Lev. 1−7; whole burnt offerings (Lev. 1.3−17); cereal offerings (Lev. 2); peace offerings (Lev. 3); sin offerings (Lev. 4.1−5.13); and guilt offerings (Lev. 5.14−6.7).

The whole burnt offering was a male animal without blemish; it could be a bull, a ram or a goat, or, for the poor, two turtle doves or pigeons. The offerer put his hand on the head of the animal and then killed it himself. The blood was taken by the priests and splashed onto the four sides of the altar. The offerer skinned the animal and cut it in pieces. The skin was given to the priests (Lev. 7.8), and the income from this leather was considerable: '[The Law] ordains that the priests who minister at the holy sacrifices should receive the hides of the whole burnt offerings, the number of which is incalculable, and this is no small gift, but represents a very large sum of money' (Philo, *Special Laws*, I.151). The legs and entrails were washed, and then the whole was burnt on the altar by the priest. This ritual effected 'atonement' (Lev. 1.4), but we do not know how this was understood. Some scholars say that the laying on of hands was a sign that guilt had been transferred to the animal, i.e. it was a substitute; others favour the idea that it established contact with God; others that it was an assertion that this was the offerer's gift, and that he should receive any benefits. Since the animal had to be pure it is unlikely that the laying on of hands was thought to transfer guilt as this would have made the animal unfit. The scapegoat offered on the Day of Atonement was loaded with the sins of Israel, and this made it unfit for sacrifice; it was driven out into the desert. What is known is that blood was believed to be life (Lev. 17.14), and that *the offering was therefore not of the death of the animal but its life*. This must affect our understanding of the New Testament.

Whole burnt offerings were offered in Israel from ancient times. Gideon offered a whole sacrifice (Judg. 6.26−8) as did Samson's father (Judg. 13.15−20). Samuel offered a whole offering (1 Sam. 7.9); so did David when the ark was brought to Jerusalem (2 Sam. 6.17—18); and Solomon offered burnt offerings three times a year in the temple (1 Kings 9.25). Elijah's offering on Carmel was a whole burnt offering (1 Kings 18.23, 33). There are hints that the whole burnt offering had once included human sacrifice. The king of Edom, for example, when he was in dire straits, offered his oldest son as a burnt offering, and the writer implies that this was effective. The Israelites who had been attacking the king were afflicted with 'great wrath' such that they had to withdraw (2 Kings 3.27). Isaac was to be offered as a whole burnt offering (Gen. 22), but the story records that Israel's tradition rejected such human sacrifice. Nevertheless the prophet Micah could still ask the question: 'Shall I give my firstborn for my transgression?' (Mic. 6.7).

The cereal offering could be of raw or baked grain. If raw, a handful of the flour was taken by the priests and burnt with oil and frankincense. The rest could be eaten by the priests. If cooked, the flour had to be baked with oil into unleavened bread. Some loaves were burnt on the altar; the rest were used by the priests. All cereal offerings had to be offered with salt and no leaven or honey was permitted because these were agents of fermentation and therefore unclean. There was also a firstfruits offering of grain, offered with oil and frankincense.

The 'peace offering' (Lev. 3.1—17; 7.11—18) is also called simply a 'sacrifice' (to distinguish it from a burnt offering). It was a meal shared between the Lord and his people. There were three types: the praise offering (Lev. 7.12—15), the freewill offering (Lev. 7.16—17), and the votive offering (Lev. 7.16—17). The animal could be any from the flock or herd, male or female. The worshipper put his hands on the animal's head, killed it and gave its blood to the priests to throw round the altar. The fat of the animal, including the kidneys, the liver and the fat tail of a sheep, were burnt. All fat, like blood, belonged to the Lord (Lev. 3.16—17). The breast and the right thigh of the animal were the priests' portion and the rest of the meat was to be cooked and eaten by the worshipper, his family and guests. A praise offering had to be accompanied by leavened and unleavened bread, one loaf of which was the priests' portion (Lev. 7.14), and the meat had to be consumed on the day it was offered. The other types of peace offering could be eaten on the following day, but on the third day anything left over had to be burnt.

THE HOUSE OF THE LORD

There is a full description of one of these sacrifices in 1 Sam. 2.12—17. The worshipper offered his sacrifice, burnt the fat and then boiled the meat in a cauldron. The priests' servant came to claim the priests' portion. The priests at Shiloh, however (and this is the point of this story) had been abusing their position, and had not even permitted the fat of the offering to be burnt. Solomon offered 'sacrifices' when the temple was consecrated. Huge numbers of animals were offered so that all the people present for the occasion could take part in the festive meal. (The numbers, however, have probably grown as the story was retold.) The king offered the burnt offering, the cereal offering and the fat of the peace offering on the great bronze altar which was too small for the occasion. The temple court was also used. (1 Kings 8.62—4). This type of offering appears in the prophets: '"What to me is the multitude of your sacrifices?" says the Lord; I have had enough of burnt offerings of rams and the fat of fed beasts' (Isa. 1.11; cf. Isa. 19.21; Amos 4.4). It is mentioned in the most ancient lawcode, the Book of the Covenant: 'You shall not offer the blood of my sacrifice with leavened bread, or let the fat of my feast remain until the morning' (Exod. 23.18). Sometimes they are called 'peace offerings'; 'David offered burnt offerings and peace offerings before the Lord' when the ark was brought to Jerusalem. He then gave food to all the people present, 'a cake of bread, a portion of meat and a cake of raisins' (2 Sam. 6.17—19). The Book of the Covenant also uses this term: 'An altar of earth you shall make for me and sacrifice on it your burnt offerings and your peace offerings' (Exod. 20.24). The combined form 'sacrifice of peace offering' is used mainly in the Priestly writings, e.g. Lev. 3.1, 'If a man's offering is a sacrifice of peace offering . . .'

The fourth and fifth types of sacrifice can be considered together, since they were very similar: the *ḥatta'th* (RSV 'sin offering') and the *'asham* (RSV 'guilt offering'). There is considerable confusion about them and the distinction between them. The only sins which could be dealt with were unwitting sins; anyone who deliberately sinned could not make a sin offering for expiation (Num. 15.27—31). The characteristic of these sacrifices was that the blood was put on the horns of the altar and the rest poured out at its base. All the fat of the animal was burnt, and the meat was eaten by the priests except when the sin offering was for a priest. In this case the animal had to be burnt outside the sanctuary on the ash heap. The type of animal offered depended on the status of the person who had sinned; the high priest had to offer a bull, the whole people had to offer a bull, the leader of the community had to offer a he-goat and anyone else offered a sheep or a she-goat. The poor could offer turtle doves or pigeons. If a bull was offered, for the sin of the high priest or for the whole people, the blood was collected and taken into the temple itself, the only time that any part of an animal sacrifice was taken inside. The blood was sprinkled seven times on the veil of the *debir*, and on the horns of the altar of incense (Lev. 4.17); the remainder was poured at the foot of the great altar before the animal was burnt. If a sheep or goat was offered, the blood was not taken inside the temple, and the meat was eaten by the priests. The *'asham*, guilt offering, was a similar rite, but was accompanied by payment of damages, if these could be estimated. A ram was offered, and the fine, plus one fifth for the priests, was paid.

It is not known if these sacrifices were ancient or not. They appear to be mentioned in the time of King Jehoash (802–786). The money from the guilt offerings and sin offerings, we are told, was given to the priests and not used for the repair of the temple (2 Kings 12.16). Hosea also mentions priests who fed on the *ḥatta'th* of the people, presumably the sin offerings (Hos. 4.8). The first time they are clearly mentioned is in Ezekiel (40.39; 42.13; 44.29) but he does not introduce them as though they were something new. It is more likely that he was describing a system with which he was familiar. The sin offering, mentioned in Isa. 53.10, of the Suffering Servant is the *'asham*, the guilt offering of the ram.

There were also the daily services of the temple. Numbers 28.2–8 describes the morning and evening sacrifices, the 'perpetual' (*tamid*) offerings which were 'taken away' from the Lord during the persecution which preceded the Maccabean revolt (Dan. 8.11, 13; 11.29). The Mishnah gives a glimpse of the daily life of the second temple as it describes how the *tamid* was to be offered. The priests, it says, slept on mattresses with their holy garments folded up under their heads. Before daybreak they were awakened by the temple officers who had the keys to the temple court. Duties were assigned by lot, and whoever had to clear the altar ashes washed his hands and feet in the great laver before climbing to the top of the altar carrying a silver firepan for the cinders. He worked in the twilight by the light of the fire which was still burning. Other priests followed with rakes and shovels to clear the ashes and save any pieces of offerings which had remained unburnt from the previous day. A new pile of wood was laid for the fire on the eastern side of the altar. There are various traditions about the wood: in the second century BC cypress, bay, almond, fir, pine, cedar, savin, fig, olive, myrrh, laurel and aspalathus were permitted and no others (Jub. 21.12); the Mishnah says that any wood but vine and olive was permitted. Another pile of wood was prepared in the southwest corner of the altar, fig wood this time to provide the hot charcoal necessary for burning incense (Mishnah, *Tamid* 2.3). No split or dark wood was permitted for the altar fires, but only what was hard and clean; nor could old wood be used, for it had no fragrance (Jub. 21.13). Both fires were relit and the unburnt offering replaced on the fire. The wood for all these fires was kept in a special chamber at the north-east corner of the court of women. Priests who had become ritually unfit for offering sacrifices were seconded to the wood shed where their duty was to examine the wood for worms 'since any wood wherein was found a worm was invalid' (Mishnah, *Middoth* 2.5).

The priests then returned to their chambers to cast lots for their other duties.

> The officer said to them, 'Come and cast lots', [to decide] which of them should slaughter, which should sprinkle the blood, which should clear the inner Altar of ashes, which should trim the Candlestick, and which should take up the Ramp the members [of the Daily Whole Offering namely] the head and the right hind leg, and the two fore legs, the rump and the [left] hind leg, the breast and the neck, and the two flanks, the inwards and the fine flour, the Baken Cakes and the wine. (Mishnah, *Tamid* 3.1)

Someone was sent to see if the dawn had come; if he could say, 'The whole east is alight as far as Hebron', the sacrifice could begin. A lamb was brought from the chamber of lambs and given a drink from a golden cup. It was inspected by torchlight to make sure that it had no impurities. The lamb was then taken to the slaughtering area north of the altar. Its blood was saved and splashed on the altar from two points; from the north-east corner it was splashed on the north and east faces, and from the opposite corner on the other two faces. The rest of the blood was poured out at the base of the altar. The animal was skinned, dismembered and the entrails washed. It was divided between six priests who took it to the altar, followed by priests carrying the fine flour, the baked cakes and the wine.

Lots were also cast for the duties inside the temple; the ashes had to be cleared from the incense altar and the great lamp refuelled. Fresh coals from the fig wood fire were then carried in a golden bowl and placed on the incense altar. Everyone in the temple area stopped to pray at the moment of the incense offering. When the priests emerged, they blessed the people from the temple steps. (This is the setting of Luke 1.8−10, when Zechariah went to burn incense and saw the angel by the altar.)

In the time of the first temple there was a burnt offering only in the morning, and a cereal offering in the evening; 2 Kings 16.15 describes the morning burnt offering and the evening cereal offering. 'The time of the cereal offering' meant the late afternoon (Ezra 9.5; Dan. 9.21). By New Testament times there were burnt offerings both morning and evening, the latter being killed at about half past two and offered an hour later (Mishnah, *Pesaḥim* 5.1). On the Sabbath there were additional offerings. Num. 28.9−10 suggests that the Sabbath offering had to be double that on any other day; '*two* male lambs a year old without blemish, *two* tenths of an ephah of fine flour . . .'.

The Passover

In the spring and autumn (originally at the time of the equinoxes, perhaps), there were two other great sacrifices, Passover and the Day of Atonement. Passover is said to have originated in Israel's nomadic days, and therefore to have been a domestic sacrifice rather than a temple ceremony, but nobody can be certain about this. A male sheep or goat less than a year old was sacrificed on the fourteenth day of the first month, i.e. at the time of the full moon. Its blood was daubed on the doorposts and its flesh eaten with herbs and unleavened bread. The animal was roasted whole and anything left over had to be burnt (Exod. 12.1−10). When the cult was centralized at the time of King Josiah's reform, it seems that Passover was made a pilgrimage feast, one to be celebrated in Jerusalem rather than at home. The most ancient list of pilgrimage feasts describes only the three harvest festivals; 'unleavened' bread (the barley harvest), 'harvest' (the wheat harvest), and 'ingathering' (the grape harvest) (Exod. 23.14—17). Passover was not included. At some stage Passover and the feast of unleavened bread were fused together, with the result that the character of the Passover altered. The Passover kept in the time of King Josiah was certainly different: 'For no such Passover had been kept since the days of the judges who judged Israel, or during all the days of the kings of Israel or of the kings of Judah' (2 Kings 23.22). The Chronicler tells a different tale; he says that there was a great temple Passover held one month late in the time of the first temple reformer, King Hezekiah (2 Chron. 30). The detail of the late Passover has a ring of authenticity, but how can one then account for the statement in 2 Kings?

By New Testament times the Passover was established as a pilgrimage festival. All those who were able to get to Jerusalem for the feast purchased their lambs and took them to the temple to be sacrificed there. Coping with such huge numbers of animals called for considerable organization. There were three separate sessions: the first group came into the temple court with their lambs and the doors of the court were closed. All the priests stood in rows carrying silver or golden bowls. There was no flat bottom to the bowls, so that they could not be put down and the blood left to congeal. There were three blasts on the ram's horn trumpets. As each man killed his own lamb, so a priest caught the blood and passed it by a chain of waiting priests to the altar where it was poured out at the base. The levites sang the Hallel Psalms (Pss. 113—118). The animals were then skinned and the sacrificial portions removed, as prescribed for the peace offering in Lev. 3.3—4. The first group left the temple court and were followed by the second and the third. All who had sacrificed lambs stayed within the temple precincts until nightfall, when they went to their homes or lodging places to roast and eat the feast (Mishnah, *Pesaḥim* 5.5—10).

Josephus has left an account of the huge numbers who attended these festivals. The final siege of Jerusalem by the Romans began during the time of the feast, with the result that huge numbers of pilgrims were trapped. Speaking of the ninety-seven thousand prisoners taken he says:

> Of these the greater number were of Jewish blood, but not natives of the place; for, having assembled from every part of

> the country for the feast of unleavened bread, they found themselves suddenly enveloped in the war, with the result that this overcrowding produced first pestilence and later the more rapid scourge of famine. That the city could contain so many is clear from the count made under Cestus ... On the occasion of the feast called Passover, at which they sacrifice from the ninth to the eleventh hour, and a little fraternity, as it were, gathers around each sacrifice, of not fewer than ten persons (feasting alone not being permitted), while the companies often included as many as twenty, the victims were counted and amounted to two hundred and fifty five thousand six hundred; allowing on average ten diners to each victim, we obtain a total of two million seven hundred thousand, all pure and holy. (*War*, VI. 420—5)

The blood of the lamb in the original account of the Passover had been painted on the doorposts to protect Israel from destruction (Exod. 12.13). A careful reading of this chapter shows that the destroying angel was the Lord. The blood of the Passover lambs thrown on the altar may have had a similar function, to protect Israel from the divine wrath.

After the Passover came the offering of the firstfruits. Leviticus says that the first sheaf of the harvest was to be brought to the priest, 'and he shall wave the sheaf before the Lord, that you may find acceptance; on the morrow after the Sabbath the priest shall wave it' (Lev. 23.11). Problems arose in later times as to when this sheaf was to be offered. The old regulations had presupposed that the feast of unleavened bread would begin on a Sabbath, which would have meant offering the sheaf on the first day of the next week. When the feast of unleavened bread was joined to the Passover, however, it could no longer start on the Sabbath since the date of Passover was determined by the moon and could fall on any day of the week. The Pharisees and Boethuseans (a Sadducean party) argued about the interpretation but reached no conclusion.

The firstfruits passed into Christian symbolism as a description of the resurrection. Easter Sunday would have been the day after the Sabbath which followed Passover, and so the risen Jesus was seen as 'the first fruits of those who have fallen asleep' (1 Cor. 15.20), the first offering which rendered the whole harvest pure (Rom. 11.16). Those who had been 'redeemed from mankind, as first fruits for God and the Lamb' (Rev. 14.4) would then represent not the total number of the elect, the exclusive few, but rather the representative offering which consecrated all mankind.

Some modern translations use a different word in these verses and in so doing cut the text off from much of its meaning. Temple imagery here, as in so many other places, has no modern equivalent; we have to explore the original image in order to grasp the meaning. There are no short cuts; simplified translations can impoverish and trivialize the New Testament.

The Day of Atonement

The earliest account of the rituals for the Day of Atonement is in Leviticus. First lots were cast over two goats; one was chosen 'for the Lord' and the other was 'for Azazel'. The latter is usually called the scapegoat (Lev. 16.8). Then a bull was offered as a sin offering by the high priest, for himself and all the other priests. He took incense into the *debir* and burnt it in front of the ark, before returning with the bull's blood. This was sprinkled seven times 'on the front of the mercy seat and before the mercy seat' (Lev. 16.14). The goat 'for the Lord' was then killed as a sin offering for the people, and its blood, too, was taken into the *debir* and sprinkled like that of the bull. None but the high priest was allowed into the temple when this was being done. Some of the blood was put on the horns of the golden altar of incense. The ritual atoned for the priests and people, but also for the holy place and the altar (Lev. 16.17, 18). The fact that it made atonement for places as well as people indicates that more was involved than just the 'forgiveness of sins' as that is understood today. The ritual made everything clean and holy again (Lev. 16.19), showing that the rite was one of restoring and renewing. When he emerged, the high priest put his hands onto the head of the goat for Azazel and by this act laid upon him all the sins of Israel. The goat was then driven into the desert, bearing all the sins 'to a solitary land' (Lev. 16.22).

Nobody knows the original significance of this ritual. Primitive though it seems to be, there is no reference to it in the earliest parts of the Old Testament. The prophets do not mention the Day of Atonement; only Ezekiel has anything which even resembles it. He describes a purification ritual involving a young bull, but says that it was to be performed twice a year, at the beginning of the first and seventh months. The blood was to purify the sanctuary, and be put on the doorposts of the temple, the corners of the altar and the posts of the gate to the inner courtyard (Ezek. 45.18—20). There is no reference to the two goats. The exiles offered several types of sacrifice in the autumn after they returned, but the Day of Atonement is not mentioned (Ezra 3.1—6).

One of the oldest parts of 1 Enoch, however, may afford a clue. Since the rituals described in Leviticus are thought to be those of the second temple, and this part of 1 Enoch is at least as old as the third century BC, the two texts were contemporary. Furthermore, 1 Enoch claims that the innovations of the second temple were impure, implying that the traditions of those who transmitted 1 Enoch were those of the older temple. The myth in 1 Enoch may have given rise to the ritual of Leviticus, which, like so many features of the older cult, was cut adrift by the upheavals both of the exile and of the reforming Deuteronomists. 1 Enoch says that evil was caused by angels who rebelled against the Great Holy One and came to earth. They abused their knowledge of heavenly secrets, and thus corrupted the creation, causing both human sin and human misery in the process. 1 Enoch 10 describes the first punishment of these fallen angels. The Most High, the Great and Holy One, sent his archangels to rescue the world from the dominion of the evil ones, one of whom was Azazel. Since he was the first to be punished and was blamed for all evil (1 Enoch 10.9), Azazel was probably the chief of the fallen angels.

> And secondly the Lord said to Raphael, 'Bind Azazel hand and foot [and] throw him into the darkness!' And he made a hole in the desert which was in Dudael and cast him there; he threw on top of him rugged and sharp rocks. And he covered his face in order that he may not see light, and in order that he may be sent into the fire on the great day of judgement. And give life to the earth which the angels have corrupted. (1 Enoch 10.4—7)

'Raphael' means 'God heals'; the ritual of the Day of Atonement was also one of healing and cleansing. Did that ritual depict the banishment of the evil one, symbolized by the goat for Azazel, and the restoration of the earth, symbolized by the purification of the temple effected by the bull and the goat for the Lord? One of the ancient Palestinian Targums, *Pseudo-Jonathan*, said of Lev. 16.21—2 that the goat was taken to Beth Chadure, which is believed to be the original name behind the 'Dudael' in the Ethiopic of 1 Enoch. (The difference is due to d and r looking very similar in Hebrew.) In other words, later legends remembered that the goat bearing the sins of Israel was sent to the place where Azazel was imprisoned; the binding of Azazel and the banishing of the scapegoat were, perhaps, the belief and its expression in ritual.

The Mishnah describes the rituals as they were in the first century AD. When the lots had been cast over the goats, a thread of crimson wool was bound on the head of the goat for Azazel. After the bullock had been slaughtered as the sin offering for the priests, the blood was collected and someone was chosen to stir it so that it did not start to congeal before the rituals could be completed. The high priest first took incense into the *debir*, passing between the two curtains. (The text says that there were two curtains before the holy place at that time, each extending the full width of the *debir*, with a space of one cubit between them.) Once in the sanctuary, he placed the fire pan of glowing charcoal on the *eben sh'tiyyah*, a great stone which stood 'higher than the ground by three fingerbreadths' (Mishnah, *Yoma* 5.2). Then he put incense onto the coals, and the whole place was filled with smoke. He went out and brought the blood into the *debir* where it was sprinkled seven times. Then the goat 'for the Lord' was killed and its blood sprinkled in the same way. When he had come out of the holy place this third time, the high priest sprinkled the blood on the curtain of the sanctuary, and then on the horns and top surface of the altar of incense. Any remaining blood was poured at the base of the great altar in the temple court. The high priest placed his hands on the head of the goat for Azazel, confessed the sins of the people and handed the goat over to those who were to lead it away. There was a causeway from the eastern gate of the temple over to the Mount of Olives, whence a special path, marked by ten halts, led out into the wilderness. If possible, the goat was led by a foreigner who was provided with refreshment at the stopping places. He went alone beyond the last place, and when he reached the appointed ravine, he took the crimson wool and tore it in half; one piece was tied to the rock and the other to the horns of the goat. The animal was pushed over the precipice, and the man who had done the deed, by this time rendered unclean through contact with the sin-bearing animal, returned to the tenth place where he remained. News that the deed was done was signalled back from halt to halt by waving flags. Meanwhile the high priest had dealt with the carcases of the sin offerings; the fat pieces of the beasts were offered on the altar, and the remainder was taken outside the temple and burnt.

The Epistle to the Hebrews offers another first-century account of the Day of Atonement (Heb. 8—9), but also an indication of what the ritual depicted. Like the Songs of the Sabbath Sacrifice, this epistle envisages a heavenly temple of which the earthly one is but a copy. The rituals of the Day of Atonement were the annual means by which the mediator was enabled to enter, briefly, the divine presence in the holy place, and thereby effect a temporary restoration of the creation to purity and wholeness. What we do not know is the heavenly reality, the 'myth' which was thought to underlie these rituals of restoration. The banishing of Azazel described in 1 Enoch accounts only for the goat sent into the wilderness; we still have to find a reason for the blood taken into the sanctuary. Is it possible that there is a hint of it in the ancient Song of Moses (Deut. 32.1—43) describing the power of the Lord? It says: 'He avenges the blood of his servants, and takes vengeance on his adversaries, and makes expiation (atonement) for the land of his people' (Deut. 32.43). Making atonement for the land of his people was one of the roles of the Lord. Were the adversaries in this song superhuman foes like those whom Jesus defeated (Col. 2.15)? Did the high priest enact a more than human role when he entered the divine presence to make expiation? Was he the earthly counterpart of the Lord in heaven? These are all questions to which there is no certain answer, but it does look as though the writer to the Hebrews was claiming that Jesus made real one of the ancient roles of the Lord. Many later texts *do* suggest that the high priest represented the visible presence of the Lord (see Chapter 3).

Jesus was also compared to the scapegoat. The Epistle of Barnabas has an early Christian commentary on the ritual.

> Now what does that signify? Notice that the first goat is for the altar, and the other is accursed; and that it is the accursed

one that wears the wreath. That is because they shall see him on that Day clad to the ankles in his red woollen robe, and will say, 'Is not this he whom we once crucified, and mocked and pierced and spat upon? Yes, this is the man who told us that he was the Son of God. But how will he resemble the goat? The point of there being two similar goats, both of them being fair and alike, is that when they see him coming on the Day, they are going to be struck with terror at the manifest parallel between him and the goat. In this ordinance, then, you are to see typified the future sufferings of Jesus. (Ep. Barnabas 7)

The Music of the Temple

Music was an important part of worship in the temple. The Songs of the Sabbath Sacrifice show that heavenly worship was the song of countless angels around the divine throne and their songs accompanied the sacrifices of the Sabbath. Worship in the temple was the counterpart of this heavenly liturgy, and thus the role of the singers was very important especially at the time of sacrifice. The Psalms were the hymns of the temple, and some of them indicate sacrifices as their original setting.

> May he remember all your offerings
> and regard with favour your burnt offerings. (Ps. 20.3)

> I wash my hands in innocence
> and go about thy altar, O Lord. (Ps. 26.6)

> I will come into thy house with burnt offerings;
> I will pay thee my vows ... (Ps. 66.13; cf. Pss. 107.22; 116.17)

The fullest picture of a sacrifice and its music in the Old Testament is recorded by the Chronicler, but this raises problems. Although the description is of the rededication of the temple in the time of King Hezekiah, it is usually thought to have been influenced by what the writer knew of the temple in his own day, several centuries later. The passage may well be a more accurate description of a sacrifice in the second temple than of one in the first.

> Then Hezekiah commanded that the burnt offering be offered on the altar. And when the burnt offering began, the song to the Lord began also, and the trumpets, accompanied by the

> instruments of David king of Israel. The whole assembly worshipped, and the singers sang, and the trumpeters sounded; all this continued until the burnt offering was finished. When the offering was finished, the king and all who were present with him bowed themselves and worshipped. And Hezekiah the king and the princes commanded the Levites to sing praises to the Lord with the words of David and of Asaph the seer. And they sang praises with gladness, and they bowed down and worshipped. (2 Chron. 29.27—30)

Other psalms list musical instruments, although it is not always possible to know exactly what each of these was; Ps. 150 lists trumpets, lutes, harps, strings, pipes, and two types of cymbals. Ps. 81.2—3 lists timbrel, lyre, harp and trumpet.

The origin of the music and the temple singers is not known. David brought the ark to Jerusalem with a musical procession, with 'songs and lyres and harps and tambourines and castanets and cymbals' (2 Sam. 6.5). There is, however, no mention of music in this writer's account of the dedication of Solomon's temple. A comparison with the Chronicler's account shows clearly that the latter had a great interest in the temple music, and mentioned it on occasions when the other account did not. Thus the Chronicler's account of the temple dedication included the information that

> all the Levitical singers, Asaph, Heman and Jeduthun, their sons and kinsmen, arrayed in fine linen, with cymbals, harps and lyres, stood east of the altar with one hundred and twenty priests who were trumpeters; and it was the duty of the trumpeters and singers to make themselves heard in unison in praise and thanksgiving to the Lord. (2 Chron. 5.11—13)

After the king's great prayer, when the sacrifices were offered, there was singing and the sound of trumpets (2 Chron. 7.6). Amos knew of such music to accompany sacrifices in the older shrines; he approved of neither the sacrifices nor the music: 'Take away from me the noise of your songs; to the melody of your harps I will not listen' (Amos 5.23).

There were three great families of temple singers, and their role in the temple was hereditary as was that of the priests. Heman, Asaph and Ethan are named as the heads of these families (1 Chron. 6.31—47). They lived in chambers in the temple and were on duty day and night (1 Chron. 9.33). One of their duties was to *'prophesy* with lyres, with harps and with cymbals' (1 Chron. 25.1). They had previously been the musicians installed by David to sing in front of the tabernacle of the tent of meeting, before Solomon had built a temple to house the ark (1 Chron. 6.31; cf. 1 Chron. 16.4—6). What they did when they prophesied can probably be deduced from the story of Saul and the prophets. Saul met a band of prophets coming down from their sanctuary 'prophesying' to the sound of 'harp, tambourine, flute and lyre' (1 Sam. 10.5). The spirit of the Lord came upon Saul; he joined in the prophesying and was 'turned into another man' (1 Sam. 10.6). This implies some sort of trance state in which the prophet received divine guidance. Elisha also prophesied in this way: 'When the minstrel played the power of the Lord came upon him. And he said, "Thus says the Lord..."' (2 Kings 3.15—16).

A state of induced trance associated with the prophets and also apparently with the temple singers, who prophesied with their music before the Lord, may account for some of the descriptions in later texts of mystical journeys and visions in a temple setting. Heavenly music, the song of the angels, was a common feature of these texts. Heman was the king's seer (1 Chron. 25.5), Asaph was a seer (2 Chron. 29.29) and some have even suggested that the writing prophets of the Old Testament were temple priests and prophesied in that role. Isaiah certainly had his call vision in the temple (Isa. 6); Jeremiah (Jer. 1.1) and Ezekiel (Ezek. 1.3) were both priests. Several other prophets have the Day of the Lord as their theme or setting, and, since the temple was the scene of this expected judgement, these too may have been temple prophets, basing their oracles on some liturgy now lost to us. Among these temple prophets one would put Joel, Nahum, Habakkuk and Zephaniah. Zechariah too has a temple setting (the high priest, Zech. 3.1; the lampstand 4.2). It is pointless to be dogmatic; since we know all too little about the liturgies of the first temple, we cannot say what did or did not influence the prophets. All we can do is note the frequency with which the temple theme appears in the work of the prophets and the curious information that the temple singers were seers and they prophesied.

The Mishnah gives several practical details about the temple music. The levites used to sing on the fifteen steps which led from the court of women to the court of Israel. Several chambers were built under the court of Israel, opening onto the court of women, and in these the levites used to play harps, lyres, cymbals and other instruments. The arrangement suggests something like an orchestra pit opening onto the court of women, with the choir on the semicircular flight of steps in the middle (Mishnah, *Middoth* 2.5–6). There was a system of signalling down from the court of the priests so that the levites knew when to start singing. When the drink offering was poured at the climax of the early morning sacrifice, 'The Prefect waved the towel and Ben Arza clashed the cymbal and the levites broke forth into singing. When they reached a break in the singing they blew upon the trumpets and the people prostrated themselves; at every break there was a blowing of the trumpet, and at every blowing of the trumpet a prostration' (Mishnah, *Tamid* 7.3). On the first day of the week they sang Ps. 24, on the second Ps. 48, on the third Ps. 82, on the fourth Ps. 94, on the fifth Ps. 81, on the sixth Ps. 93 and on the Sabbath Ps. 92. The levites sang the Hallel psalms (Pss. 113–18) during the slaughter of the Passover lambs (Mishnah, *Pesaḥim* 5.7).

The Letter of Aristeas describes the temple in the second century BC and says that the time of the actual sacrifice was one of complete silence:

> The ministration of the priests is in every way unsurpassed both for its physical endurance and for its orderly and silent service . . . The most complete silence reigns so that one might imagine that there was not a single person present though there are actually seven hundred men engaged in the work, besides the vast number of those who are occupied in bringing up the sacrifices (Letter of Aristeas 92, 95).

Presumably, as the Mishnah says, the singing began *after* the offerings had been placed on the altar. The account of Hezekiah's sacrifice may reflect a different practice, or it may mean that the singing began as the offering began to burn, in which case there would always have been a time of silence during the actual presentation on the altar.

The Revelation of John is set in the heavenly liturgy. He hears the singing of angels after the great sacrifice of the lamb as the elders offer the prayers of the saints in their golden bowls of incense (Rev. 5.6–10). The four living creatures never cease to sing (Rev. 4.8); the twenty-four elders before the throne sing (Rev. 4.11) and the saints sing the song of the Lamb (Rev. 15.3—4).

The End of the Temple

The Jewish wars against Rome culminated in the sack of Jerusalem in AD 70; the destruction of the city was a part of the earliest Christian expectation, and the Gospels record that Jesus himself predicted it. The temple was to be utterly destroyed (Mark 13 and parallels). Jesus had seen the destruction that was to come and he wept over the city before driving the moneylenders out of the temple (Luke 19.41—6). The evil city of Revelation had originally been Jerusalem, the harlot seated upon many waters (Rev. 17.1). She had become drunk with the blood of the saints and with the blood of the martyrs of Jesus (Rev. 17.6). The terrifying picture of destruction was later used of Rome also, but originally it was a description of a city *attacked* by Rome. The ten horns attacked the harlot and made her desolate, devoured her and burned her with fire (Rev. 17.16). This is not the description of the great fire of Rome but of war and deliberate destruction.

The church historian Eusebius, who wrote early in the fourth century, recorded that the fall of the city was a direct result of the martyrdom of James, the brother of Jesus (Eusebius, *The History of the Church*, 2.23). Quoting extracts from Hegesippus and Josephus, he described how Ananus the young high priest, who was a fanatical Sadducee, brought James to trial.

> So he assembled a council of judges and brought before it James, the brother of Jesus known as Christ, and several others, on a charge of breaking the law, and handed them over to be stoned . . . [The destruction of the city] happened to the Jews in requital for James the Righteous, who was a brother of Jesus known as Christ, for though he was the most righteous of men, the Jews put him to death.

(Some of this is from our text of Josephus, *Antiquities* XX, but the second extract is no longer extant except here and in a quotation in Origen.) Eusebius also quoted from a fuller and slightly different account in Hegesippus. James was preaching from the parapet of the temple at the time of the Passover when some Scribes and Pharisees threw him down. He survived the fall, so they stoned and clubbed him to death. 'Such was his martyrdom. He was buried on the spot, by the sanctuary, and his headstone is still there by the sanctuary. He has proved a true witness to Jews and Gentiles alike that Jesus is the Christ. Immediately after this Vespasian began to besiege them.' Terrifying portents announced the end of the temple: there was a strange sword-shaped star which appeared over the city and a comet which lasted for a year; a bright light appeared around the altar and the sanctuary in the small hours of one night in April; a cow about to be sacrificed gave birth to a lamb in the temple court itself; the great eastern gate of the inner court opened of its own accord at midnight and the temple guard had great difficulty in closing it again. On 8 June 'before sunset throughout all parts of the country chariots were seen in the air and armed battalions hurtling through the clouds and encompassing the cities' (Josephus, *War*, VI. 299).

Shortly after this 'at the feast which is called Pentecost, the priests on entering the inner court of the temple by night, as their custom was in the discharge of their ministrations, reported that they were conscious, first of a commotion and a din, and after that of a voice as of a host, "We are departing hence"' (*War*, VI. 299). A prophet named Jesus son of Ananias had appeared in the city and for seven years and five months had proclaimed 'Woe to Jerusalem' until he was finally killed by a missile in the siege.

After a siege which reduced the people to starvation and cannibalism, both city and temple were destroyed. Josephus has left a vivid account of these times, but it is somewhat biased since he wrote to show that the dreadful events had been brought about by an unrepresentative minority of zealots, and that the Romans had acted reasonably under the circumstances. The following passages are all taken from his *Jewish War*, Book VI.

> Titus, now that he saw that his endeavour to spare a foreign temple led only to the injury and slaughter of his troops, issued orders to set the gates on fire (228).
> The troops were by now setting fire to the gates, and the silver melting all around quickly admitted the flames to the woodwork, whence they spread in dense volumes and caught hold of the porticoes. The Jews, seeing the fire encircling

them, were deprived of all energy of body and mind; in utter consternation none attempted to ward off or extinguish the flames; paralysed, they stood and looked on (232—3).
At this moment, one of the soldiers awaiting no orders and with no horror of so dread a deed, but moved by some supernatural impulse, snatched a brand from the burning timber and, hoisted up by one of his comrades, flung the fiery missile through a low golden door, which gave access on the north side to the chambers surrounding the sanctuary. As the flames shot up, a cry as poignant as the tragedy arose from the Jews who flocked to the rescue, lost to all thought of self-preservation, all husbanding of strength, now that the object of all their past vigilance was vanishing (252—3).
On all sides was carnage and flight. Most of the slain were civilians, weak and unarmed people, each butchered where he was caught. Around the altar a pile of corpses was accumulating; down the steps of the sanctuary flowed a stream of blood and the bodies of the victims killed above went sliding to the bottom (259).
During these same days one of the priests named Jesus son of Thebuti, after obtaining a sworn pledge of protection from Caesar, on condition of his delivering up some of the sacred treasures, came out and handed over the wall of the sanctuary two lampstands similar to those deposited in the sanctuary, along with tables, bowls and platters, all of solid gold and very massive; he further delivered up the veils, the high priests' vestments, including the precious stones, and many other articles used in public worship. Furthermore the treasurer of the temple, by name Phineas, being taken prisoner, disclosed the tunics and girdles worn by the priests, an abundance of purple and scarlet kept for necessary repair to the veil of the temple, along with a mass of cinnamon and cassia and a multitude of other spices which they mixed and burnt daily as incense to God (387—90).

The treasures were taken as spoils to Rome where they were carried in a triumphal procession. These extracts are from Book VII:

The spoils in general were borne in promiscuous heaps; but conspicuous above all stood those captured in the temple in Jerusalem. These consisted of a golden table, many talents in weight, and a lampstand likewise made of gold but constructed on a different pattern* from those we use in ordinary life. Affixed to a pedestal was a central shaft, from which there extended slender branches arranged trident fashion, a wrought lamp being attached to the extremity of each branch; of these there were seven, indicating the honour paid to that number among the Jews. After these, and last of all the spoils, was carried a copy of the Jewish Law (148—50).

Josephus continued: 'The triumphal ceremonies being concluded and the empire of the Romans established on the firmest foundation, Vespasian decided to erect a temple of Peace . . . Here he laid up the vessels of gold from the temple of the Jews on which he prided himself; but their Law and the purple hangings of the sanctuary he ordered to be deposited and kept in the palace' (158—62). Such a disaster was devastating; many thinkers tried to explain why God had allowed this to happen to his temple. One book from the time is 2 Baruch, written as though describing the destruction of the city by the Babylonians in the sixth century. The Baruch of the title is Jeremiah's scribe (Jer. 36.32), and he describes a vision not unlike Ezekiel's, when the angels of destruction came upon the temple (Ezek. 9).

> And lo! suddenly a strong wind raised me, and bore me aloft over the wall of Jerusalem. And I beheld, and lo! four angels standing at the four corners of the city, each of them holding a torch of fire in his hands. And another angel began to descend from heaven and said unto them: 'Hold your lamps and do not light them until I tell you. For I am first sent to speak a word to the earth and to place in it what the Lord the Most High has commanded me.' And I saw him descend into the Holy of Holies, and take from thence the veil and the holy ark and the mercy seat and the two tables and the holy raiment of the priests and the altar of incense and the forty-eight precious stones wherewith the priest was adorned and all the holy vessels of the tabernacle. And he spake to the earth with a loud voice:

---

*The Law did not allow anyone to have a seven-branched candlestick in his home; it was a sacred design. The Talmud says: 'A man may not make . . . a candlestick after the design of the candlestick [in the temple]. He may, however, make one with five, six or eight branches, but with seven he may not make one, even though it be of other metal (b.*Menahoth* 28b).

THE HOUSE OF THE LORD

'Earth, earth, earth, hear the word of the mighty God,
And receive what I commit to thee.
And guard them until the last times,
So that, when thou art ordered, thou mayest restore them,
So that strangers may not get possession of them.
For the time comes when Jerusalem also will be delivered for a time,
Until it is said that it is again restored for ever.'
And after these things I heard that angel saying unto those angels who held the lamps:
'Destroy, therefore, and overthrow its wall to its foundations, lest the enemy should boast and say:
"We have overthrown the wall of Zion,
And we have burned the place of the mighty God."'
... Now the angels did as he had commanded them, and when they had broken up the corners of the walls, a voice was heard from the interior of the temple after the wall had fallen, saying:
'Enter ye enemies, and come, ye adversaries;
For he who kept the house has forsaken it.' (2 Bar. 6.3—8.2)

As in the sixth century, the fall of the city was seen as a work of the Lord, not as the triumph of an enemy over Jerusalem. The fall of Jerusalem was the result of sin: 'Hast thou seen all this people are doing to me? ... for this reason behold I bring evil upon this city and upon its inhabitants' (2 Bar. 1.1, 4). Cf. the passage in Lamentations describing the disaster in the sixth century:

> The Lord gave full vent to his wrath,
> he poured out his hot anger;
> and he kindled a fire in Zion,
> which consumed its foundations.
> The kings of the earth did not believe,
> or any of the inhabitants of the world,
> that foe or enemy could enter
> the gates of Jerusalem.
> This was for the sins of her prophets
> and the iniquities of her priests,
> who had shed in the midst of her
> the blood of the righteous. (Lam. 4.11—13)

54 THE GATE OF HEAVEN

2 Baruch adds that the destruction was the beginning of the last judgement;

> Therefore have I now taken away Zion,
> That I may the more speedily visit the world in its season.
> And then I will show thee the judgement of my might,
> And my ways which are unsearchable. (2 Bar. 20.2, 4)

4 Ezra was another book written at this time of disaster; in many ways it resembled 2 Baruch, but it had a more pessimistic outlook. If the disaster had been caused by the sins of the people, what use was it to offer them the hope of a future life, since they would not merit that either? 'Who of the earth born is there that has not transgressed thy covenant? And now I see that the coming Age shall bring delight to few, but torment unto many. For the evil heart has grown up in us, which has estranged us from God and brought us into destruction' (4 Ezra 7.47—8). The destruction of the temple had long been thought of as part of the judgement; Jesus warned his followers that the stones of the temple would be thrown down as the prelude to the last judgement and the coming of the Son of Man (Mark 13.2—37). Luke's version of the discourse is even more specific; no stone of the temple would be left standing and armies would surround Jerusalem (Luke 21.5—36). Some scholars have doubted that such a detailed hope for the end of the city could have been part of the earliest Christian traditions, and prefer to think that it was added after the actual end of Jerusalem, as a way of explaining the disaster. But 1 Enoch, written some two centuries before the Gospels, describes the destruction of the temple as the climax of the judgement:

> Then I stood still looking at that ancient house being transformed: all the pillars and all the columns were pulled out; and the ornaments of that house were packed and taken out together with them and abandoned in a certain place in the south of the land. I went on seeing until the Lord of the sheep brought about a new house, greater and loftier than the first one, and set it up in the first location which had been covered up; all its pillars were new, the columns new; and the ornaments new as well as greater than those of the first. (1 Enoch 90.28—9)

THE HOUSE OF THE LORD 55

Mysteries surround the ultimate fate of the treasures from the temple. Josephus says that he was given some holy books:

> Again, when Jerusalem was on the point of being carried by assault, Titus Caesar repeatedly urged me to take whatever I would from the wreck of my country, stating that I had his permission. And, now that my native place had fallen, having nothing more precious to take as a solace for my personal misfortunes, I made request to Titus for the freedom of some of my countrymen; I also received by his gracious favour a gift of sacred books. (*Life*, 417–18)

In 1952 archaeologists found at Qumran a copper scroll (3Q15). It was in a poor state, but, when it was eventually unrolled, proved to be a list of sixty-four hiding places in Jerusalem and elsewhere in which gold, silver, spices, scrolls, etc. were buried. Enormous sums are described; one estimate is that over three thousand talents of silver and one thousand three hundred talents of gold were deposited, together with gold bars, six hundred and eight pitchers of silver, and hundreds of gold and silver vessels. In all it is estimated that there were twenty-six tons of gold and sixty-five tons of silver. Some scholars think that the scroll was a work of fiction; others have said that it was too detailed and sober an account to have been fiction. The hoard could have been the temple treasure, or perhaps funds collected to rebuild the temple.

In 410, Rome was sacked by the Visigoths under Alaric. A history of the times records that he had taken, as part of the booty, 'the treasures of Solomon the King of the Hebrews, a most noteworthy sight. For the most of them were adorned with emeralds; and they had been taken from Jerusalem by the Romans in ancient time' (Procopius, *History of the Wars*, V. xii.41). The Jews observed perpetual mourning; the Babylonian Talmud says: 'When the temple was destroyed for the second time, large numbers in Israel became ascetics, binding themselves neither to eat meat nor to drink wine.' They were advised that this was too extreme, and a middle way was adopted:

> Not to mourn at all is impossible, because the blow has fallen. To mourn overmuch is also impossible because we do not impose on the community a hardship which the majority cannot endure . . . The Sages therefore ordained thus. A man

may stucco his house but he should leave a little bare . . . A man may prepare a full-course banquet, but he should leave out an item or two . . . A woman can put on all her ornaments, but leave off one or two . . . For so it says, 'If I forget thee O Jerusalem, let my right hand forget, let my tongue cleave to the roof of my mouth if I remember thee not, if I prefer not Jerusalem above my chief joy.' (*Baba Bathra* 60b)

CHAPTER TWO

THE GARDEN

Solomon built the temple as a garden sanctuary; the walls of the *hekal* were decorated with golden palm trees and flowers, set with precious stones; the bronze pillars were decorated with pomegranate patterns and the great lamp was a stylized almond tree. But the temple was also built in accordance with a heavenly plan to represent on earth the garden of God. 'On earth as it is in heaven' could well describe both the structure of the temple and its rituals. The Garden of Eden was the first dry land created in the midst of the primeval waters and so the temple was the centre of the created order and the key to its wellbeing. The presence of the temple, as we have seen, was believed to suppress and control the waters deep underground which threatened the creation, and yet from the garden of Eden there flowed other waters in the four rivers which gave life to the creation. These rivers appear in the mythology of the temple where they were wisdom flowing from the divine throne to renew the creation. It may well be that the streams of life and the suppression of the threatening waters are an expression of the highly sophisticated attitude to wisdom which is expressed elsewhere in the myth of the fallen angels; wisdom apart from God is the cause of evil and destruction.

As we explore the significance of the garden temple, we find ourselves led onto many paths, back and forth through ancient texts. A remarkably consistent picture emerges of beliefs about the created world, the role of the Messiah in the restoration of the creation, the role of the Spirit as the bringer of life and the way in which the Lord was thought to be present with his people.

The temple is like an ancient tapestry; in some parts the picture has faded, in others the threads are no longer clear. In the remaining part of this book I shall try to explain how some of the threads were woven together. This is a destructive process in the first instance, examining individual threads in a great work of art. To appreciate the temple and its symbolism as a whole, one must stand back at the end of the process of examination and let all the images blend together again.

Time and Place

> Change and decay in all around I see,
> O thou who changest not abide with me.
>
> H. F. Lyte

How did the temple function? To answer this question it is necessary to look at the traditions associated with it. What stories were told of the temple? What happened there? By this I do not mean: What did the high priests do? or, How were sacrifices performed? but, What were the beliefs which gave rise to those stories and those actions? In order to understand how the temple functioned we must first look at how those who worshipped there understood space and time. Modern ideas of space and time are very different, and if we are not aware of this, everything about the temple seems strange and almost ridiculous. It is impossible to understand the temple using twentieth-century post-enlightenment ways of thinking and it is of little value to study the temple simply as a marvel of ancient architecture or the setting for colourful ritual. The point of studying a temple is to understand what was being expressed there. We have to try to stand where they stood, think as they thought, look where they looked, and then, perhaps, we shall glimpse what they saw. What they saw of God and the ways in which they expressed this underlie much early Christian thought. It is only at that point of vision that we can begin to disentangle the 'message' from the manner in which it was expressed.

There are several ways in which this other view of space and time has been described; the commonest is *mythical*. The mythical way of understanding the world presupposed another 'world', beyond what we experience as space and time, which both explained and determined our world. Experience of the material world is made possible by our perception of the three dimensions of space and solidity, i.e. an object or a place has

THE GARDEN 59

length, breadth and height; and by the dimension of time, i.e. how long something lasts. The mythical world envisages another manner of being, a dimension in which there is neither spatial limitation nor time in our sense, but one which shares with this world the invisible forces of love, hate, obedience, rebellion and so forth. This other world is often called Eternity, which does not mean an unbelievably long span of time but rather an existence *without* time, something which, because it lies outside our experience of time, actually underlies in its entirety every perception that we have of time. It could perhaps be called a belief in certain basic principles on which the world was based, principles which could be compared to the laws of science in that they were used to interpret the experiences of life and to predict what was likely to happen. In the same way eternal space was present in its entirety in any one sacred place and so the temple, an area of some three hundred square metres, represented the whole world.

These underlying principles covered both the natural and the moral order, but instead of being expressed in formulae or dogma, they were expressed in stories or visions. We need two separate words here, but the Hebrews had one word *parable* which covered both. A parable could be a story with another meaning or it could be a vision of the heavenly world which corresponded to or represented (that is the basic meaning of parable/*mashal* in the Hebrew) a situation on earth. Of course such a comparison with scientific laws cannot be pressed too far; but it is likely that these structuring stories and visions originated in observation of the natural and moral order, because they dealt with scientific subjects such as astronomy as well as theological issues like the origin of evil. They were modified in the light of experience. One of the most important myths described the fall of the angels from heaven but it had at least two quite different forms: one said that the heavenly knowledge brought to earth by the angels was fundamentally evil (this is the version in 1 Enoch 6–11); the other said that it was good but abused by human kind (this is the version in Jubilees 4). Here we have an observed situation; it was agreed that heavenly knowledge resulted in evil on earth, but was this due to the knowledge itself or to those who used it? The disagreement was expressed in different versions of the one myth. This important myth appears in the Old Testament only at Genesis 6, where there is a brief account which scholars have long suspected was the residue of something longer. The same is true of all the myths; only traces are left in the canonical texts, sometimes as no more than a figure of speech. Some have argued that these 'traces' were the basic material upon which the later mythology grew and that early Israel had no real mythology. A study of temple texts, however, makes a 'late mythology' view unlikely. The temple was the centre and setting of their complex mythology, and those who reformed the temple and its cult are more likely to have removed the mythology than to have encouraged the growth of something which had formerly not existed.

The myth of the garden of Eden also exists in two forms (Ezek. 28 and Gen. 2–3), showing that it was reworked to cope with altered circumstances. The post-exilic teachers emphasized individual responsibility, essential for a culture based upon the keeping of the Law. Eden had formerly been a tale of the fall from heaven, a myth. It became the story of the first human sin, history. There will be several points at which a comparable process is seen as the temple is explored. Myth became history and its function changed. It dealt with the past and no longer with the present. If the myths and symbols of the ancient temple are viewed in this way, as a description of the eternal present, they begin to seem less bizarre.

Once a basic principle for the understanding of life had been expressed in story or picture form, it was possible by ritual to interact with this story or vision and to make it 'work' for the worshipper. Conversely, neglect of these things led to disaster. Religious observance was not an optional extra; it was a vital part of maintaining the fabric of the created order. The form that this interaction should take was debated; should it be ritual and sacrifice, or should it be the keeping of various divine commands? The result of failure was the same in each case. Neglect resulted in disaster. Joel illustrates this dilemma well; in a time of drought (Joel 1.17) the people had opted for temple rituals (Joel 1.9, 13–14), but the prophet had said it was divine commands which had been broken: 'Rend your hearts and not your garments' (Joel 2.13). We tend to opt for the prophet's point of view, but the majority of his hearers probably opted for the rituals. Why else did the prophets speak out and why else were their words traditionally ignored?

The temple in Jerusalem was in mythical space and time. It was not just a highly decorated building, but rather a place where the eternal and the earthly were one. The decorations represented the heavenly world, but it was more than just representation. In some respects the temple *was* the heavenly world, and there are several instances where the decorations of the temple actually came alive; e.g. in the Songs of the Sabbath Sacrifice the angel figures on the temple walls are alive because the songs describe the heavenly temple. Nor is it always possible to know whether the setting is the earthly temple or the heavenly court of the Holy One, due to the fact that, whereas we always want to separate heaven and earth, the ancient writers did not. The rituals of the temple were performed on earth but were a part of an eternal, heavenly reality. Thus space and location were ambiguous. Time was similarly ambiguous; the stories which we read as having taken place in time, albeit in the remotest past, were believed by them to be another aspect of the present, perpetually there. The myths were not primitive history, but statements of current principles in symbolic or narrative form. The great complex of myth which describes the fallen angels, for example, was not only understood as a description of some event which had happened once in the past, and its sequel, the last judgement, as something which would only happen once in the future. Both past and future were combined in the one myth. The fall and the judgement had originally been statements of a principle which was believed to underlie the created order, a pattern by which it could be interpreted and understood. Thus in Revelation John hears an angelic voice saying, 'Come up hither and I will show you what must take place after this' (Rev. 4.10). *After this* can also mean *beyond this*, meaning here that John will see what has to happen behind the earthly drama he sees in his own times and this will include what is to happen in the future because it is a glimpse of the eternal. That evil should end was a fundamental principle derived from the belief that God was good; a pagan god who was believed to be powerful but not necessarily good did not give his worshippers the problem of evil. Thus the fall and the judgement were continually being actualized in history, the fallen angels and their judgement were an eternal present. Thus the Second Isaiah spoke as though the judgement had passed (Isa. 40.1–2) but the Third Isaiah saw a judgement yet to come (Isa. 66.6). This idea of the eternal dimension, the beyond which is perpetually present, underlies both the symbolism and myth of the temple, and the actions of the priests in appropriating the stability of the eternal dimension for the benefit of their people. The mediators who passed between the two worlds were vital to the cult.

The temple was the centre, the key point of both space and time; it was the holiest place on earth. The notion of concentric areas of holiness meant that pilgrims travelling to Jerusalem were going up, in both senses, to the presence of God. The holiness of the temple meant that it was a place of purity; everything, as we have seen, had to be perfect and whole. Elaborate preparations, including several ritual washings, were necessary before the high priest could enter the holy of holies wearing a special robe of white linen. Temple personnel could become unclean by contact with anything dead or even by visiting the lavatory. Women who had recently given birth were not allowed into even the outer parts of the sacred place.

Holiness also meant that it was a place of power, and power could be life or death. Wrongly approached it brought death, as happened when Uzzah touched the ark on the way to Jerusalem (2 Sam. 6.6–7), but it also brought supernatural fertility, as in the stories told of the ark's causing dry wood to sprout and golden trees to bear real fruit. In the days of the Messiah, when the relationship between heaven and earth would be restored to its proper state of harmony, the land itself would produce miraculous crops: 'And he who plants a vine upon it will produce wine for plenitude. And every seed that is sown on her, one measure will yield a thousand [measures] and one measure of olives will yield ten measures of presses of oil' (1 Enoch 10.19). Until that time the point of communication had to be maintained with the cult of the temple, which culminated in the awesome blood ritual of the Day of Atonement. Then and only then, in a state of absolute purity, the high priest went into the holy of holies, to the heart of space and time, and there he sprinkled blood, i.e. life. This was the turning of the year, the rite of renewal, the turning of history.

The Melchizedek text from Qumran described the heavenly high priest Melchizedek on the Great Day of Atonement when Ps. 82 would be fulfilled: 'God has taken his place in the divine council; in the midst of the gods he holds judgement' (Ps. 82.1). This means that in New Testament times the rites were still seen as a part of the great day of judgement when the powers of heaven would be judged in the heavenly court. It also shows that God was deemed to act through his high priest Melchizedek. The blood ritual and judgement at the heart of time were followed by the great Feast of Tabernacles and the enthronement of the Lord's anointed in triumph over the judged and defeated powers of evil. This was represented in the Melchizedek text by a quotation from Isaiah: 'How beautiful upon the mountains are the feet of the messenger who proclaims peace, who brings good news, who proclaims salvation, who says to Zion: Your ELOHIM [reign]s' (Isa. 52.7; 11QMelch). After the enthronement the creation was renewed. All this was claimed by the first Christians as giving the truest expression of the meaning of the death and resurrection of Jesus. The fulfilment of the blood ritual was explored in the Epistle to the Hebrews with Jesus as the new Melchizedek, in Col. 2.15 with its assertion that the powers of evil had been defeated, and in Revelation with the ascension, enthronement and renewal of creation.

Since the temple was a statement about the natural order, it was closely associated with the myth of the creation. Again, this was not only a description of how the world was formed long ago, but also a description of how the world was continually formed and maintained. The temple was at the intersection of earth and heaven, and, as such, the first place from which the material world was ordered. In the ancient East this place was usually envisaged as a cosmic mountain which held heaven, earth and underworld together. It was the home of the gods; the temple of the great creator god was built at the top of the cosmic mountain. In the myths of Mesopotamia, for example, Marduk triumphed over the forces of chaos to establish the ordered creation, and his triumph was marked and sealed by the erection of his great temple on the ziggurat, a massive artificial mountain (Gray, *N.E.M.*, p. 32). The holiest place in Egyptian temples was regarded as the first mound of earth which surfaced from the primeval waters (*Bib. Arch.* [1944], p. 78). In Canaan, the triumph of Baal over the unruly sea was a sign that he had established order in the creation, and this was marked by the erection of his temple. In Genesis, however, when the Lord had finished the work of creation he made for himself not a temple but a garden. It has often been observed that the garden of Eden in Israel's tradition replaced the temple of the other creation myths, and this is certainly true of the Old Testament in its present form. There is, however, a great deal which suggests that the garden of Eden and the temple had at one time been one and the same. When the Lord triumphed over chaos and ordered the creation he *did* establish his temple in Jerusalem, according to the creation story presupposed by the Psalms. This temple 'was' the garden of God on the summit of the holy mountain.

Each sacred mountain in the ancient Near East was the home of a divinity. In Canaanite myth, Baal lived on Mount Zaphon and had his temple there; Anat, the chief goddess, lived on mount *Innb* and El lived on a mountain in the far north named *Hrsn*, world mountain, beneath which the cosmic waters rose up. It was situated 'at the sources of the two rivers, in the midst of the fountains of the double deep' (UM I.5—6, quoted Cross, p. 36). All this was said of the temple in Jerusalem. Furthermore, he lived in a tabernacle where the gods met and feasted (cf. Exod. 24.11, where the elders of Israel ascended Sinai, 'beheld God, *and ate and drank*'). In the Old Testament these mountains were known, but the mountain of Baal and the mountain of assembly were one and the same. When the Day Star, son of Dawn, boasted, he said:

'I will ascend to heaven above the stars of God
I will set my throne on high;
I will sit on the mount of assembly *in the far north*;
I will ascend above the heights of the clouds,
I will make myself like the Most High'. (Isa. 14.13—14)

In the far north is better rendered *in the recesses of Zaphon*, i.e. the two mountains were not distinguished. Mt Zion is also identified with Mt Zaphon;

His holy mountain, beautiful in elevation,
Is the joy of all the earth,
Mount Zion *in the far north*
the city of the great king. (Ps. 48.2)

Again *in the far north* is better rendered *in the recesses of Zaphon*. It is hard to imagine any standpoint in Israel from which Zion could have been called the mount of the far north! What we have here is Zion named as the mountain of God. Ezekiel mentions a 'holy mountain of God', but says that it was 'Eden, the garden of God' (Ezek. 28.13—14). In other words,

Israel had similar but not identical ways of describing the dwelling of God. It was only when the reformers of Israel's religion sought to suppress much of the older mythology that the garden of God became the more familiar Eden of Genesis, and the temple was presented simply as a place of prayer and sacrifice.

The Great Sea

> Thou, whose almighty word
> Chaos and darkness heard,
> And took their flight.
> J. Marriott

Before examining this Eden motif in greater detail, it is necessary to look at the overall plan of the temple to see how it was thought to represent the firmament set in the seas from which the creation arose. There was an enormous bronze basin in the temple courtyard which must have dominated the area since it was half the width of the temple itself. It was, significantly, called 'the sea' and probably represented the primeval waters in ritual. There was an established belief that the courtyard 'was' the sea surrounding the stable earth. A tradition attributed to Rabbi Pinhas ben Ya'ir, who lived in the second century AD describes the temple thus: 'The house of the holy of holies was made to correspond to the highest heaven. The outer Holy House was made to correspond to the earth, and the courtyard was made to correspond to the sea . . .' (Quoted in Patai, *Man and Temple*, p. 108). The interpreters of the Pentateuch said, 'The court surrounds the temple just as the sea surrounds the world' (*Numbers Rabbah* XIII.19). The Babylonian Talmud remembers that the white and blue marble of the temple walls looked like the waves of the sea (b. *Sukkah* 51b). All these are later texts, written after the temple had been destroyed, but Josephus, who knew the temple, also said that the outer courtyard represented the sea. He said that the tabernacle on which it was modelled, was divided into three parts: 'and giving up two of them to the priests, as a place approachable and open to all, Moses signifies the earth and the sea since these too are accessible to all; but the third portion he reserved for God alone because heaven also is inaccessible to men' (*Antiquities*, III. 181). Furthermore, texts which undoubtedly refer to Solomon's temple associate the temple with the seas subdued before the creation, and thus it is very possible that the complex symbolism found in first-century writers such as Philo and Josephus was not a later interpretation but a memory of the original. Ps. 93, for example, describes the Lord enthroned and robed in majesty, established as mightier than the floods and the waves of the sea. Ps. 29.10 is similar:

> The Lord sits enthroned over the flood;
> the Lord sits enthroned for ever.

Since the throne was in the temple, this is a picture of the creator who has triumphed and is literally enthroned in his sanctuary over the floods he has subdued. Ps. 24 says that the Lord has established the world upon the seas, and immediately asks: 'Who shall ascend the hill of the Lord?' (Ps. 24.3), implying that the established place is the holy hill, the place of security for his people. The ancient poem now incorporated into Exodus (The Song of the Sea, Exod. 15) tells of the Lord bringing his people through a terrifying sea (hence its inclusion in this story) but it does not end with the rest of the Exodus story. In its original setting it did not describe the events of the Exodus. The poem in fact tells the ancient story of the creation:

> Thou wilt bring them in, and plant them on thy own mountain,
> the place, O Lord, which thou hast made for thy abode,
> the sanctuary, O Lord, which thy hands have established.
> (Exod. 15.17)

This, incidentally, is a good example of myth at work; the events of history are set in an existing framework, and the creation of the chosen people as a result of the Exodus is told in terms of the creation of the world from the primeval seas. There are many other descriptions of the Lord subduing the seas, e.g. Pss. 33.7; 74.13; 89.9; Jer. 5.22, and the stories about King David subduing the subterranean waters before building the temple are a variation on the same theme.

The sea surrounding the temple, the place of the divine throne, also appeared in several of the prophetic visions which had the temple as their setting. Daniel's vision of the one like a son of man (Dan. 7) was a vision based upon the ancient rituals of enthronement. (That these had been remembered right until the second century BC is another indication that the original symbolism of the temple had not been forgotten.) Before the man-like figure was enthroned and given dominion, four monstrous beasts rose from 'the great sea' (Dan. 7.2—7). One was killed, the rest were allowed to live for a time but their power was taken away (Dan. 7.11—12). In this context the four beasts stood for four empires, but their antecedents had been the chaos monsters whom Yahweh had tamed (cf. Job 41) or defeated (cf. Isa. 51.9). The old myth was being reinterpreted for a new situation (Dan. 7.17), suggesting that it had a certain status within the tradition. In time of crisis, this was how events were explained. It was neither new nor alien as is sometimes implied.

A similar temple vision is recorded in 4 Ezra. A man figure rises from the sea and makes for himself a great mountain on which he stands to wage war against the encroaching enemies. This is the ancient creation myth, the formation of the holy mountain from the midst of the sea, but here it is interpreted for the reader, showing that this writer too was using an existing tradition and applying it to his situation. The mountain is Zion, we are told, and the battle is against the enemies of the chosen people. The expected pattern of creation, i.e. the myth underlying every situation, is here applied to the creation (or rescue) of God's people from the situation of chaos in which they currently find themselves.

Paradise, whether described as the garden or as the place of the heavenly throne, was also surrounded by sea. A text from the first century AD described how Adam was led back to Paradise by the archangel Michael. He froze the waters around Paradise, so that they could cross (Life of Adam and Eve 28.4). More familiar is the sea around the heavenly throne in Revelation: 'and before the throne there is as it were a sea of glass, like crystal' (Rev. 4.6) or in front of the heavenly temple: 'And I saw what appeared to be a sea of glass mingled with fire, and those who had conquered the beast and its image and the number of its name, standing beside the sea of glass with harps of God in their hands' (Rev. 15.2). The temple, the place of God's throne, stood in the midst of the seas, and represented/was the firmament which the creator had established and continued to maintain for his people.

The Temple as Eden

The *hekal* was decorated with golden trees and flowers; it was jewelled like Ezekiel's garden of God, and when the Paradise theme occurs in the Old Testament, it must not be separated from the temple with which it was synonymous. Nor must there be a crude, historical understanding of the Eden myth. The prophets looked forward to a time when the End would be like the Beginning, and everything would be restored to its original state, but this was not so much their view of linear history as an expression of their belief that the material creation was perpetually out of harmony with the divine original, and that it was constantly necessary to re-establish the correspondence. The future and the past were perpetually and potentially present.

Eden was often linked with Jerusalem as the ideal it would one day attain. Thus Isaiah hoped for the time when Zion would enjoy the harmony of the holy mountain, ruled by the Davidic king (Isa. 11). The Second Isaiah hoped for the time when the desert of Zion would become Eden, the garden of the Lord (Isa. 51.3). The Third Isaiah hoped for the time when Jerusalem would be recreated as the new holy mountain (Isa. 65.17—25), a time when the serpent of the Genesis Eden would have no power ('and dust shall be the serpent's food', Isa. 65.25). As late as the first century AD the same ideas were employed. When Jerusalem had been destroyed by the Romans, 2 Baruch recorded one of the many explanations of the disaster. The earthly Jerusalem had not been the true city, he said; this was in heaven, the city revealed to Adam in Paradise before he sinned, to Abraham when he offered the covenant sacrifices, and to Moses on Sinai (2 Bar. 4.2—7). Jerusalem was thus identified with the mountain-top garden of the Lord, and this in turn was represented by the temple. That the whole city was seen as an extension of the temple can be seen in the enormous dimensions of the outer courtyard of the temple envisaged in the Temple Scroll.

There are numerous indications that the temple represented Eden, both in the descriptions of the first temple, and in the way that later writers describe heaven both as Eden and as the temple. According to Genesis 2, Eden was the garden of God, a place of trees, rivers, cherubim and an evil snake. When Adam and Eve were cast out, cherubim and a flaming sword were

THE GARDEN 69

placed to guard the gate. There is nothing to suggest in this account that they had been driven from a temple. Descriptions of the *temple*, however, do suggest that it was Eden. Ezekiel described a temple built on a high mountain (Ezek. 40.2), whose courtyards were decorated with palm trees (Ezek. 40.31, 34). The interior was decorated with palm trees and cherubim (Ezek. 41.17ff.), and from the temple flowed a river which brought supernatural fertility (Ezek. 47.1 – 12). Ezekiel did not invent these Eden-like features; each is mentioned elsewhere in the Old Testament. The temple on a high mountain was the theme of Isa. 2.2 – 4 and Mic. 4.1 – 3; the righteous were described as the trees of the house of the Lord (Ps. 92.13), a metaphor which would have been pointless had there been no trees there; 1 Kings 6.29 described the palm trees, cherubim and flowers carved on the temple walls; and several prophets looked forward to the day when waters would flow from the temple (e.g. Zech. 14.8; Joel 3.18). Hezekiah had removed a bronze serpent from the temple (2 Kings 18.4), and the seven-branched candlestick, as we shall see presently, was remembered as the tree of life. Ezekiel, it seems, had a vision of a garden sanctuary like those known elsewhere in the ancient Near East, but it was also an accurate description of the temple he had known in Jerusalem.

Despite the reworking, the memory of Eden as the temple survived. Jubilees described how Adam was created outside the garden and only put there later to tend it. He had to wait until forty days after his creation, and Eve had to wait eighty days (Jub. 3.9). Why? The answer lies in the purity laws of Leviticus 12.1 – 5. A woman who had given birth was unclean for forty days if she had borne a son, and eighty days if it was a daughter. Only then could she go to the temple and offer her sacrifices. One of the characteristics of Jubilees was to put the origin of Jewish laws back into primeval times. Here it was implied that Adam and Eve were the reason for the impurity laws, when in fact the reverse was the case. But why did the writer of Jubilees think it appropriate to associate Adam and the temple? When he left the garden, Adam offered an incense offering; not the frankincense of the courtyard sacrifices, but the special compound incense *only used in the sanctuary* (see p. 28): 'He offered as a sweet savour an offering, frankincense, galbanum, and stacte and spices in the morning with the rising of the sun' (Jub. 3.27). Enoch was taken up into the Garden of Eden and installed as the scribe of the great judgement (Jub. 4.23). Enoch also burnt incense there: 'He burnt the incense of the sanctuary, sweet spices acceptable before the Lord on the Mount' (Jub. 4.25). The writer of Jubilees must have identified temple and Eden. Another account of the expulsion in the Apocalypse of Moses says that when Adam was cast from Paradise he was permitted to take with him the herbs and spices necessary to make *incense* and seeds to grow plants for food (Ap. Mos. 29.5—6). A commentary on Genesis 3.22 (*Genesis Rabbah* XXI.8) linked the expulsion from Eden to the expulsion from the sanctuary and the destruction of the temple. Later still, Jewish folklore said that heaven was surrounded by three concentric walls of fire, defining areas allocated to various classes of the righteous. This must have been a memory of the temple courts. Another tradition remembered Eden as a series of houses, the first two built of cedar, the third of precious metals and the fourth of olive wood. In the third house was the tree of life from which flowed the four rivers of Paradise.

The Place of Judgement

> Judge Eternal, throned in splendour,
> Lord of lords and King of kings,
> With thy living fire of judgement
> Purge this realm of bitter things.
>
> H. S. Holland

Beyond the *hekal* was the holy of holies, the place of the cherub throne, and this too was reflected in the mythology. We tend not to associate the garden of Eden with the last judgement; they occur at opposite ends of our view of things, because we have 'historicized' myth. Even those who deny that myth has any place in their thinking will usually admit that the judgement happens at the end and Eden at the beginning. Our thinking has been historicized. There is *a* judgement theme in the Genesis story of Eden, a vestige of the older myth, but there is no throne. In the Apocalypse of Moses, however, there *is* the chariot throne in the garden of God, from which judgement is passed on Adam: 'And when God appeared in Paradise, mounted on the chariot of his cherubim, with the angels proceeding before him and singing hymns of praises, all the plants of Paradise . . . broke into flowers. And the throne of God was fixed where the tree of life was' (Ap. Mos. 22.3−4). This Apocalypse is a relatively late text, but there is a description of Eden in Ezekiel 28, almost certainly older than that of Genesis, which is also a judgement scene and from which we can deduce that his Eden was the temple. Ezekiel's garden is very different from that of Genesis; it is on the mountain of God, a place of precious stones and cherubim. The text of this chapter is notoriously difficult to read at certain points, but what it seems to describe is the judgement of an *angel* figure who was also the King or Prince of Tyre. This angel prince had lived in the garden of Eden, but had sinned and so was thrown down from the mountain. His sin was pride and violence. This, I suggest, is a glimpse of the original Eden, the place of the great judgement.

By piecing together allusions in several texts we can also deduce that this heavenly garden was the temple. The angel prince had had a 'covering' (Ezek. 28.13), which probably means some sort of shrine, a *sukkah*. In Hebrew there are several words similar to the one here translated 'covering'. One occurs in Ps. 27, where the worshipper has asked to dwell in the house of the Lord, to behold the beauty of the Lord, and to inquire in his temple:

> For he will hide me in his *shelter* in the day of trouble;
> he will conceal me under the cover of his tent,
> he will set me high upon a rock. (Ps. 27.5)

Another is in Ps. 18 where the Lord flew on the cherub and the wings of the wind:

> He made darkness his covering around him,
> his *canopy* thick clouds dark with water. (Ps. 18.11)

(Cf. Job 36.29; Pss. 31.20; 76.2; Jer. 25.38.) It is not hard to see where this imagery originated; it was in the holy of holies, where the Lord could set his servant firm upon the rock and hide him in his sanctuary. The sanctuary of the Lord was the guarantee of the people's safety. Isaiah too bewailed the loss of this sanctuary on the day when the Lord punished his people: 'He has taken away the *covering* of Judah' (Isa. 22.8). Amos looked forward to a time of restoration, when 'the *booth* of David' would be raised up again (Amos 9.11). The booth here must have been the place of the king, just as the angel/king of Tyre had had his *covering*.

Amos implies that the *booth* had been destroyed and with it, Israel. In Ezekiel's oracle, the angel/king of Tyre was thrown from his sanctuary and thus the prosperity of Tyre was ended. The Greek of Ezekiel 28.18 suggests that it may once have read 'I profaned you from your sanctuary', which would confirm that the covering was a sanctuary. Becoming mortal was the punishment, just as it had been when the gods, the sons of the Most High, were judged in the divine council (Ps. 82.6—7). The king of Tyre was no longer a god. There is in the Old Testament one curious reference to the princes of Israel which suggests the same belief. When the Second Isaiah was explaining how his people had come to suffer such disasters at the hands of the Babylonians, he said:

> Your first father sinned,
> and your mediators sinned against me.
> Therefore *I profaned the princes of the sanctuary*,
> I delivered Jacob to utter destruction
> and Israel to reviling. (Isa. 43.27—8)

The imagery is the same, the punishment is the same, but Isaiah linked *sanctuary* and judgement, as did the psalmist (Ps. 73.17), whereas Ezekiel linked *Eden* and judgement. In the second century BC the subjugation of Jerusalem by Antiochus Epiphanes and the desecration of the temple were described in the same way. The 'Prince of the Host' had a sanctuary at Jerusalem; his burnt offerings were taken away and his *sanctuary* was overthrown (Dan. 8.11).

Now the *covering* of the king of Tyre was made of gold and precious stones, even though it was in the garden of Eden. Ezekiel's garden must have been a place of golden shrines and judgement, of guardian cherubim and stones of fire. This older Eden may explain two otherwise inexplicable features of the temple; when describing the holy of holies, the Chronicler says that Solomon 'overlaid the *upper chambers* with gold' (2 Chron. 3.9); these can hardly have been store rooms. Similarly, in the Songs of the Sabbath Sacrifice, there seem to have been seven sanctuaries in the heavenly temple each of which is the place of a chief angel (4Q 403). Solomon's golden upper chambers are nowhere explained; it is possible that they were the smaller sanctuaries surrounding the holy of holies, the side chapels, so to speak, and these were depicted in the *Songs of the Sabbath*

Sacrifice as the sanctuaries of the seven angels. It would have been from one of these golden places, or rather from the heavenly reality it represented, that the king of Tyre was thrown down when he was judged. He was thrown into the sea, presumably both the primeval sea which surrounded the holy mountain as well as the Mediterranean into which his city did fall.

The King in Eden

> Hail the day that sees him rise, Alleluia!
> To his throne above the skies; Alleluia!
>
> C. Wesley

Ezekiel's oracle against Tyre shows the Eden cult in its natural setting as the regulator of the politics of the day. It raises an important question: if Ezekiel believed that the nations round about Israel had angel princes who walked on the holy mountain, must he not also have believed that Israel had an angel prince? Since Ezekiel was a priest in the temple (Ezek. 1.3), this is an important indication of what the ancient cult believed about the king; he would have been both an earthly king and a heavenly patron, an angelic being. This may be what was meant by the coronation oracle which survives in Ps. 2:

> 'I have set my king on Zion, my holy hill.'
> I will tell you of a decree of the Lord:
> He said to me, 'You are my son,
>   today I have begotten you.' (Ps. 2.6−7)

We cannot be certain what this meant. It could have referred only to the ceremony of establishing the king in Jerusalem, or it could imply that some divine status for the king was a part of the temple cult. In view of Ezekiel's otherwise inexplicable oracle, the latter seems more likely. Ps. 89 also presupposes a similar belief; it depicts the king in Jerusalem as the first-born of the Lord, the highest of the kings of the earth. It also tells of an ancient vision and of a chosen one who has been *raised up* from the people (Ps. 89.20). What does *raised up* imply? The last words of David are also significant:

> The oracle of David, the son of Jesse,
>   the oracle of the man who *was raised on high*,

>   the anointed of the God of Jacob,
>   the sweet psalmist of Israel:
>   The *Spirit of the Lord speaks by me*,
>   his word is upon my tongue. (2 Sam. 23.1–2)

Was the king simply 'exalted' in our sense of that word, or was he raised to the holy mountain, where, in a mystical experience, he became the embodiment of the Lord? Both Ps. 2 and 2 Sam. 23 imply that the king was possessed by the Spirit of the Lord and thus was his son. We know from the prophets that speaking in the name of the Lord was accompanied by a claim to have stood in the council of the Lord, before the heavenly throne (e.g. Isa. 6.1; Amos 3.7). If his words were decrees of the Lord, was it in fact the king who spoke to Israel from the throne between the cherubim, since the cherubim were his throne too? (see Chapter 4). Isa. 41.8 also needs this mountain setting: 'You are my servant, I have chosen you and not cast you off.' Cast off from where? The obvious comparison is with the other angel princes of the nations who had been judged and thrown from the holy mountain. If Israel had had a similar belief about her kings, it would explain a great deal of the later visionary material which describes the ascent of a human figure to a throne in heaven. The one like a son of man in Daniel 7 would have been based on this tradition, as would the Son of Man in the Similitudes of Enoch who had been appointed by the Most High as the heavenly judge. The ascended Christ of Revelation was also this royal figure enthroned in heaven; again, the context is judgement and although there are no Eden motifs at this point in Revelation, the whole vision is set in the temple and there are Eden motifs elsewhere. The ascent of the king was probably expressed by entering the holy of holies and sitting on the throne of the Lord (1 Chron. 29.23). Entering the holy of holies symbolized entering heaven, and several later texts imply that entering the sanctuary conferred angelic status (see Chapter 3).

The Genesis Eden is an adaptation of the older royal myth to suit the changed circumstances of the post-exilic period when there were no more kings, and the earthly king could no longer be the centre of the temple cult. Many of the older beliefs were democratized and what had formerly been the role of the king became that of the whole people or of the individual; all were chosen, all were the sons of God (e.g. Deut. 14.1–2), and all were the holy priesthood (Exod. 19.6). The rest of the royal theology either became the messianic hope: the divine ruler, the heavenly judge, the restorer of the creation and the one to protect the chosen people from their enemies; or it passed the Moses legends, where the Lawgiver was described as both god and king (see Meeks, 'Moses as God and King'). Thus the Genesis Eden describes not the pride of an angelic king, but the disobedience of man. This was the Eden myth modified for an era when the Law was becoming more important in Israel's faith, and individual responsibility was recognized. Older traits are still discernible. The ancient angel princes had wanted to be higher than God Most High (e.g. Isa. 14.12—15) and were punished with mortality for their aspirations; Adam and Eve were driven from the garden for obeying the serpent who had promised they would be *like God* if they ate the fruit. They too were punished with mortality. In Genesis 1, man was made in the image of God, a phrase which has exercised the ingenuity of commentators ever since it was written. It too is a memory of older myths, for in the ancient Near East the king was often described as the image of God. Here the king has become the man, but the older royal associations were not forgotten. Philo was later to use it of the Logos, the second God, and Paul used it of Jesus: 'He is the image of the invisible God, the first born of all creation' (Col. 1.15). The early hymn quoted in Philippians 2 shows that this myth of the proud angels was very much a part of the first Christians' world view: '. . . though he was in the form of God did not count equality with God a thing to be grasped' (Phil. 2.6). Like the angel prince, man was thrust from the garden, lest, with his knowledge of good and evil, he should also acquire immortality and become like God (Gen. 3.22).

The Source of Life

> To all life thou givest, to both great and small;
> In all life thou livest the true life of all.
>
> W. C. Smith

Since the temple was the place of creation, it was also the source of life. There are many examples in later texts of the life-giving powers of the holy place.

> The rod of Aaron, after it had lain for a night in the sanctuary, 'brought forth buds, and bloomed blossoms, and even yielded almonds'. The cedars that Hiram, king of Tyre, sent to Solomon for the building of the temple, as soon as the incense of the sanctuary reached them, thrilled green anew, and throughout centuries bore fruits, by means of which the young priests sustained themselves. Not until Manasseh brought the idol into the Holy of Holies, did these cedars wither and cease to bear fruit. The third incident ... was the stretching of the staves of the Ark when Solomon set them in the Holy of Holies, and the staves, after having been part of the Ark for four hundred and eighty years, suddenly extended until they touched the curtain. (L. Ginzberg, *The Legends of the Jews*, vol. 3, p. 162)

They also remembered that the sanctuary played a vital role in the stability of the created order. Ginzberg has collected a veritable mosaic of legendary material associated with the temple, and the following passage shows as well as any how, in all their elaborations upon the theme, later expositors did not lose sight of the original significance of the temple. When Moses was receiving instructions about the building of the sanctuary, he wanted to know how God could dwell in such a small place. The Lord said that he did not demand what was due to him, but only such as his people could offer him. He would bring his presence into the sanctuary for their sake. Ginzberg's account continues:

> God was indeed anxious to have a sanctuary erected to Him, it was the condition on which he led them out of Egypt, yea, in a certain sense the existence of all the world depended on the construction of the sanctuary, for when the sanctuary had been erected, the world stood firmly founded, whereas until then it had always been swaying hither and thither. Hence the tabernacle in its separate parts also corresponded to the heaven and the earth, that had been created on the first day. As the firmament had been created on the second day to divide the waters which were under the firmament from the waters which were above, so there was a curtain in the Tabernacle to divide between the holy and the most holy. As God created the great sea on the third day, so did he appoint the laver in the sanctuary to symbolize it, and as he had on that day destined the plant kingdom as nourishment for man, so did he now

require a table with bread in the Tabernacle. The candlestick in the Tabernacle corresponded to the two luminous bodies, the sun and the moon, created on the fourth day; and the seven branches of the candlestick corresponded to the seven planets, the Sun, Venus, Mercury, the Moon, Saturn and Mars. Corresponding to the birds created on the fifth day, the Tabernacle contained the Cherubim, that had wings like birds. On the sixth, the last day of creation, man had been created in the image of God to glorify his creator, and likewise was the high priest anointed to minister in the tabernacle before his Lord and creator. (*Legends*, vol. 3, p. 150)

The earliest reference to the temple as the source of fertility is in the sixth-century prophet Haggai. He addressed the newly returned exiles who had concentrated on building their own homes and had not restored the temple. There had been a drought and a bad harvest. The prophet diagnosed the fault:

You have looked for much, and, lo, it came to little; and when you brought it home, I blew it away. Why? says the Lord of hosts. Because of my house that lies in ruins, while you busy yourselves each with his own house. Therefore the heavens above you have withheld the dew, and the earth has withheld its produce. And I have called for a drought upon the land and the hills, upon the grain, the new wine, the oil, upon what the ground brings forth, upon men and cattle, and upon all their labours. (Hag. 1.9—11)

The existence of the temple and its rituals was vital for the wellbeing of the land: 'The latter splendour of this house shall be greater than the former, says the Lord of hosts; and in this place I will give prosperity, says the Lord of hosts' (Hag. 2.9). In the time of the monarchy the king had also played a part in maintaining the fertility of the land; he had been the channel of God's justice and gift of prosperity:

> May he judge thy people with righteousness,
>   and thy poor with justice!
> Let the mountains bear prosperity for the people,
>   and the hills, in righteousness. (Ps. 72.2—3)

In the time of the Messiah, it was believed that both justice and fertility would return.

The Eternal Covenant

> Bind us together Lord,
> Bind us together,
> With cords that cannot be broken.
>
> B. Gillman

Fundamental to all ancient Israel's thought about the creation, life and fertility was their belief in one underlying principle which they called the Eternal Covenant (Isa. 24.5) or the Covenant of Peace (Num. 25.12; Isa. 54.10). The meaning of this might be better expressed by the term *Cosmic Covenant*, even though this name is never used for it in the English translations. Eternal for us means 'lasting a long time' whereas for Israel it meant something which belonged to the other order of existence, the one outside time and space which influences every aspect of our existence. 'Cosmic' conveys this meaning better, but since the English translations use 'Eternal', I shall also. The Eternal Covenant underlies all the covenants with Noah, with Abraham, with Moses and with David, since these were but individual examples of the one underlying covenant. When Jeremiah spoke of a new covenant, he related the promise for Israel's future to the Eternal Covenant:

> Thus says the Lord,
> who gives the sun for light by day
>   and the fixed order of the moon
>   and the stars for light by night,
> who stirs up the sea so that its waves roar –
>   the Lord of hosts is his name:
> 'If this fixed order departs from before me, says the Lord,
> then shall the descendants of Israel cease
>   from being a nation before me for ever.' (Jer. 31.35–6)

The Eternal Covenant expressed the belief that all things visible and invisible were a part of one great system and bound by this great covenant. When anyone or anything, human or divine, rebelled against this fixed order, then the covenant was damaged and creation became distorted. Both moral and physical order began to disintegrate. There were two major sins against the covenant; one was pride which resulted in false claims to supreme power (as in Isa. 14) and the other was abuse of divine knowledge, the knowledge of the secrets of creation. There had been tales of proud heavenly beings punished for their pride (Isa. 14; Ezek. 28) and of others who abused their knowledge; thus they had destroyed the fertility, harmony and peace of creation. One very early list of this knowledge occurs in 1 Enoch 7—8, where we find that magic, medicine, metalwork to make weapons, cosmetics, astronomy and astrology, when misused, all contributed to the 'lawlessness' which destroyed the earth. A second broadly similar list appears in the Parables of Enoch, but the significance of this list is that it leads directly into a description of the restoration of the great 'oath', clearly the same as the biblical 'Eternal Covenant'. A part of this great oath was a hidden name which bound together the natural order; it kept heaven and earth in place, the sea within its bounds and the stars in their courses. Unfortunately the text does not seem to be complete, but there is enough extant to show that this *was* the Eternal Covenant, the Covenant of Peace. The Enochic account gives the additional detail that the Son of Man, the royal figure at the centre of Enoch's visions, had a 'name' which, when revealed, both effected the judgement and restored the creation. Since this Son of Man was derived from the ancient king, we have in these visions a glimpse of one of his roles.

In the Old Testament the Eternal Covenant was the basis for the messianic/Eden oracle in Isa. 11.1—9. A king would come possessed by the Spirit of the Lord and he would bring justice to the earth, judgement to the wicked and peace and harmony to the holy mountain. The Eternal Covenant was something for the future; Isaiah knew that he was not describing what *was*, but what could and should be.

Another passage in Isaiah will serve to illustrate what happened when the Covenant was broken:

The earth mourns and withers,
 the world languishes and withers;
 the heavens languish together with the earth.
The earth lies polluted
 under its inhabitants;
for they have transgressed the laws,
 violated the statutes,
 broken the everlasting covenant.

> Therefore a curse devours the earth,
> and its inhabitants suffer for their guilt . . . (Isa. 24.4–6)

The whole of Isaiah 24–27 describes the distortion and desolation of a world ready for judgement and the appearance of the Lord.

> On that day the Lord will punish
> the host of heaven, in heaven,
> and the kings of the earth, on the earth.
> They will be gathered together
> as prisoners in a pit;
> they will be shut up in a prison,
> and after many days they will be punished.
> Then the moon will be confounded,
> and the sun ashamed;
> for the Lord of hosts will reign
> on Mount Zion and in Jerusalem
> and before his elders* he will manifest his glory. (Isa. 24.21–3)

There are many places in the Old Testament where the Eternal Covenant is either mentioned or assumed (e.g. Gen. 9.16; Ezek. 16.59; Hos. 2.18).

This covenant was a part of the judgement–enthronement–renewal cycle associated with the autumn festivals of the Day of Atonement and Tabernacles, and yet neither Leviticus 16 nor the Mishnah associated these festivals with this covenant. Indirect allusions, however, do suggest that the Eternal Covenant was particularly connected with the priests and their role in the temple. In Numbers we read that Phineas the priest turned back the wrath of the Lord from the people and made atonement for them; he was given the Covenant of Peace: 'Therefore say, "Behold I give to him my covenant of peace; and it shall be to him, and to his descendants after him, the covenant of a perpetual priesthood, because he was jealous for his God, and made atonement for the people of Israel"' (Num. 25.12). Malachi links the corruption of the priesthood to the breaking of this covenant:

> My covenant with [Levi] was a covenant of life and peace, and I gave them to him that he might fear; and he feared me, he stood in awe of my name. True instruction was in his mouth,

---

*The Syriac version here has Holy Ones, i.e. angels.

and no wrong was found on his lips. He walked with me in peace and uprightness, and he turned many from iniquity. For the lips of a priest should guard knowledge, and men should seek instruction from his mouth, for he is the messenger* of the Lord of Hosts. But you have turned aside from the way. (Mal. 2.5—8)

It is interesting that Malachi links the broken covenant to the priest's role as the angel of the Lord, and implies that he is a fallen angel because he has given false teaching, led men astray and thus caused the covenant to be broken. It has been suggested that the fallen angel themes of 1 Enoch were in fact an attack upon the corrupt priesthood of the second temple period (see Suter, 'Fallen Angel, Fallen Priest').

This covenant with the priests had also been linked with atonement (Num. 25.12). Do we have here echoes of a belief found in later texts, but in fact very ancient, that the priest as the angel/messenger of the Lord made atonement for the people on the Day of Atonement because he had been entrusted with the Eternal Covenant? The writer to the Hebrews also links the Day of Atonement to a new covenant (Heb. 9.15); and one wonders if it was *this* covenant, the Eternal Covenant, centred originally on the messianic priest-king, the angel of the Lord, who was to judge the wicked and renew the creation, which became the basis for the Christians' New Covenant? Early preaching suggests that it was. Peter's sermon in Acts 2 was based on Joel 2.28; he saw in this prophecy the explanation of what had happened at Pentecost. Now the earlier parts of Joel had described the process of judgement and renewal in the Eternal Covenant, even though that covenant was not named. He had described the desolation and despair which preceded the Lord's intervention to save his people, and the proof that the Lord was in their midst again would be an outpouring of the Spirit upon all. It was this gift of the Spirit which Peter had claimed, the sign that the eternal covenant had been renewed. Paul too knew that the giving of the Spirit would result in the renewal of the creation (Rom. 8.12—21). All these themes in the New Testament derive ultimately from the myths of Eden and from their enactment in temple ritual. Certain aspects of this myth have become so

---

* The Hebrew word is the one usually translated 'angel'.

familiar (e.g. Pentecost, Romans 8) that they have come to stand in their own right as component parts of the Christian picture and no context is thought necessary. Returned to their temple setting, however, these passages are much enriched.

The Gift of Rain

> He shall come down like showers
> Upon the fruitful earth,
> And love, joy, hope, like flowers,
> Spring in his path to birth.
>
> J. Montgomery

The garden temple was the place of creation and recreation. It was the source of fertility which, in Palestine, meant rain. Although there is no direct evidence for rain rituals in the first temple, there were certainly such rituals at a later period and indications that they were of ancient origin. The rain rituals were associated with the Feast of Tabernacles which celebrated the Lord's kingship over all the earth. We do not know when rain rituals came to be practised at Tabernacles; the best we can do is piece together information and allusions in earlier texts, to see if there is anything which could have been such a ritual even though the possibility falls short of proof.

In Zechariah there is a reference to rain at Tabernacles as the reward for faithful worshippers. A familiar pattern of judgement (which was a development of the older triumph over chaos), kingship and then fertility is apparent in his vision of the day of the Lord; this must have derived from the older cult. From what is known of the prophet's visions, they are more likely to have been set within a well-known pattern of ideas than to have been complete innovations. What was new was the prophet's use of those ideas and images. Having described the supernatural portents on the day when the Lord becomes king over all the earth and the judgement upon his enemies, the prophet goes on to describe the great Feast of Tabernacles (booths) which follows: 'Then everyone that survives of all the nations that have come against Jerusalem shall go up year after year to worship the King, the Lord of hosts, and to keep the feast of booths. And if any of the families of the earth do not go up to Jerusalem to worship the King, the Lord of hosts, there will be no rain upon them' (Zech. 14.16—17). One wonders why drought was considered an appropriate punishment, unless the belief was traditional.

The Deuteronomists had said that rain was a reward for loving the Lord and keeping his Law: 'And if you will obey my commandments which I command you this day, to love the Lord your God, and to serve him with all your heart and with all your soul, I will give the rain for your land in its season, the early rain and the later rain, that you may gather in your grain and your wine and your oil' (Deut. 11.13—14). There is no association with tabernacles or even the temple here but, if there had been a ritual for rain-making in the temple, such a thing would have met with the Deuteronomists' disapproval, and would not have survived in their texts. Solomon's prayer at the dedication of the temple, although probably expanded into its present form by the Deuteronomists, and therefore full of their teaching, *does* preserve a hint that the temple was associated with rain: 'When heaven is shut up and there is no rain because they have sinned against thee, if they pray toward this place, and acknowledge thy name . . . grant rain upon thy land which thou hast given to thy people as an inheritance' (1 Kings 8.35—6). It was prayers *to the temple* which helped in time of drought.

Apart from this, there are references in the Psalms which are open to several interpretations. The most interesting is Psalm 68, which associates the themes of judgement and rain-giving. The Lord scatters his enemies, gives protection to the weak and rain to all his people.

> God gives the desolate a home to dwell in;
>   he leads out the prisoners to prosperity;
>   but the rebellious dwell in a parched land . . .
> Rain in abundance, O God, thou didst shed abroad;
>   thou didst restore thy heritage as it languished. (Ps. 68.6, 9)

The whole sequence is set in the temple because the psalmist describes the great triumphal procession into the temple: singers, minstrels, and princes of the tribes (Ps. 68.24—7). It would be hard to see this as other than an ancient judgement, kingship and rain-giving pattern associated with temple ritual, and if the pattern was ancient, it would have been the basis for Zechariah's vision of the future Day of the Lord: judgement, kingship and rain.

84 THE GATE OF HEAVEN

In the second temple period there was a rain ritual associated with the Feast of Tabernacles which has been recorded in minute detail in the Mishnah. Every day the pilgrims went out and gathered long (about four metres) willow branches which were placed upright all around the great altar in the temple court. When the altar was completely covered with greenery the ram's horn trumpet was blown, and then the worshippers walked around the altar, each carrying his *ethrog* (a citrus fruit) and his *lulab* (a bundle of palm, myrtle and willow, in accordance with Lev. 23.40). On the seventh day they walked round seven times. Each time the procession sang:

> Save us, we beseech thee, O Lord,
> O Lord, we beseech thee, give us success! (Ps. 118.25)

The psalm continues,

> Bind the festal procession with branches,
> up to the horns of the altar! (Ps. 118.27)

(There is an unmistakable similarity to Palm Sunday; the crowds waved branches and cheered, and they chanted a Hosanna [i.e. *Hoshi'ahnna'* which is the Hebrew for 'Save us', Ps. 118.25], and then, 'Blessed is he who comes in the name of the Lord', which is Ps. 118.26.)

Both Psalm and Mishnah show that this festival was a time of great rejoicing; it was said, 'He that has never seen the joy at the water drawing has never in his life seen joy' (Mishnah, *Sukkah* 5.1). As darkness fell great candelabra were lit in the court of women. Each had four lamps, and they were so high (the Talmud says fifty cubits, i.e. about twenty-two metres!) that the lamps had to be refuelled by means of ladders. The light could be seen all over Jerusalem. A carnival atmosphere transformed the temple; men danced with burning torches and the levites played their various instruments. When the first cock-crow was heard the priests sounded a trumpet blast, and the merriment ceased. A procession formed to follow the priests out through the eastern gate of the temple, the Water Gate, to Siloam, where the priest filled a golden flagon with water. The procession then returned to the temple, where the priest ascended the ramp at the side of the great altar and offered two libations, one of water and the other of wine. He poured both liquids simultaneously into the shafts which went beneath the altar on the western side, the side from which the rain clouds appeared. By this time it was dawn and time for the morning sacrifice. What was the significance of this dawn ritual? R. Akiba, who belonged to the 'third generation' of rabbis, i.e. he flourished between AD 120 and 140, when temple rituals would still have been within living memory, gave this reason for the libation: 'Bring the libation of water at the Feast of Tabernacles, that the showers may be blessed to thee. And accordingly it is said, that whosoever will not come up to the Feast of Tabernacles shall have no rain' (Tosefta, *Sukkah* 3.17). The people who performed this ritual, then, associated it with the rain promised by Zechariah, and they must have seen themselves as perpetuating an ancient practice.

Of the three great Jewish festivals, Passover, Weeks and Tabernacles, only two have passed into the Christian year: Passover became Easter and Weeks became Pentecost. A great mystery surrounds the fate of Tabernacles; it was important for the first Christians since both Hebrews (12.22—4) and Revelation (7.9—12) have Tabernacles as the setting for the triumph of the saints in heaven. The *Shepherd* of Hermas also includes a parable based on Tabernacles in which the angel of the Lord gives out willow branches, and when they are returned to him, their condition, green or withered, indicates the state of the bearer — faithful or apostate, sinner or saved: 'And the angel of the Lord commanded crowns to be brought and crowns were brought, made, as it were of palm leaves, and he crowned the men who had given up their sticks with buds and some fruit and sent them away into the tower ... And all who went into the tower had the same clothing, white as snow' (*Parable* 8,ii, 1, 3). The tower here is the Church, but it had formerly been a common description of the temple or the holy of holies. The white robes are the robes of glory, the dress of the angels (see Chapter 3). The great angel is said to be Michael (8.iii.3), which suggests that this vision, like that of Revelation, had pre-Christian roots. In both there are duplicate namings of the great angel: here he is Michael but later he is the son of God (9.xii,8); in Revelation the warrior is Michael (Rev. 12.7—8), and also the Word of God (Rev. 19.13). This is not a sign of confusion in the text, but rather proof of just how much the first Christians took wholesale from the Judaism which produced the apocalypses. The underlying vision in Hermas was a judgement vision based on the Feast of Tabernacles where the great angel of Israel admitted the chosen to the heavenly temple. The revealing of the Messiah and the judgement were the twin themes of this type of vision (see Chapter 4). These themes were not lost in the Church. They survived as Advent and Epiphany; Advent is the time when we think of the judgement, and Epiphany is the time when the Messiah was revealed to the world. The Eastern Churches still bless the waters at Epiphany, commemorating now the baptism of Jesus, but more anciently rooted in the blessing of the waters in the temple.

The Rivers of Paradise

> See the streams of living water,
>   Springing from eternal love,
> Well supply thy sons and daughters,
>   And all fear of want remove.
>
> J. Newton

From Eden there flowed a great river which watered the garden and then divided into four to water the whole earth (Gen. 2.10). This aspect of the Eden myth occurs many times in the older temple texts; the temple was always associated with a supernatural river which flowed out to give life to the world. One early reference is in Ps. 36:

> The children of men take refuge in the shadow of thy wings.
> They feast on the abundance of thy house,
>   and thou givest them drink from the river of thy delights.
> For with thee is the fountain of life;
>   in thy light do we see light. (Ps. 36.7−9)

Another is Ps. 46:

> There is a river whose streams make glad the city of God,
>   the holy habitation of the Most High. (Ps. 46.4)

The rivers are also a part of one of the more difficult chapters of Isaiah. Isaiah 33 comes from a time of crisis; the people are waiting for the Lord's help against their enemies. There then follows what seems to be a vision of heaven; someone ascends the holy mountain and stands amidst the eternal fires (Isa. 33.14). The next verse resembles Ps. 24.4, the description of the man who can stand in safety on the holy mountain; it would make sense to read this Isaiah passage in the same way. The one who stands on the holy hill 'sees the king in his beauty' (Isa. 33.17) and with his majesty there is a place of broad rivers and streams (Isa. 33.21). Burning fires, the Lord in majesty as judge and flowing streams from before the throne occur much later in the Similitudes of Enoch, where they are a part of the vision of heaven: 'Furthermore in that place I saw the fountain of righteousness, which does not become depleted and is surrounded completely by numerous fountains of wisdom' (1 Enoch 48.1). Nobody is prepared to date the material in 1 Enoch, but this passage in Isaiah is probably from the eighth century BC, early evidence for streams coming from the heavenly throne. Joel, too, expected a fountain to flow from the temple on the Day of the Lord (Joel 3.18).

The most detailed description of this river is found in Ezekiel's vision of the restored temple, a vision which occurred at New Year, i.e. at the time of the Feast of Tabernacles (Ezek. 40.1). Ezekiel saw water flowing from the door of the temple (Ezek. 47.1) and out towards the east. It flowed to the Dead Sea and made the waters sweet again (Ezek. 47.8). Fishermen worked there, and trees grew on the river banks which bore fruit every month 'because the water for them flows from the sanctuary' (Ezek. 47.12). This is an early reference to the fertility motif which occurs in so many later texts. Ezekiel associated this fertility with the Lord's return to the temple; the glory of the Lord came into the temple through the eastern gate (Ezek. 43.4).

Zechariah also associated the water of the temple with the time of the Lord's coming. Zech. 14 describes the battle of the Lord against his enemies as he stands east of the city on the Mount of Olives: 'On that day living waters shall flow out from Jerusalem, half of them to the eastern sea and half of them to the western sea; it shall continue in summer as in winter. And the Lord will become king over all the earth; on that day the Lord will be one and his name one' (Zech. 14.8–9). The chapter ends with all the nations coming up to Jerusalem to celebrate Tabernacles. John's Revelation also had the Feast of Tabernacles as its setting (Rev. 7.9), the heavenly reality which the temple rituals shadowed. At the end of his vision, John saw the river of life, 'bright as crystal, flowing from the throne of God and of the Lamb through the middle of the street of the city; also, on either side of the river, the tree of life with its twelve kinds of fruit, yielding its fruit each month; and the leaves of the tree were for the healing of the nations' (Rev. 22.1−2). He then saw the great light in the temple, not the huge candelabra of the temple courtyards, but the light of the Lord God in their midst.

Jesus had had this vision of the great fulfilment of Tabernacles; he was obviously the source of John's inspiration in this as in all else. The Fourth Gospel records an incident at the Feast (John 7.14) when he was teaching in the temple using the Tabernacles theme: 'On the last day of the feast, the great day, Jesus stood up and proclaimed, "If any one thirst, let him come to me and drink. He who believes in me, as the scripture has said, 'Out of his heart shall flow rivers of living water.'" Now this he said about the Spirit, which those who believed in him were to receive' (John 7.37−9). John here is not giving his own private interpretation of the rivers as the Spirit, since by New Testament times the waters of Eden *had* come to symbolize the Spirit of God or, more often, the Wisdom of God, which was almost synonymous with the Spirit. 'Had come' begs a question, since it implies that the waters of Eden had acquired that meaning; it is possible that they had always symbolized the spirit of Wisdom which gave life to the creation. The idea of the Spirit as the agent of creation (Gen. 1.2; 2.7) or of recreation (Joel 2.23−8) was very old. Similarly, Wisdom was the agent of creation (Prov. 8.22−31), and of recreation (Wisd. 7.27). Sirach describes Wisdom in terms drawn from the temple, and concludes by comparing it to the four rivers of Paradise: 'In the holy tabernacle I ministered before him' (Ecclus. 24.10). 'Like cassia and camel thorn I gave forth the aroma of spices, and like choice myrrh I spread a pleasant odour, like galbanum, onycha and stacte, and like the fragrance of frankincense in the tabernacle' (Ecclus. 24.15). The Law is then compared to Wisdom: 'It fills men with wisdom, like the Pishon, and like the Tigris at the time of the first fruits. It makes them full of understanding like the Euphrates, and like the Jordan at harvest time. It makes instruction shine forth like light, like the Gihon at the time of vintage' (Ecclus. 24.25−7).

Apart from the Jordan, these are the four rivers into which the river of Eden divided itself as it flowed to water the earth (Gen. 2.10−14). Sirach continues: 'I went forth like a canal from a river, and like a water channel into a garden. I said, "I will water my orchard and drench my garden plot"; and lo, my canal became a river and my river became a sea' (Ecclus. 24.30—31). This is Ezekiel's river from the temple. Wisdom flowed out like the rivers from Eden and like the waters from the temple.

Two passages in the Similitudes of Enoch confirm this association. In the second vision of the heavenly throne and the Son of Man, Enoch saw before the throne: 'Furthermore, in that place I saw the fountain of righteousness, which does not become depleted and is surrounded completely by numerous fountains of wisdom' (1 Enoch 48.1). From before the Son of Man on the throne, 'So wisdom flows like water and glory is measureless before him forever and ever' (1 Enoch 49.1). But this throne was also the tree of life; both *Genesis Rabbah* and 2 Enoch say that the streams flowed from the foot of the tree of life:

> The tree of life covered a five hundred years' journey, and all the primeval waters branched out in streams under it. (*Gen. Rab.* XV.6)
>
> And in the midst of them was the tree of life, at that place where the Lord takes his rest . . .
> and two streams come forth, one a source of honey and milk, and a source which produces oil and wine. And it is divided into four parts . . . (2 Enoch 8.3, 5)

In Christian interpretations of Genesis, the river which divided into four streams to water the earth was a symbol of Christ who, through the four Gospels, brought life to the earth (e.g. in Hippolytus' *Commentary on Daniel* I.17). The streams flowing from the sanctuary passed into the Christian liturgy; at the end of the service in the Coptic Church, the priest stands at the south side of the altar and throws water down onto the congregation, representing the river of Ezekiel which flowed from the south of the altar in the temple (Ezek. 47.1). The streams flowing from the tree of life passed into Christian art: the great twelfth- or thirteenth-century mosaic in the apse of San Clemente depicts the cross as the tree of life with four streams flowing from the foot; the great mosaic in San Giovanni in Laterano shows the four streams flowing from the foot of the cross; the throne of St Mark in St Mark's Venice depicts the tree of life with the lamb at its foot, and from it flow four streams.

The Tree of Life

> Fulfilled is now what David told
> In true prophetic song of old,
> How God the heathen's king should be;
> For God is reigning from the tree.
>
> Venantius Fortunatus, tr. J. M. Neale

In the temple stood a seven-branched candlestick, the *menorah*. The account of the temple in 1 Kings does not mention it, neither does the account in 2 Chronicles. From this it would be all too easy to conclude that there was no *menorah* in Solomon's temple. Zechariah, however, who prophesied when Haggai was exhorting the people to rebuild the temple (i.e. before the second temple had been built, Zech. 1.1; cf. Hag. 1.1) had a temple setting for his visions and he saw a seven-branched lamp. This must have been something he remembered from the older temple. He also saw angels standing among trees (Zech. 1.7), heavenly horses (Zech. 1.8; 6.1–8), and Satan standing by the angel of the Lord (Zech. 3.1); these must also have been part of the temple he had known. The seven-branched lamp stood between two olive trees. Twice the prophet says that the lamp represents the Lord: the seven lamps are the seven eyes of the Lord which range through the whole earth (Zech. 4.10) and the two olive trees stand by the Lord of the whole earth (Zech. 4.14). The question raised by Zechariah is this: If he could envisage a seven-branched lamp representing the Lord, angels among the trees, presumably of the heavenly garden, heavenly horsemen and Satan, was he a dangerous innovator or was he, as a priest, remembering accurately the ways of the older temple? The seven-branched lamp, the angels and Satan are all thought to be later, post-exilic additions to temple lore, but Ezekiel too was a priest and he, our best source of information for the chariot throne, is also difficult to domesticate into reconstructions of the ancient temple.

The Psalmist had praised the Lord as his lamp, and later as his rock (2 Sam. 22.29, 32). This linking of lamp and rock does suggest that it was the temple lamp he had in mind. Later tradition remembered this association of the lamp with the presence of the Lord; R. Jacob b R. Jose said: 'The Holy One, Blessed be He, was constrained to dwell with mortals in the light of a lamp' (*Numbers Rabbah* XV.9). Some remembered that the lamp was 'God who gives light, and the Torah' (*Exodus Rabbah* XXXVI.16) and said that the lamp was one of the five things which would be restored to the temple in the age of the Messiah, along with the fire, the Spirit, the ark and the cherubim, all things which had been absent from the second temple. Now there *was* a seven-branched lamp in the second temple, which suggests that there was something important about the earlier one which its replacement no longer had.

The sages who compiled commentaries on the holy books, especially on the Torah, loved to find significance in every little detail, but they were curiously silent about the *menorah*. The lamp was described in great detail in Exodus, and yet there was virtually no teaching built upon it. Modern scholars (e.g. Goodenough) have suggested that the silence was because the lamp had become the subject of mystical speculation, and this was not encouraged. If it had formerly been a symbol of the presence of God, such mystical speculation is very likely.

Almost contemporary with Zechariah are the two specifications for the seventh-branched lamp of the tabernacle in Exod. 25.31—40 and 37.17—24, both of which describe a tree-like object using words such as 'branch', 'flower', 'almond-like'. It was to be made of pure gold and all its associated utensils were to be of pure gold. No dimensions are given, which is unusual, since the ark (Exod. 25.10; 37.1), the mercy seat (Exod. 25.17; 37.6), the table of shewbread (Exod. 25.23; 37.10) and the incense altar (Exod. 37.25) all have measurements given. The measurements of the lamp of the second temple are recorded in the Talmud: 'Samuel said in the name of an old scholar, The height of the candlestick was eighteen handbreadths' (b. *Menaḥoth* 28b). In his vision of the heavenly world (written in the third or second century BC) Enoch saw the great tree:

> This tall mountain which you saw whose summit resembles the throne of God is (indeed) his throne, on which the Holy and Great Lord of Glory, the Eternal King, will sit when he descends to visit the earth with goodness. And as for this fragrant tree, not a single human being has the authority to touch it until the great judgement, when he shall take vengeance on all and conclude everything forever. This is for the righteous and the pious. And the elect will be presented with its fruit for

life. He will plant it in the direction of the north-east, in the direction of the house of the Lord, the Eternal King. (1 Enoch 25.3—5)

2 Enoch also described a great tree in Paradise which was also in the sanctuary, since it was the place where the Lord rested. It was a golden, fiery tree of enormous size: 'And in the midst (of them was) the tree of life . . . And that tree is indescribable for pleasantness and fine fragrance and more beautiful than any other created thing that exists. And from every direction it has an appearance which is gold-looking and crimson with the form of fire' (2 Enoch 8.3—4). This book exists in two slightly different versions; one adds at this point: 'And another tree is near it, an olive, flowing continually with oil'. Whoever wrote this version of 2 Enoch identified the tree of life with the seven-branched lamp of Zechariah's vision, which was also fed by olive trees at its side. This lamp was said to be 'the Lord of the whole earth' (Zech. 4.11—14). Although 2 Enoch has survived only in an Old Slavonic translation, it is thought to have come originally from Egypt at the end of the first century BC or perhaps a little later; and a contemporary, Philo, also implied that the *menorah* represented the tree of life. He applied the same astronomical symbolism to both (*Questions on Genesis*, I.10). (This complex system need not concern us here except to note that the seven branches were the seven planets, and in Zechariah's vision they had been the seven eyes of the Lord, the seven agents. These seven must have been stars as well as angels, which is exactly what we find both in the later apocalypses and in the Old Testament. Great angelic figures had/were stars: e.g. Num. 24.17, the messianic ruler rises as a star, Isa. 14.12 the king of Babylon is the Day Star, Matt. 2.2 the new star means a new king of the Jews.) What is important at the moment is the twofold association; that the lamp represented the Lord and that the lamp represented the tree of life.

There are indications of yet a third strand; that the lamp represented the king. Ahijah the prophet prophesied to Jeroboam that he would rule ten of the tribes, but that Solomon's son would keep one: 'That David my servant may always have a lamp before me in Jerusalem, the city where I have chosen to put my name' (1 Kings 11.36). Similarly 2 Sam. 21.17 says that David's men begged him not to venture into battle, 'lest you quench the lamp of Israel' (2 Sam. 21.17). The Lord did not destroy Jehoram the evil king of Judah, 'for the sake of David his servant, since he promised to give a lamp to him and his sons forever' (2 Kings 8.19). The lamp, I suggest, was the great lamp of the temple which had this threefold significance; it was equally the presence of God with his people and the symbol of the dynasty, since God was present with his people in the king; Immanuel, 'God with us', was the name to be given to the royal child whose birth would prove God's continuing presence with his people (Isa. 7.14).

In the traditions of the ancient Near East there is 'a garden of paradise where a gardener supervises the Tree of Life growing at the Water of Life, a tree from whose branches he has taken a twig which he carries as his rod or sceptre. But the idea of the Tree of Life has other, still more important implications, for it has been seen by other scholars that this Tree of Life is nothing but a mythic-ritual symbol of both god and king' (Geo Widengren, *The King and the Tree of Life in Ancient Near Eastern Religion*, p. 42). Not all the evidence is as unambiguous as it might be, but there are certainly several texts which suggest that this was the case even in the Old Testament tradition. In Jerusalem, the royal house was the tree of Jesse, from which the anointed branch (*nezer*) would grow (Isa. 11.1). Branch (*tsemah*) was a messianic title in Isa. 4.2; Zech. 3.8; and Zech. 6.12; Jeremiah speaks twice of the king as a righteous branch (*tsemah*; Jer. 23.5; 33.15); Jotham's parable about monarchy was a tale about trees (Judges 9). The Testament of Judah describes the Messiah as, 'This Branch of God Most High, And this fountain giving life unto all' (Test. Jud. 24.4). Note that the royal figure is both Tree and Fountain.

The lamp was made with 'almond work' (Exod. 25.33—4), which presumably means that the *menorah* was a stylized almond tree of some sort. Now the almond tree did have a particular association with the presence of the Lord: Aaron's rod blossomed and bore almonds (Num. 17.8) and Jeremiah saw a blossoming almond tree which he recognized as a sign that the Lord was watching his people (Jer. 1.11—12). There is word play in the Hebrew here, it is true, ('almond' being *shaqed* and 'watching' being *shoqed*), but it would be hard to imagine that Jeremiah's association of the almond with the watching Lord, and Zechariah's association of the *menorah* with the watching Lord were unconnected.

The branches of the *menorah* are called *qanim* (Exod. 25.32), which means 'reeds' and is probably a technical term to describe their being hollow. The Servant of the Lord is also associated with a reed and the wick of a lamp (Isa. 42.3). The Hebrew here can be read, 'a bruised reed he will not be broken, a dimly burning wick he will not be quenched'. Since this Servant would not 'burn dimly' or 'be bruised' (Isa. 42.4) until he had brought justice and law to the world, and since he was also the Chosen One on whom the Spirit of the Lord rested, it looks very much as though this poem was describing the fate of a king using the imagery of a broken *menorah*. The Second Isaiah was the prophet of the exile; the poem could well have been inspired by the sight of the broken lamp being taken away by the Babylonians. Whatever its inspiration, it associates the royal figure with the branching lamp.

Philo records that the central shaft of the seven-branched lamp represented the Word (*Who is the Heir?* 215), whom he also called the archangel (*Who is the Heir?* 205), the mediator and judge before the face of God (*Questions on Exodus*, II.13), the viceroy of God (*On Dreams*, I.241), the high priest and king (*On Flight*, 118). The whole creation, said Philo, was 'like some flock under the hand of God, its King and Shepherd. This hallowed flock he leads in accordance with right and law, setting over it his true Word and Firstborn Son who shall take upon him its government like some viceroy of a great king; for it is said in a certain place: Behold I AM, I send my angel before thy face to guard thee in the way' (*On Agriculture*, 51). Most of these titles are immediately recognizable as those of the ancient kings; the others were probably derived from the same source. Philo, after all, knew a good deal more about temple imagery than we do, and he used this as the basis for all his expositions. The information he gives, which is not explicit in the Old Testament, though implied there, is that the king was believed to be an angelic being, the high priest and the central shaft of the *menorah*, which symbolized the presence of God. When John describes the glorified Jesus, he uses exactly the same imagery: 'I saw seven golden lampstands, and in the midst of the lampstands, one like a son of man' (Rev. 1.12–13). Here we see the seven lamps with the angelic King figure in the midst of them, in other words the ancient Eden/temple symbolism right at the heart of the early Christian vision of heaven.

Wisdom, which was the feminine aspect of the Lord, was also described as a tree of life (Prov. 3.18), and the early Palestinian Targum to Genesis said that the tree of life was the Torah whose fruits nourished the just. The fruits of the tree of life were to be an important theme in early Christian poetry, as we shall see, when they became the Body of Christ in the Eucharist. What is important is to notice the continuity and consistency in the traditions; the Law was both *menorah* and tree, Jesus was both Light and Vine.

Clement of Alexandria described Jesus as the *menorah* and he too linked the lamp to the royal tree; Jesus was the lamp as the means of light, but also because there was something in the *shape of the lamp*, which was important for understanding him: 'The golden lamp conveys another enigma as a symbol of Christ, not in respect of form alone, but in his casting light . . . And they say that the seven eyes of the Lord are the seven spirits resting on the rod that springs from the root of Jesse' (Isa. 11.2) (*Stromata*, V.6). Irenaeus had a similar understanding, suggesting that this was a widely used image of Jesus:

> But the earth is encompassed by seven heavens, in which dwell Powers and Angels and Archangels . . .
> That is why the Spirit of God in his indwelling is manifold, and is said by the prophet Isaiah to rest in seven forms on the Son of God, that is, on the Word in his Incarnation . . .
> And Moses revealed the pattern of this in the seven-branched candlestick. (*Proof*, 9)

In Christian art Christ is represented as the central stem of the tree of life which is also the cross, as for example in the San Clemente mosaic or in the early fourteenth-century Italian painting by Pacino da Bonaguido, *Christ on the Tree of Life*. The lamp itself was also *combined* with the cross, another indication that the tree and the lamp were one. (Yarden, *The Tree of Light*, p. 20, gives several examples of this from the early Christian period.)

Odes and Hymns

The early Christians often described the Church as Paradise; their writings are full of ideas such as the saints being the trees of Eden or the four rivers being the four Gospels. Irenaeus said those who had received the Spirit were 'planted as it were in the Paradise of the King' (*Against Heresies*, V.10.1). Hippolytus saw the Church as a garden, the earthly garden pointing to the heavenly reality. In his *Commentary on Daniel*, I. 17, he mixes together quite naturally the imagery of the heavenly garden and the imagery of the plan for the tabernacle revealed to Moses on the mountain. This is why the ark had to be made of wood which did not decay (the Greek version of Exod. 25.10 which he would have used says that the ark was made of incorruptible wood). The ark was part of the heavenly world. Hippolytus' thoughts pass naturally from the heavenly Eden to the heavenly glory revealed and represented by the tabernacle, and then to the Church as this spiritual garden. There is one place where the older temple traditions clearly break through; the Church, he said, was 'the spiritual *house* of God, planted in Christ as in the East where may be seen all sorts of trees' (*Commentary on Daniel*, I.17). Commentaries on the text assume that this *house* of God is a mistake for the *garden* of God, and translations are adjusted accordingly. But the ancient house of the Lord *was* the Garden of Eden, and the earliest Christian writers knew this.

Similar descriptions can also be found in pre-Christian writings such as the Psalms of Solomon, showing that this was an unbroken tradition: 'The Paradise of the Lord, the trees of life, are his pious ones, Their planting is rooted for ever' (Ps. Solomon 14.2—3). In these texts there is nothing to suggest that they were drawing on a tradition which linked Paradise to the temple. Others, however, do show this link; there are passages in the Qumran texts where the Plantation of the righteous is a *holy building for the priesthood*, and, although the words 'temple' and 'Eden' are not used, the association of ideas is striking. Thus the *Manual of Discipline* describes the Council of the Community as

> an Everlasting Plantation, a House of Holiness for Israel, an Assembly of Supreme Holiness for Israel . . .
> It shall be a Most Holy Dwelling for Aaron . . . and shall offer

up sweet fragrance. (IQS VIII)
He has joined their assembly
to the Sons of Heaven
to be a Council of the Community,
a foundation of the Building of Holiness,
an eternal Plantation throughout all ages to come. (IQS XI)

This older belief of Eden as temple passes into the hymns of the Syriac-speaking Christians as the association of Eden and Church. In several places ideas and allusions are put together in such a way that the old temple symbolism must have been in the writer's mind.

The *Odes of Solomon* is a collection of early hymns in Syriac, possibly written for baptismal rites. All are steeped in Jewish tradition to such an extent that it is not always easy to distinguish Christian from Jewish elements. Ode 11 describes the believer's recovery of Paradise; what is remarkable is that Paradise was described with allusions to the temple and to traditions about it not found in the Bible. The believer was 'carried to his Paradise' where he 'worshipped the Lord on account of his glory' and 'the Lord was like the Sun shining on the face of the land'. Speaking waters from the fountain of the Lord touched his lips and he was 'established upon the rock of truth'. He was clothed in a garment of the Lord and '[he] possessed me by his light and from above he gave me rest in incorruption'. Elsewhere he said: 'I was clothed with the raiment of thy spirit and thou didst remove from me my raiment of skin' (Ode 25). Adam had been given a raiment of skin, i.e. mortality, when he left Eden. The high priest (see Chapter 3) also wore robes which symbolized the material world, but these were changed for garments symbolizing the angelic state when he entered the holy of holies, the presence of the Lord. This changing of garments was an important piece of temple symbolism, and it is interesting that the believer who has changed his garments is called elsewhere 'a priest of the Lord' (Ode 20).

Ode 36 seems to have derived directly from the older beliefs about the ascent of the king to the heavenly garden where he was installed as the Lord's son and spoke as his messenger:

> I rested on the Spirit of the Lord: and the Spirit raised me on high: and made me stand on my feet in the height of the Lord, before his perfection and his glory, while I was praising him

by the composition of his songs. The Spirit brought me forth before the face of the Lord: and, although a son of man, I was named the Illuminate, the Son of God: while I praised among the praising ones, and great was I among the mighty ones. For according to the greatness of the Most High, so he made me: and like his own newness he renewed me; and he anointed me from his own perfection: and I became like one of his neighbours; and my mouth was opened like a cloud of dew; and my heart poured out as it were a gushing stream of righteousness, and my access to him was in peace; and I was established by the Spirit of his government.
Hallelujah.

This ascent into the heavenly council to receive illumination is also found in the Qumran Hymns, another indication of the unbroken Eden/temple tradition:

> Thou hast raised me up to everlasting height.
> I walk on limitless level ground,
> and I know there is hope for him
> whom thou hast shaped from the dust
> for the everlasting council.
> Thou hast cleansed a perverse spirit of great sin
> that it may stand with the host of the Holy Ones,
> and that it may enter into the community
> with the congregation of the sons of heaven. (IQH III)
> Through me Thou hast illumined
> the face of the congregation
> and thou hast shown thine infinite Power.
> For thou hast given me knowledge
> through thy marvellous mysteries
> and thou hast shown thyself mighty within me
> in the midst of thy marvellous council. (IQH IV)

There is a remarkable memory of the older temple traditions in another of the *Odes of Solomon* which begins: 'I went up into the light of truth as if into a chariot; and the truth took me and led me' (Ode 38). The chariot, as we shall see in Chapter 4, was the throne of God in the holy of holies, the place of illumination to which the chosen ascended and where they were transformed into angelic beings, often to return as 'messengers' from God, 'messenger' and 'angel' being the same word in Hebrew.

Richest of all their explorations of the Paradise theme are St Ephrem's *Hymns on Paradise*, written in the middle of the fourth century. His Paradise was a mountain divided into three levels, the lowest for penitents, the next for the righteous and the highest for the triumphant. At the summit of the mountain was the Glory of God. We are reminded immediately of the cosmic mountain, the mountain garden of Ezekiel's Eden, the mountain of the throne of God in 1 Enoch and then of the temple with its concentric areas of holiness rising up the temple mount to the holy of holies at the highest central place (*Hymn* 2.11). His Paradise was also the Church where formerly it had been the temple. Eden/temple became Paradise/Church in which life-giving fruit was picked daily and given to all.

> The assembly of saints
> bears resemblance to Paradise;
> in it each day is plucked
> the fruit of Him who gives life to all. (*Hymn* 6.8)

Jesus was the tree of life in Ephrem's Garden just as the Lord had been the *menorah* in the temple. The imagery of the tree was developed to carry various teachings about the sacraments, but it must have derived from the older tree/lamp in the Eden/temple which was the presence of the Lord with his people in the person of the king. 'The Tree of Life in it [Paradise] is the type of Christ as source of the Church's life, with reference both to the eucharist and to the sacraments of anointing, especially the pre-baptismal signing. This means that the Tree of Life is represented simultaneously as vine and as olive' (Murray, p. 125). The tree/lamp as the symbol of the Lord also accounts for the tree of life being described as the 'Sun of Paradise' to which all the other trees bowed down:

> Perhaps that blessed tree,
> the Tree of Life,
> is, by its rays,
> the sun of Paradise;
> its leaves glisten,
> and on them are impressed
> the spiritual graces
> of that Garden.

> In the breezes the other trees
> bow down as if to worship
> before that sovereign
> and leader of the trees. (*Hymn 3.2*)

This hymn continues by comparing the tree of knowledge to the veil of the temple. Adam tasted from the tree, just as king Uzziah went through the veil of the temple (2 Chron. 26.16—21). As a result, both saw the forbidden glory and both were punished (*Hymns*, 3.14; 12.4). Later mystics were also to describe the fate of those who glimpsed the Glory; of the four rabbis who entered Paradise in their vision, only one survived the sight of the throne (see Chapter 4).

> In the very midst he planted
> the Tree of Knowledge,
> endowing it with awe,
> hedging it with dread,
> so that it might straightway serve
> as a boundary to the inner region of Paradise. (*Hymn* 3.3)

> In the midst of Paradise God had planted
> the Tree of Knowledge
> to separate off, above and below,
> sanctuary from Holy of Holies.
> Adam made bold to touch,
> and was smitten like Uzziah;
> the king became leprous,
> Adam was stripped.
> Being struck like Uzziah,
> he hastened to leave;
> both kings fled and hid,
> in shame at their bodies. (*Hymn* 3.14)

The trees of Paradise were like the angels who covered their faces before the Lord:

> the seraphs with their wings,
> the trees with their branches,
> all cover their faces so as not to behold their Lord.
> (*Hymn* 3.15)

Christ was the heavenly high priest, presumably in Eden just as Enoch had been the priest in Eden. He saw the fate of Adam and came down to purify him so that he could re-enter Paradise:

> The Garden cast him from its midst;
> all shining it thrust him forth.
> The High Priest, the Exalted One,
> beheld him
> cast from Himself:
> He stooped down and came to him,
> He cleansed him with Hyssop,
> and led him back to Paradise. (*Hymn* 4.4)

Just as the ancient angels had had their shrines, so the sons of light had their heavenly tabernacles (*Hymns*, 1.6; 5.6), each adorned according to the good works of its occupant. Each had a chariot of clouds, and we recognize the ancient chariot of the cherubim who had originally represented the clouds. The Songs of the Sabbath Sacrifice had mentioned many such glorious chariots in the heavenly realms which the temple represented; for Ephrem they were the chariots of the children of light when they descended into the world which had persecuted them:

> The clouds their chariots
> fly through the air;
> each of them had become the leader
> of those he has taught:
> his chariot corresponds to his labours,
> his glory corresponds to his followers. (*Hymn* 1.7)

Had we but the Genesis account of Adam in Eden we should have no means of understanding what this rich and complex poetry expresses. With a knowledge of the traditions and beliefs about the temple and Eden which have survived only in other sources, however, it is possible to begin to appreciate some of the insights of the earliest Christian teachers who wrote within the original Jewish heritage of Christianity. So much of this faded when Christianity passed into a non-Jewish setting and took on Greek ways of thinking. Theology then became more a matter of words and less of pictures. Definition replaced vision.

The temple was Eden and its rituals will have interacted with this fundamental belief about the creation. The temple itself, like Eden, was between heaven and earth with access to both the divine and material worlds: 'And paradise is in between corruptibility and incorruptibility' (2 Enoch 8.3−5). Thus it was the place from which the material world took form because it could at this point be permeated by the creative power and presence of the divine. Around Eden was the primeval sea whence monsters rose who lacked human form because they lacked the image of God. The sea was the unformed chaos of mortality from which, according to Genesis 1, the Spirit of God drew forth the stable creation. The bizarre accounts of the creation in the later gnostic texts have their roots in this temple mythology, and they told of a heavenly being who had come through *the veil* separating the upper and lower worlds and had formed for himself a created order from the chaos which he found in the lower world: 'The ruler separated the watery substance to one region and the dry substance he separated to another region. And from the [one] matter he created a dwelling place for himself. He called it heaven. And from the [other] matter the ruler created a footstool. He called it earth' (*On the Origin of the World* CG II 5 101). Could this have been the memory of an older belief that the divine presence passed from the heavens, through the veil of the temple and out onto the watery chaos which surrounded the sanctuary? In the gnostic systems the divine being who passed through the veil was evil and his creation, as a result, was also evil; this is usually regarded as a gnostic invention. But a careful reading of the first chapter of Genesis shows that the emphasis of this creation story is that the material world is good. Is there an element of polemic in this chapter? Had there been another view, the remotest ancestor of the gnostics', that the material world outside the Eden sanctuary was evil? Hints of the 'evil' view of creation have survived. Those who lived in Eden were the angels and therefore immortal; those expelled from Eden, like the prince of Tyre (Ezek. 28.9), became mortal and perished. Adam and Eve were clothed with garments of skin (which later commentators said meant clothed with flesh) and they were destined to return to dust once they had left Eden (Gen. 3.19−20). The world outside the garden was a place of thorns, thistles, and pain. One could hardly have said that it was good.

At the heart of Eden was the tree of life which represented the presence of God. Its branches were the spirits of God who walked on the earth, as Zechariah saw in his vision. The king was one of these, their chief, and thus Jesus could say, 'I am the vine and you are the branches' (John 15.5). The first Christians thought of themselves as the branches of the true vine, but also as the new generation of the sons of God, angels upon earth living the life of eternity whilst still in this world. The leaves of this tree of life were to heal the nations (Rev. 22.2).

The anointed king was also the bond of the eternal covenant which held all things in their appointed place. I strongly suspect that this eternal covenant was renewed at the great autumn festival for the new year. The life of the king, symbolized by the life-blood of the substituted animal, was the sign of the divine presence on earth and this life was used to join together again the spiritual and the material worlds by means of the sprinkling of blood on each side of the temple curtain.

Speculating on the basis of a tentatively reconstructed myth must be the least exact of all disciplines, but it may well prove more fruitful than the monstrous exercise of asserting that myth is factual history. It is sad that people have set out on expeditions to remote parts in order to find where the garden of Eden might once have been long ago, and thus prove in some way that the story was true. Eden is not in space and time, but is the ever present ideal, the beyond. To speak of the End being like the beginning as though there were some process of history is to misrepresent this myth. Two sayings of Jesus in the *Gospel of Thomas* show the real meaning of Eden:

> The disciples said to Jesus, 'Tell us how our end will be'. Jesus said, 'Have you discovered, then, the beginning that you look for the end? For where the beginning is there will the end be. Blessed is he who will take his place in the beginning; he will know the end and will not experience death.' (Thomas 18)

> His disciples said to him, 'When will the kingdom come?' [Jesus said], 'It will not come by waiting for it. It will not be a matter of saying "Here it is" or "There it is". Rather, the Kingdom of the Father is spread out upon the earth, and men do not see it.' (Thomas 113)

CHAPTER THREE
THE VEIL

At the western end of the *hekal* was the great curtain, the veil which concealed the cherub throne. Neither 1 Kings nor Ezekiel mentions it even though Exodus and the Chronicler describe it in detail. It became the means of expressing many beliefs about the limits of human experience. The veil itself, simply as a piece of needlework, must have been something of a masterpiece, and it is not surprising that it was carried off as loot along with gold and bronze treasures whenever the temple was sacked. Inseparable from the veil were the vestments of the high priest, elaborately woven and embroidered in almost the same way as the veil. Veil and vestments were complementary imagery; the veil symbolized all that stood between human perception and the vision of God, and the vestments symbolized the clothing of the divine in that same material world which also concealed it. Thus the veil and the priestly vestments provided the first Christians with ready imagery to convey what they meant by the incarnation. The linen robes worn by the high priest in the sanctuary were also the dress of the angels, those who had left the life of this world and lived in the immediate presence of God. They became the white clothing of the newly baptized.

As with the garden of Eden, all these pictures must be allowed to function *as pictures*, mellowed perhaps and faded so that the detail is no longer clear. What the pictures conveyed was, and still is, more vivid than any number of words. It is only by following the imagery to and fro that the full extent of its influence can be seen and appreciated.

Between Heaven and Earth

> Jesus these eyes have never seen
> That radiant form of thine;
> The veil of sense hangs dark between
> Thy blessed face and mine.
>
> R. Palmer

The *hekal* represented the earth and the *debir* the heavens; between them was the veil which separated the holy place from the most holy (Exod. 26.33). The veil represented the boundary between the visible world and the invisible, between time and eternity. Actions performed within the veil were not of this world but were part of the heavenly liturgy. Those who passed through the veil were the mediators, divine and human, who functioned in both worlds bringing the prayers and penitence of the people to God and the blessing and presence of God to his people. All this was expressed by means of intricate symbolism. As with everything else about the temple, it has to be reconstructed from the surviving fragments, which means that there are many gaps in our knowledge. In this Chapter I shall assemble such parts of the picture as remain, from which it will be seen that the veil seems to have been the earliest expression of the idea of incarnation, the presence of God on earth in a material form. This passed directly into Christian usage: 'Therefore, brethren, ... we have confidence to enter the sanctuary by the blood of Jesus, by the new and living way which he opened for us through the curtain, that is, through his flesh' (Heb. 10.19—20). At the moment of his death the flesh and the veil were both torn and the way was opened into the heavens, into the presence of God (Mark 15.38). 'We have a great high priest who has passed through the heavens' (Heb. 4.14). The symbolism passed into early liturgy:

> We thank thee, O Lord our God, that thou hast given us boldness for the entrance of thy holy places, which thou hast renewed to us as a new and living way through the veil of the flesh of thy Christ. We therefore, being counted worthy to enter into the place of the tabernacle of thy glory, and to be within the veil, and to behold the Holy of Holies, cast ourselves down before thy goodness.
> (Liturgy of James)

The History of the Veil

> Holy, Holy, Holy! though the darkness hide thee,
>   Though the eye of sinful man thy glory may not see,
> Only thou art holy, there is none beside thee,
>   Perfect in power, and love, and purity.
>
> R. Heber

There is no description of the temple veil in the account of Solomon's temple in 1 Kings 6—8, but it is mentioned in the corresponding passage in 2 Chron.: 'And he made the veil of blue and purple and crimson fabrics and fine linen, and worked cherubim on it' (2 Chron. 3.14). Nothing is said of its significance. The curtain of the desert tabernacle is similarly described: 'And you shall make a veil of blue and purple and scarlet stuff and fine twined linen; in skilled work [*hoseb* work] shall it be made, with cherubim' (Exod. 26.31; cf. Exod 36.35). Again, nothing is said of its meaning. There was some debate after the temple had been destroyed about whether there had been a curtain at all in the first temple. The Mishnah says that on the Day of Atonement the high priest had to walk between the two curtains until he reached the ark. But, says the commentary on this passage: 'To what are we referring here? If it be the first sanctuary, was there then a curtain? Again, if it is to the second, was there then an ark?' (b. *Yoma* 52b). From this it can be seen that there was a tradition of two curtains in the second temple, and they were said to have hung one cubit apart, so that a narrow walkway existed between them: 'The outer curtain was looped up on the south side and the inner one on the north side. He went along between them until he reached the north side; when he reached the north side he turned round to the south and went on with the curtain on his left hand until he reached the ark' (Mishnah, *Yoma* 5.1). There must have been several of these great temple curtains; such a piece of fabric would have been very valuable. 'The veil was one handbreadth thick and was woven on a loom having seventy-two rods, and over each rod were twenty-four threads. Its length was forty cubits and its breadth twenty cubits; it was made by eighty-two young girls and they used to make two in every year' (Mishnah, *Shekalim* 8.5). If the veil contacted any uncleanness, it had to be washed; this must have been quite an undertaking. Two hundred square metres of wool and linen fabric would have been very heavy when wet. We are told that it required three hundred priests to immerse it.

> If the veil of the temple contracted uncleanness from a derived uncleanness, it may be immersed within the temple court and forthwith brought in again; but if from a primary uncleanness, it must be immersed outside and spread out on the Rampart since it must await sunset to be wholly clean. If it is new it must be spread out on the roof of the portico that the people may see how fine is the craftsmanship thereof. (Mishnah, *Shekalim* 8.4)

Both Antiochus and Titus took a temple veil among their spoils. In 169 BC Antiochus Epiphanes came against Jerusalem 'with a strong force. He arrogantly entered the sanctuary and took the golden altar, the lampstand for the light, and all its utensils. He took also . . . the curtain' (1 Macc. 1.21−2). This veil may have ended its days in the temple of Zeus; Antiochus rededicated the Jerusalem temple to Olympian Zeus (2 Macc. 6.2), and in the second century AD Pausanias described thus a curtain offered in the great temple of Zeus at Olympia: 'In Olympia there is a woollen curtain, adorned with Assyrian weaving and Phoenician purple, which was dedicated by Antiochus' (Pausanias, *Description of Greece*, V. 12.2). There is no proof that this was the Jerusalem curtain, but the possibility is tempting. Similarly, in AD 70 Titus took the curtain of the temple among his spoils together with a great quantity of blue and purple wools. He ordered that the curtain be kept in his palace in Rome (Josephus, *War* VII.162), where a second-century Rabbi saw it. He also saw on it the bloodstains from the Day of Atonement sprinklings: 'Said R. Eleazar b. R. Yose, "I myself saw it in Rome and there were drops of blood on it. And he told me, 'These are the drops of blood from the Day of Atonement'"' (Tosefta, *Kippurim* 2.16). Of its ultimate fate nothing more is known.

The Symbolism of the Veil

> O tell of his might, O sing of his grace,
> Whose robe is the light, whose canopy space.
>
> R. Grant

More important for our purposes is what the veil was thought to represent. There is no direct reference to this in the Old Testament, although there are places where the idea seems to be presupposed. The Second Isaiah described the place of God as a tent and a curtain, but the Lord's tent was really the heavens, and there was a curtain before him which concealed him.

> It is he who sits above the circle of the earth,
>   and its inhabitants are like grasshoppers;
> who stretches out the heavens like a curtain,
>   and spreads them like a tent to dwell in. (Isa. 40.22)

The tent of the Lord, his tabernacle, was in reality high above the earth, with the heavens stretched out as its curtain. There is nothing here to link the idea specifically to the sanctuary, but other texts do suggest that this was imagery associated with the form of the sanctuary. Psalm 104 describes the Lord's tent and his palace established over the waters, his chariot of clouds and his host of heavenly messengers, creatures of flame and fire. These are the heavenly temple and were depicted in the furnishings of the sanctuary. The tabernacle must have been intended by: 'Thou . . . who hast stretched out the heavens like a tent' (Ps. 104.2). The equally dramatic poem in 2 Sam. 22 (which is the same as Ps. 18) described the Lord riding upon his cherub, enveloped in a canopy of clouds (2 Sam. 22.12). In these three texts are the roots of several later ideas associated with the curtain, but whether the texts represented the ideas in an earlier form, or whether they were the basis of a later speculation about the curtain, we cannot know. Later tradition certainly *did* associate the tabernacle curtain with the high place from which the Lord (or his prophet) could look down and see the earth; the curtain was decorated with patterns to represent the heavens, according to one source, and the idea of the enveloping clouds was probably depicted by the cherubim even on the curtains of the desert tabernacle.

In the first century AD Josephus knew that the veil represented the created world:

> Before these [doors] hung a veil of equal length, of Babylonian tapestry, with embroidery and fine linen, of scarlet also and purple, wrought with marvellous skill. Nor was this mixture of materials without its mystic meaning: it typified the universe. For the scarlet seemed emblematical of fire, the fine

linen of the earth, the blue of the air and the purple of the sea; the comparison in two cases being suggested by their colour and in that of the fine linen and the purple by their origin as the one is produced by the earth and the other by the sea. On this tapestry was portrayed a panorama of the heavens, the signs of the Zodiac excepted. (*War*, V. 212—13)

This is the description of the outer curtain; he says that the inner veil was the same. What is not known is the origin of this symbolism; was it a recent addition to temple lore, or was it ancient? His description of the veil of the desert tabernacle is similar: 'The tabernacle was covered with curtains woven of fine linen, in which the hues of purple and blue and crimson were blended . . . This curtain was of great beauty, being decked with every manner of flower that earth produces, and interwoven with all other designs that could lend to its adornment, save only the forms of living creatures' (*Antiquities*, III.124, 126). The tapestries woven of four materials denote the natural elements: 'Thus the fine linen appears to typify the earth, because from it springs up the flax, and the purple the sea, since it is incarnadined with the blood of fish; the air must be indicated by the blue and the crimson will be the symbol of fire' (*Antiquities*, III.183). The whole tabernacle represented the universe in its different aspects: 'In fact, every one of these objects is intended to recall and represent the universe' (*Antiquities*, III.180).

Philo also mentions this symbolism: 'The highest, and in the truest sense the holy, temple of God is, as we must believe, the whole universe, having for its sanctuary the most sacred part of all existence, even heaven, for its votive ornaments the stars, for its priests the angels' (*Special Laws*, I.66). Elsewhere he says that the weaving of the curtain represents the created world:

> What is spoken about is the workmanship of the materials woven together, which are four in number and are symbols of the four elements, earth, water, air and fire, of which sublunary things are made, while the celestial sphere [is made] of a special substance, of the very most excellent things which have been brought together . . . And so he thought it right that the divine temple of the Creator of all things should be woven of such and so many things as the world was made of, [being] the universal temple which [existed] before the holy temple. (*Questions on Exodus*, II.85)

(This glorious Babylonian tapestry appears in less flattering light in Revelation 17, where it is the garb of the great harlot. The second temple was held by many to be an impure place, not least because of its corrupt priesthood. The first Christians were savagely persecuted in Jerusalem and they took for themselves the ancient descriptions of Jerusalem as the great harlot to be punished by the Lord (e.g. Ezekiel 23, the tale of Oholibah the great harlot, or Isa. 57. 7ff., the new temple as the bed of the great harlot). Like all prophecies, this one in Rev.17 was re-used and applied to the city of Rome, but in origin it was almost certainly against Jerusalem. The woman was 'arrayed in purple and scarlet, and bedecked with gold and jewels and pearls' (Rev. 17.4); she was drunk with the blood of the saints and the blood of the martyrs of Jesus (Rev. 17.6) and she was enthroned upon many waters which represented the nations of the earth (Rev. 17.15), just as they had done in the older descriptions of the Lord triumphing over his enemies, and just as they did in the almost contemporary vision of the man from the sea (4 Ezra 13.5) where the threatening deeps of the old creation story have become the nations threatening the people of God. All the details of Rev. 17 are elaborately interpreted, a sure sign that this is a traditional piece being re-used.)

Philo says a great deal about the role of the veil which separated earth from heaven in that it separated *hekal* from *debir*; 'For in the universe, heaven is a palace of the highest sanctity, and earth is the outer region, estimable indeed in itself, but when it comes into comparison with ether, as far inferior to it as darkness is to light and night to day and corruption to incorruption and mortal man to God' (*Life of Moses*, II.194). It separated the changing from the unchanging: 'It indicates the changeable parts of the world, which are sublunary, and undergo changes of direction, and the heavenly region which is without transient events and is unchanging' (*Questions on Exodus*, II.91).

The furnishings of the *hekal* such as the table and the *menorah* represented the heavenly world in the world of the senses: 'And they are placed outside the veil because the things in the inner recess are invisible and intelligible, whereas those which are external are visible and sense perceptible' (*Questions on Exodus*, II.95). The lamp was made of gold because this was a symbol of the purest substance, heaven (*Questions on Exodus*, II.73).

Clement of Alexandria drew upon the colour symbolism when explaining the mystic meaning of the tabernacle: 'And the covering and the veil were variegated with blue and purple and scarlet and linen. And so it was suggested that the nature of the elements contained the revelation of God. For purple is from water, linen from the earth; blue, being dark, is like the air, as scarlet is like fire' (*Stromata*, V.6). The curtain also appeared in the writings of the Jewish mystics. In the Hebrew Book of Enoch (3 Enoch) Metatron revealed to R. Ishmael the secrets of the great curtain spread before the Holy One. Since this writing was the account of a heavenly ascent, the curtain was described from the other side, so to speak; this was what the curtain looked like for those who saw it from the heavens. The picture is that of Isaiah, where the Lord sits and sees the inhabitants of the earth like grasshoppers. The Hebrew Book of Enoch is a late text, perhaps from the fifth century AD, but it serves to show the continuing influence of temple mythology. The veil divided this world from the beyond; Philo used it in the material sense, and showed how the veil was the boundary between the visible and the invisible creations; the writer of 3 Enoch used it in the temporal sense and showed how the veil represented all history simultaneously in the world beyond time. All the components of history could be seen on the veil just as all the elements of the created world could be seen. This view of history from beyond is important for understanding prophetic and apocalyptic texts (in reality, the same thing). Their view of the future was the view from eternity, a glimpse of the reality underlying time. John, for example, saw what was 'beyond' as well as 'after' his own time of persecution (Rev. 4.1). He was taken up and placed before the heavenly throne.

The High Priest

> Thou within the veil hast entered,
> Robed in flesh, our great high priest.
>
> W. Chatterton Dix

The only person who passed through the veil was the high priest on the Day of Atonement. The texts which describe his vestments show that these were made in exactly the same way as the temple curtain and that they also represented the creation. Their construction is described in Exod. 28: the high priest had a robe of blue with a trimming of blue, purple and scarlet pomegranates around the hem, interspersed with gold bells; over this he wore the ephod of blue, purple, scarlet and fine linen interwoven with gold, clasped at the shoulder with two engraved onyx stones. Over this again was the breastplate, set with twelve precious stones to represent the twelve tribes. On his head he wore a linen turban surrounded by a plate of gold on which was engraved 'Holy to the Lord'.

The symbolism is explained by both Josephus and Philo. Josephus says:

> The high Priest's tunic likewise signifies the earth, being of linen, and its blue the arch of heaven, while it recalls the lightnings by the pomegranates, the thunder by the sound of the bells. His upper garment too denotes universal nature, which it pleased God to make of four elements; being further interwoven with gold in token, I imagine, of the all-pervading sunlight. (*Antiquities*, III.184)

Philo says the vestments are very complicated:

> In this it would seem to be a likeness and copy of the universe. This is clearly shown by the design. In the first place it is a circular garment of dark blue colour throughout, a tunic with a full-length skirt, thus symbolising the air, because the air is both naturally black and in a sense a full-length robe stretching from the sublunar region above to the lowest recesses of the earth. Secondly, on this is set a piece of woven work in the shape of a breastplate which symbolises heaven. For on the shoulder points are two emerald stones, a kind of substance which is exceedingly valuable. There is one of these on each side and both are circular, representing the hemispheres, one of which is above and one under the earth. Then on the breast are twelve precious stones of different colours, arranged in four rows of three each, set in this form in the model of the zodiac. (*Special Laws*, I.84—7)

> Such is the form in which the sacred vesture was designed, a copy of the universe, a piece of work of marvellous beauty to the eye and the mind ... For it expresses the wish first that the High Priests should have in evidence upon him an image

of the All . . . The High Priest of the Jews makes prayers and gives thanks not only on behalf of the whole human race but also for the parts of nature, earth, water, air, fire. (*Special Laws*, I.96−7)

The Wisdom of Solomon says simply: 'For upon his long robe the whole world was depicted, and the glories of the fathers were engraved on the four rows of stones, and thy majesty on the diadem upon his head' (Wisd. 18.24). The priest offered incense on the incense altar outside the veil, and once a year, on the Day of Atonement, the high priest took incense into the *debir*. The four spices of the incense, like the robe, symbolized the worship of the creation:

> Now these four, of which the incense is composed, are, I hold, a symbol of the four elements out of which the whole world was brought to its completion.
> . . . so that while in outward speech it is the compound formed by the perfumer's art which is burned as incense, in fact it is the whole world, wrought by divine wisdom, which is offered and consumed morning and evening in the sacrificial fire. (*Who is the Heir?* 197, 199)

The high priest dressed to represent the universe when he functioned in the *hekal*, the earth, but when he passed through the veil into the holy of holies, into heaven, he wore linen garments (Lev. 16.4). Leviticus does not say why he had to wear a different garment, but it almost certainly signified a different role. It is unlikely that the vestments of the *hekal* were highly symbolic and those of the *debir* not. In the *debir* he no longer represented the created world, but was deemed one of the heavenly entourage. The white linen garment was the dress of the angels, given to favoured human beings upon their ascent to heaven. Frequently in both the Old Testament and the later apocalypses, the 'men in white' were the angels, often the archangels. Thus Ezekiel saw a man clothed in linen (Ezek. 9.2), when judgement was brought upon Jerusalem. Daniel saw a man clothed in linen, who was clearly angelic as his face was shining and his limbs gleamed like bronze (Dan. 10.5). Enoch saw white men coming from heaven (1 Enoch 87.2); they were archangels bringing the judgement. Enoch later saw the seven white men executing judgement on the fallen angels (1 Enoch

90.21–2). Enoch himself was dressed in a glorious robe when Michael brought him before the throne of the Lord: 'And the Lord said to Michael, "Go and extract Enoch from his earthly clothing. And anoint him with my delightful oil, and put him into the clothes of my glory." And so Michael did just as the Lord had said to him. He anointed me and he clothed me ... And I looked at myself and I had become like one of his glorious ones' (2 Enoch 22.8, 10). Enoch the man had become Enoch the angel; he was not only robed but also anointed, the sign of a king or a high priest. John saw the elders in white before the throne (Rev. 4.4) and a multitude in white robes (Rev. 7.9). In the Ascension of Isaiah, the prophet was taken up through the seven heavens; throughout this text angelic status is described in terms of the robe. The companion angel told Isaiah: 'You will receive the robe which you will see ... and then you will be equal to the angels who are in the seventh heaven' (Asc. Isa. 8.14–15). 'The holy Isaiah is permitted to come up here, for his robe is here' (Asc. Isa. 9.2). When he reached the seventh heaven, Isaiah saw the heavenly host; 'And there I saw Enoch and all who [were] with him, stripped of their robes of the flesh; and I saw them in their robes of above, and they were like the angels who stand there in great glory' (Asc. Isa. 9.8–9). Thus Isaiah and the ancient worthies had been transformed from men into angels; they had received their robes. Philo hints at this belief that the linen robe symbolizes the heavenly state when he says that the high priest wears a white robe in the sanctuary: '... when he enters the shrine to offer incense, because its fine linen is not, like wool, the product of *creatures subject to death*' (*Special Laws*, I.84). There is one curious incident in the Old Testament which may refer to this custom of robing the high priest for the sanctuary. When Zechariah had a vision of the high priest, he saw him standing before the Lord with Satan at his right hand to accuse him (Zech. 3.3). The high priest was then stripped of his filthy garments and robed in clean garments at the command of the Lord. After rerobing he was told that he had the 'right of access among those who are standing here' (Zech. 3.7). Since the whole vision was set in the heavenly court, this must refer to access to the angelic places, once he had received his robe and sworn to walk in the ways of the Lord.

Philo's Logos

> Almighty Son, Incarnate Word,
> Our Prophet, Priest, Redeemer, Lord.
> E. Cooper

In order to understand the role of the high priest we have to find what was intended by these different vestments, but unfortunately there is no extant text which deals directly with the meaning of the high priesthood. All that remains are the many descriptions of the robes and the rituals. Philo, however, has left us his own characteristic interpretation of the high priest's role, and this is the nearest we can get to any contemporary understanding. Throughout his writings, Philo was transforming Jewish beliefs into something comprehensible to his educated Greek contemporaries in Alexandria. *But he was transforming, not inventing.* He himself remained a leading figure in the Jewish community, and this would not have happened had he been an arch-heretic. He must have been transforming contemporary Jewish belief. The question then is: *What* was he transforming for his contemporaries? He was using temple symbolism, but instead of talking about the heavenly and the earthly temple, he talked about the universe and the individual, each man in some way a temple of God. In order to recover the first-century understanding of high priesthood, we have to extract from his writings the temple symbolism with which he began.

Philo talks of a heavenly high priest who had an earthly counterpart, which is quite consistent with what is known elsewhere of the temple. His heavenly high priest was called the Logos, the Word, of God. What is surprising is that this heavenly high priest figure was described as a *second God* who was the intermediary between the Most High God and his world. Man was made in the image of this second God, 'For nothing mortal can be made in the likeness of the Most High One and Father of the Universe, but only in that of the *second God who is his Logos*' (*Questions on Genesis*, II.62). This second God was the high priest of the universe, 'For there are, as is evident, two temples of God: one of them this universe in which there is also as high priest his Firstborn, the Divine Logos, and the other the rational soul, whose priest is the real man' (*On Dreams*, I.215). Here we have the idea of a heavenly high priest who was the Firstborn of God, a second God. Presumably this was part of Philo's own belief about the high priest, which means that the high priest in the temple must have depicted in some way the role of this second God. What he says about the cosmic significance of the Logos must have been the original significance of the high priest and whatever he represented.

Since the true high priest was a heavenly figure, he originally passed through the veil not *to* but *from* the presence of God. As he passed through the veil so he took form from it and thus became visible, robed in the four elements of the created order: 'Now the garments that the supreme Logos of him that IS puts on as raiment are the world, for he arrays himself in earth and air and water and fire and all that comes forth from these' (*On Flight*, 110). The high priest, he says, is the outward, visible image who: 'offers prayers and sacrifices handed down from our fathers to whom it has been committed to wear the aforesaid tunic which is a copy and replica of the whole heaven, the intention being that the universe may join with man in the holy rites and men with the universe' (*On Dreams*, I.215). The high priest was thus the second God in his earthly manifestation, who passed back into the presence of God as the mediator. Philo gives other passing allusions to the high priest's role; he says he was 'appointed judge and mediator' (*Questions on Exodus*, II.13). When he went through the veil he divested himself of the multicoloured garb of the material world and put on the glorious robe of the angels, of which he was the chief. 'To his Logos, his archangel, the Father of all has given the special prerogative to stand on the border and separate the creature from the creator. This same Logos both pleads with the immortal as suppliant for afflicted mortality and acts as ambassador of the ruler to the subject' (*Who is the Heir?*, 205). This Logos was a royal figure, 'he who is at once high priest and king' (*On Flight*, 118). He took human form, 'God's Man, the Logos of the Eternal' (*On the Confusion of Tongues*, 41). Finally, Philo describes the Logos as the agent of God on earth: 'This hallowed flock he leads in accordance with right and law, setting over it his True Logos and Firstborn Son who shall take upon him its government like some viceroy of a great king; for it is said in a certain place: Behold I AM, I send my angel before thy face to guard thee in the way' (*On Agriculture*, 51). The Logos, the high priest, was the angel of the Lord who bore the name of the Lord on his forehead, just as did the chosen who survived the judgement (Ezek. 9.4; Rev. 7.3; 14.1) to enter the presence of God. Philo says that the high priest wore on his turban a golden band, not inscribed 'Holy to the Lord' as we read in Exod. 28.36, but simply with the four letters of the sacred name, 'four incisions showing the name which only those whose ears and tongues are purified may hear or speak in the holy place and no other person nor in any other place at all. That name has four letters' (*Life of Moses*, II.114). In other words, the high priest bore the name Yahweh. The Letter of Aristeas says this too: 'On his head he wore a tiara, as it is called, and upon this in the middle of his forehead an inimitable turban, the royal diadem full of glory with the name of God inscribed in sacred letters on a plate of gold' (Aristeas 98).

All these descriptions of the Logos high priest are reminiscent of the old royal titles; Philo's high priest seems to have inherited the ancient role of the anointed king, and the Logos can best be explained as the memory of the heavenly ideal on which the monarchy was based. The Logos archangel was the patron angel of Israel who walked in the garden of Eden and had his shrine in the heavenly temple. In Philo's writings, however, we discover another aspect; he was made visible when he passed through the veil into the temple. The veil was the means of revelation. This is not wholly unexpected; Amos had seen the Lord standing by the altar (Amos 9.1); Malachi prophesied that the angel of the covenant would appear in the temple (Mal. 3.1); Zechariah saw the angel of the Lord standing by the incense altar in the temple, i.e. in front of the veil (Luke 1.11). What Philo says in no way contradicts what other writings imply. The information he adds is that the high priest 'was' in some way the great archangelic mediator. The Dead Sea Scrolls often mention priests as angels; this is not explained, simply assumed. Thus in the blessing of the sons of Zadok, the priests, we find: 'May you be as an Angel of the Presence in the Abode of Holiness to the glory of the God of [Hosts] . . . May you attend upon the service in the Temple of the Kingdom and decree destiny in company with the Angels of the Presence' (1 QSb IV). The *Songs for the Sabbath Sacrifice* also describe angelic priests: 'to be for him the priests of [the inner Temple in his royal sanctuary], ministers of the Presence in his glorious innermost Temple chamber' (4Q 400); 'the sovereign Princes of the [wonderful] priest[hood] . . . the seven priest[hoods] in the wonderful sanctuary for seven councils of holiness' (4Q 403).

The texts are all too fragmented for any certain conclusions to be drawn, but what remains is consistent with Philo's picture. No Qumran text describes his heavenly high priest, but if the priests 'were' the angels of the sanctuary, it is not unreasonable to suppose that the chief priest should have been the chief angel, exactly as Philo says, and this chief angel took a visible form when he passed through the temple veil and arrayed himself in the elements of the material world.

Some Gnostic Texts

The veil represented the division between the material and spiritual worlds, between the visible and the invisible, and in this respect it *concealed* the divine. But it also *revealed* the divine in that the veil was the robe of the heavenly high priest when he passed into the visible world. All these ideas were used in the early Christian centuries both by those whom history remembers as Christians and those whom it has labelled heretics. Of the heretics, the most important for our purposes were the Gnostics who developed a highly sophisticated form of Christianity which survived for many centuries and reappeared in the twelfth century in southern France with the Cathars. Nobody can be certain of the origin of the Gnostics, but the imagery used in many of their texts suggests that there was at the very least a Jewish grandmother in the family, with whom they had had a violent disagreement. Their use of Jewish themes went hand in hand with a determination to show that the Jewish God was evil. This accounts for some of the more peculiar twists in their writings. Gnosticism was a great threat to Christianity in its earliest years, and it was some time before the two systems really became distinct. Irenaeus, who wrote towards the end of the second century in southern France, left a systematic condemnation of their teachings and it is from his accounts that we gain a great deal of our information about them.

A library of gnostic books was found in December 1945 at Nag Hammadi in Egypt. Of the texts found there, two clearly use the ancient temple themes. These gnostic texts are thought to date

THE VEIL 119

from the third century AD, and they are obviously related to each other. The nature of this relationship need not concern us here; what is important is the way they both employ the old temple themes albeit in their own characteristic way. The Gnostics held that the creator God of the Old Testament was a second deity, and that there was a higher divine being. This is exactly what is implied in the writings of Philo, namely that there was a Most High God and then a second divinity, his Firstborn, his Word, the deity who was made visible in the world below the temple veil. Where the Gnostics differed from Philo is that they said the creator God was evil, and this belief of theirs explains some of the alterations they made to the traditions. As with Philo, we have in these gnostic texts an interpretation of an underlying tradition, or rather, a scheme which uses elements from the older pattern. In so far as we are dependent upon so little to reconstruct the 'original' scheme of temple belief, it is not easy to say what is a new construction using the old materials, and what is actually a development of earlier ideas. Here I shall simply pick out familiar motifs.

The first of these texts, *The Nature of the Archons* (CG. II.4), demonstrates the reality of the great angelic rulers of the universe by giving an esoteric interpretation of the first six chapters of Genesis. Norea, the daughter of Eve, encountered the Great Angel, a being clothed in white whose appearance was like fine gold (CG. II.4/93). This Great Angel was one of the four Light-Givers who stood in the presence of the Great Invisible Spirit. (We recognize here the four archangels.) He assured her that the Rulers would have no power over her, and that they would one day be bound. He then told her of the upper world: 'Within limitless realms dwells Incorruptibility. Sophia (Wisdom) . . . wanted to create something alone without her consort, and her product was a celestial thing' (CG. II.4/94). (We recognize here the creative power of Wisdom and the belief in a world beyond matter and time.) The angel then explained the creative process: 'A veil exists between the world above and the realms that are below; and a shadow came into being beneath the veil; and that shadow became matter; and that shadow was projected apart. And what she had created became a product in the Matter, like an aborted foetus.' (Here there is the divine being passing through the veil and taking material form). Philo had called the Logos the Shadow: 'God's shadow is his Logos, which he made use of like an instrument and so made the world' (*Allegorical Interpretation*, III.96). This divine being looked around him and declared that he was the only God. He was androgynous and created for himself seven androgynous offspring. (Here we recognize the creator of Genesis who made male and female in his own image [Gen. 1.27]. There were also the seven archangels and the seven eyes of the Lord who were upon the earth as his agents. Finally, there was the hostility to Judaism which characterizes the gnostic writings; the God of the Old Testament is here depicted as arrogant, claiming to be unique. Whatever the interpretation, the underlying tradition is immediately obvious; the God of the Old Testament was as bad as any of the fallen angels who were condemned for their pride.) The divine being who took material form and became arrogant was named Sabaoth. He later repented of his arrogance and was installed by Wisdom as ruler of the seventh heaven which was 'below the veil between above and below' (CG. II.4/95): 'And he is called the God of the Forces, Sabaoth, since he is up above the Forces of Chaos, for Wisdom established him' (CG. II.4/96). (Here we recognize the ancient enthronement of the Lord over the waters of chaos. The enthronement of the arrogant Sabaoth is only possible because he repented; this is the gnostic element in the account, in order to bring their peculiar views about the God of the Old Testament back into line with the tradition of Sabaoth as the ruler.) Finally this Sabaoth 'made himself a huge four-faced chariot of cherubim and infinitely many angels to act as ministers, and also harps and lyres' (CG. II.4/96). The source of this is unmistakable; Sabaoth was the Lord of Hosts (*Yahweh Sabaoth* in Hebrew) and the whole episode must have been the gnostic version of the temple myth of the creation, with the added refinement that they wished to depict the creator God of the Old Testament as essentially evil. According to the tradition underlying this account, *it was the Lord himself who passed through the veil to take material form* and create the world. Perhaps this is why the high priest wore on his head the sacred name Yahweh; he represented the Lord. Had he inherited the role of the ancient king, as seems likely, this would be consistent with the idea that the king had been the visible manifestation of the Lord, the patron deity of Israel.

The second of these texts is an untitled work usually known as *On the Origin of the World* (CG. II.5). It also deals with primeval times and says that Chaos was the original Shadow, the Darkness. After the immortals had been created Sophia (Wisdom) wished to create something from the light, that is from the upper world, the world above the shadow: 'Immediately her wish appeared as a heavenly likeness, which possessed an incomprehensible greatness, which is in the middle between the immortals and those who came into being after them, like what is above, which is *a veil which separates men and those belonging to the sphere above*' (CG. II.5/98). The upper world, called the aeon of truth, was a place of immeasurable light and therefore had no shadow, i.e. no matter, within it. The shadow then realized that it was not the greatest power (cf. Sabaoth recognizing a higher power), and Wisdom realized what horrors resulted from a creation which existed without her: 'Then she turned to it and [breathed] into its face in the abyss [which is] beneath all the heavens' (CG.II. 5/99). (This is the creation story of Genesis, but the Spirit on the face of the waters is named Wisdom as so often happens in the intertestamental texts.) She then gave the power of the upper world of light to the ruler of chaos: 'Now when Faith-Wisdom desired [to cause] the one who had no spirit to receive the pattern of a likeness and rule over the matter and all its powers, a ruler first appeared out of the waters, lion-like in appearance, androgynous and having great authority within himself, but not knowing whence he came into being' (CG. II.5/100). This creature organized matter and created the heaven for himself and the earth for his footstool. He then created seven androgynous beings (the seven eyes of the Lord, the seven archangels), and created for each of them a glorious heavenly place with a chariot throne and angelic servants. (This is the picture of the heavens implied in the *Songs of the Sabbath Sacrifice*, where there are the seven angelic Princes with their sanctuaries.) In this version of the story it is the Father of the seven sons who becomes arrogant and is condemned, but the tale then continues with the familiar repentance of Sabaoth, one of the seven sons, who is then endowed with great light by Faith–Wisdom and given power over Chaos. The earlier description of the father God and this one of his son Sabaoth seem to be variants of the same belief, namely that one essentially evil being was endowed by Faith-Wisdom with light which enabled him to rule Chaos/matter. Sabaoth is taken up to the seventh heaven by Faith–Wisdom and then makes for himself, 'a great throne on a four-faced chariot called cherubim ... And seven archangels stand before him' (CG. II.5/105). Sabaoth thus sits in the seventh heaven as the creator, the one who rules over Chaos; he is the second God. He had been a part of the world of matter/chaos, elevated to heaven by the power of Wisdom.

A third Nag Hammadi text, *A Valentinian Exposition*, is too fragmented to be read with any certainty, but it seems to introduce a concept known elsewhere in gnostic texts, that of the Limit, Horos, which divided the material world from the upper world: 'And Limit [is the separator of the All] ... completely ineffable to the All, and he is the confirmation and [the] hypostasis of the all, the silent [veil], the [true] High Priest [the one who has] the authority to enter the holy of holies revealing the glory of the aeons' (CG XI.2/25—6).

Another gnostic writer who used temple themes was Theodotus, a Valentinian Gnostic who was teaching towards the end of the second century. Clement of Alexandria made a collection of quotations from his teaching, possibly as the basis for a book; these survive as the *Excerpts from Theodotus*. It is not always possible to tell which sections were from Theodotus and which were Clement's comments, but this need not concern us overmuch. What is important is the temple imagery used and what it reveals of the role of the veil in the temple cult:

> The priest on entering within the second veil removed the plate at the altar of incense,* and entered himself in silence with the Name engraved upon his heart, indicating the laying aside of the body which has become pure like the golden plate and bright through purification ...
>
> Now he discards this body, the plate which had become light, within the second veil, that is, in the rational sphere the second complete veil of the universe, at the altar of incense, that is, with the angels who are the ministers of the prayers carried aloft. Now the souls, stripped by the power of him who has knowledge, as if it had become a body of the power, passes into the spiritual realm and becomes now truly rational and high priestly. (*Excerpt* 27)

Beneath the gnostic peculiarities we see the more ancient belief

---

* Nothing is known of this custom from other sources.

that passing through the veil was passing into heaven, and that this dangerous journey could only be made by the high priest.

A second extract uses *TOPOS*, the Greek equivalent of the Hebrew *MAQOM*, one of the many circumlocutions for the Divine Name. It means 'the place'.

> A river goes from under the throne of [Topos] and flows into the void of the creation which is Gehenna, and it is never filled, though the fire flows from the beginning of the creation. And [Topos] itself is fiery. Therefore, he says, it has a veil in order that things may not be destroyed by the sight of it. And only the archangel enters it, and to typify this, the high priest every year enters the holy of holies. From thence Jesus was called and sat down with Topos. (*Excerpt* 38)

Here we see the angelic role of the high priest who enters on the Day of Atonement into the presence of the fiery throne.

Clement also records that these Gnostics knew of a Limit (*Horos*) which separated the upper world from the lower. It is clear, even from their highly stylized use of the idea, that this too originated with the temple veil. The soul of the Gnostic goes to meet its heavenly counterpart, its angel bridegroom: 'then they enter the bridal chamber within Horos and attain to the vision of the Father' (*Excerpt* 64). When Jesus came into the world he 'went forth outside Horos' (*Excerpt* 35), and the cross became 'a symbol of Horos in the Pleroma, for it divides the faithful from the unfaithful just as the latter separates the world from the Pleroma' (*Excerpt* 42).

There were angels baptized for their gnostic believers, 'in order that we too . . . may not be held back and prevented by Horos and the Cross from entering into the Pleroma' (*Excerpt* 22). When Jesus said 'I am the door' (John 10.7) he meant: 'up to the Horos where I am, you will come, you who belong to the superior seed' (*Excerpt* 26).

These gnostic writings, for all their apparent confusion, allow the older beliefs to show through. The setting for all the drama of creation and redemption is the temple with its angels and its two worlds, the upper world of the light, the Pleroma, and the lower material world. The second God is the one who has a place in both worlds; *The Nature of the Archons* says he came through the veil and became matter, *The Origin of the World* seems to emphasize rather his origin in matter and elevation by Wisdom.

Either way, this creator God was a divine being who could have a material form and who passed through the veil separating the world of light and incorruptibility from the world of darkness and matter. He was enthroned in the seventh heaven, on the cherub throne of the temple sanctuary. The *Excerpts* on the other hand, emphasize the high-priestly role rather than that of the creator. The roots of all three are beyond doubt in the temple.

The Early Christian Writings

> Veiled in flesh the Godhead see!
> Hail the incarnate Deity!
> C. Wesley

The veil of the temple was used by Christians from the beginning to describe the incarnation. Further, they used not only the veil but also the robe of the high priest, which symbolized the second divine being robed in the material world of the veil. The first Christians knew the intimate connection between the two. The earliest reference to the veil is in Hebrews where the curtain is the flesh of Jesus, and Jesus the High Priest takes his own blood through the veil into the sanctuary (Heb. 10.19−21). The Gospels record that the veil was torn in two at the moment of Jesus' death, a graphic illustration of the identity of flesh and veil (Matt. 27.51; Mark 15.38; Luke 23.45).

Melito of Sardis, who wrote about AD 170−80, composed a homily on the Pascha. Pascha has no exact English equivalent; it can mean either the Passover or the Christian Holy Week and Easter which replaced it but kept many of its themes. Speaking of the moment when the temple veil was torn at the crucifixion, Melito said: 'For when the people did not tremble, the earth quaked; when the people were not terrified, the heavens were terrified; when the people did not tear their clothes, the angel tore his; when the people did not lament, the Lord thundered out of heaven and the Highest gave voice' (*On the Pascha*, 98). The veil of the temple is the robe of the angel. Melito says *the* angel as though his hearers would have known which angel was meant. It must have been the angel who was present in the temple. In a fragment of his work which has survived only in a Georgian translation, he also described the crucifixion: 'Stars withheld their light, the sun was darkened, and angels horrified quit the temple, and seraphim cried out with their noise, [the veil] was torn, and shadows filled all the earth' (*New Fragment* II, 101–6). This is similar to the account in Josephus of the angels leaving when the temple was about to fall to the Romans (see Chapter 1), and a different version of the tradition is in a Christian addition to the Testaments of the Twelve Patriarchs: 'And the veil of the temple shall be rent, and the Spirit of God shall pass on to the Gentiles as fire poured forth' (Test. Benjamin 9.4).

Clement of Alexandria, who wrote at the end of the second century, knew that the robe and the veil depicted the incarnation. This, he said, was particularly for the benefit of those people who could not cope with the world beyond that of the five senses: 'But the knowledge of God is a thing inaccessible to the ears and like organs of this kind of people. Hence the Son is said to be the Father's face, being the revealer of the Father's character in the five senses by clothing himself with flesh... Now the high priest's robe is the symbol of the world of sense.' Only those who bore the sacred name were able to pass through the veil and enter the sanctuary. Every item of the high priest's vestment represented some aspect of Jesus' ministry; the three hundred and sixty bells on the robe were the days of the acceptable year of the Lord, the golden mitre was the sign of princely rule, the breastplate by which oracles were given signified the Word as prophet and judge, and so forth. 'And they say that the robe prophesied the ministry in the flesh, by which he was seen in closer relation to the world. So the high priest, putting off his consecrated robe ... washes himself and puts on the other tunic, a holy of holies one, so to speak, which is to accompany him into the adytum.' This linen robe is 'the bright array of glory' and the one who wears it 'is now replenished with insatiable contemplation face to face'. 'But in one way, as I think, the Lord puts off and puts on by descending into the region of sense; and in another, he who through Him has believed puts off and puts on, as the apostle intimated, the consecrated stole' (all these are from *Stromata*, V.6). Justin knew a different tradition; he said that there were twelve bells which represented 'the twelve Apostles who were dependent on the Power of Christ the everlasting Priest' (*Trypho*, 42). When Irenaeus described the incarnation in his *Proof of the Apostolic Preaching*, he used language which must have come from this setting:

So he united man with God and brought about a communion of God and man, we being unable in any other wise to have a part in incorruptibility, had it not been for his coming to us. For incorruptibility, while invisible and imperceptible, would not help us; so he became visible, that we might be taken into full communication with incorruptibility. (*Proof*, 31)

He also spoke of the shadow: 'and shadow means His body, for as a shadow is made by a body, so too Christ's body is made by His Spirit' (*Proof*, 71). He elaborated the shadow image in several ways, but the fact that the shadow of the Spirit becomes the visible body shows that he was using the traditional description of the second God coming through the veil.

St Ephrem the Syrian, who wrote in the middle of the fourth century, used the veil and the robe to describe the incarnation:

> The firstborn was clothed in the body;
>   it was the veil of his glory.
> The immortal Bridegroom
>   will shine forth in this robe.
> The guests in their robe
>   will be like that robe of his;
> [their] bodies, their garments will shine. (*Nisibene Hymns* 43. tr. Murray in *Symbols of Church and Kingdom*, p. 76)

In one of his *Hymns on the Nativity* he wrote: 'Blessed is He Who made our Body a tabernacle for His unseen Nature... Blessed be He Who dwelt in the womb and wrought therein a perfect Temple, that He might dwell in it, a Throne that he might be in it, a garment that He might be arrayed in it' (*Hymn* 11). In his *Hymns on Paradise* he spoke of the veil differently (see Chapter 2). He compared the sin of Adam and the sin of King Uzziah, who took the incense and went into the temple, despite the protests of the priests (2 Chron. 26.16—21) and was punished with leprosy. Ephrem compared the veil which should not have been penetrated by Uzziah with the tree whose fruit should not have been tasted by Adam. Both veil and tree separated what was above from what was below (*Hymn* 3.14). It is easy to see why he said this: the fruit of the tree gave man knowledge so that he became like one of the *elohim* (Gen. 3.22), and the vision beyond the veil also transformed the beholder, but in each case there was death for anyone who did this unlawfully. Ephrem must have known that the holy of holies was the place of transforming vision, which rendered the human divine, or he could not have made the comparison.

The *Book of James* was first mentioned by Origen in the early third century and must record very early material about the infancy of Jesus. One of its stories tells how Mary had been a temple weaver; the mother of the holy child was weaving a new temple veil as she carried him in her womb.

> Now there was a council of the priests and they said: Let us make a veil for the temple of the Lord . . . And they brought [seven virgins] into the temple of the Lord and the priest said: Cast me lots, which of you shall weave the gold and the undefiled [the white] and the fine linen and the silk and the hyacinthine and the scarlet and the true purple. And the lot of the scarlet and the true purple fell unto Mary and she took them and went unto her house. (Book of James X)

As she was working, Gabriel came and told her she was to have the holy child. She continued her work and then brought the purple and scarlet wool back to priests in the temple.

The veil of the temple is thus a means of revelation as well as of concealment. The divine becomes visible when it is veiled in the material world. In the earliest biblical texts this is implicit: 'And let them make a sanctuary *that I may be seen among them*' (Exod. 25.8, translated from the Greek version). It was this Greek version which inspired Origen's understanding of the tabernacle: 'God wishes, therefore, that we make a sanctuary for him. For he promises that if we make a sanctuary for him, *he can be seen by us*' (*Homily on Exodus*, IX).

Beyond the Veil

> . . . till before my Father's throne,
> I shall know as I am known.
>   J. E. Leeson

Beyond the veil was the world outside time and thus the sanctuary was the place for visions from eternity and of eternity. What was eternal was concealed; the Hebrew words for 'eternity' and 'conceal' come from the same root *'lm*. Sometimes these were visions of judgement, sometimes they were panoramic views of history. Sanctuary visions in later texts often describe how the seer looked down from a high place and saw the whole creation, both in time and space, simultaneously before him.

The clearest example of this tradition is in the Hebrew Book of Enoch, a late text, but one which undoubtedly incorporates many old ideas. R. Ishmael had been taken up through the heavens by the great angel Metatron, who had formerly been the seer Enoch. He recorded his experience, one of which was seeing the heavenly veil: 'R. Ishmael said: Metatron said to me: Come and I will show you the curtain of the Omnipresent One which is spread before the Holy One, blessed be He, and on which are printed all the generations of the world and all their deeds, whether done or to be done, till the last generation' (3 Enoch 45.1). There follows a long description of Israel's history from earliest times until the days of the Messiah yet to come. 'All the rest of the leaders of every generation and every deed of every generation both of Israel and of the gentiles, whether done or to be done in the time to come, to all generations, till the end of time, were all printed on the curtain of the Omnipresent One' (3 Enoch 45.6). The veil filtered out all the limitations of time and space and gave a view of the creation from the divine throne. Those who passed beyond the veil passed beyond the limitations imposed by what it represented. Having described Jesus as the true High Priest who veiled himself in flesh and then passed back through the heavens, the writer to the Hebrews could conclude that Jesus was a part of the world beyond the veil: 'Jesus Christ is the same yesterday and today and forever' (Heb. 13.8). Many of the prophetic visions in the Old Testament may have had such a setting; the prophets claimed a special insight into the ways of God: 'Surely the Lord does nothing without revealing his secret to his servants the prophets?' (Amos 3.7).

The earliest certain reference to a panoramic view of history from the height of the sanctuary is in 1 Enoch. Three of the archangels grasped Enoch by the hand, 'and took me from the generations of the earth, lifted me up into a high place, and showed me a high tower above the earth and all the hills were small. One of them said to me, "Stay here until you see everything that will happen"' (1 Enoch 87.3—4). *The tower* was a common description of the sanctuary. The oldest reference to the tower as a place of vision is in Habakkuk:

THE VEIL 129

> I will take my stand to watch,
> and station myself on the tower,
> and look forth to see what he will say to me,
>   and what I will answer concerning my complaint.
> And the Lord answered me
> 'Write the vision;
>   make it plain upon tablets,
>   so that he may run who reads it.
> For still the vision awaits its time;
>   it hastens to the end – it will not lie.
> If it seem slow, wait for it;
>   it will surely come, it will not delay.' (Hab. 2.1–3)

For the Psalmist the tower was the sanctuary, even though there is no question of a vision in this text:

> Lead thou me to the rock that is higher than I;
> for thou art my refuge,
>   a strong tower against the enemy.
> Let me dwell in thy tent forever!
>   Oh to be safe under the shelter of thy wings! (Ps. 61.2–3)

In 1 Enoch, the returning exiles built a high tower and offered bread on the table before the tower (1 Enoch 89.73). This bread must have been the shewbread which was set out in the *hekal* before the sanctuary. In the Assumption of Moses we read: 'the God of heaven will make the court of his tabernacle and the tower of his sanctuary' (Ass. Mos. 2.4). Isaiah's Song of the Vineyard (Isa. 5.1–7) said that the vineyard of the Lord of Hosts was the house of Israel; an interpretation attributed to R. Yosi in the early second century AD adds, 'And he built a tower in the midst of it . . . this is the sanctuary' (Tosefta, *Sukkah*, 3.15). In Hermas the Church is described as a great tower, but the imagery has obviously been taken over from the earlier temple. The tower is built of people, the living stones of 1 Peter 2.5, built upon water (*Parable* 3.ii.4) and also built over a great rock (*Parable* 9.iii.1). A glorious man, whom we have been told was the Son of God, is the Lord of the tower (*Parable* 9.vii.1), and also the rock on which it is built (*Parable* 9.xii.1). None could enter the tower, also called the kingdom of God, unless he had received the name of the Son of God (*Parable* 9.xii.8). This tower is the sanctuary of the temple, with the great rock beneath it, the primeval waters around it, and the name of the Lord upon all who could enter.

It was from this tower that Enoch had his vision; he was caught up by archangels and saw the whole history of Israel as an animal fable, from the time of the garden of Eden until the time of the Last Judgement. Jesus' visions during his temptations are very similar in form; 'And the devil took him up and showed him all the kingdoms of the earth in a moment of time . . . And he took him to Jerusalem and set him on the pinnacle of the temple' (Luke 4.5, 9). There is a similar panoramic vision in the Apocalypse of Abraham. At the time of his covenant sacrifice (Gen. 15) Abraham was taken by the angel Iaoel up to the divine throne where he saw the heavenly beings and heard their song. The Eternal Mighty One spoke to him:

> Look now beneath your feet at the firmament and understand the creation that was depicted of old on this expanse, and the creatures which are in it and the age prepared after it. And I looked beneath the firmament at my feet and I saw the likeness of heaven and the things that were therein. And [I saw] there the earth and its fruit and its moving things, and its things that had souls . . . And I saw there the sea and its islands and its cattle and its fish and Leviathan and his realm and his bed and his lairs. (Apoc. Abraham 21.1—5)

Abraham too saw all of Israel's history until the time of the Messiah.

The visions in the Apocalypse of Baruch were given in the sanctuary. When Baruch was questioned about the disaster which had befallen Jerusalem he said: 'Far be it from me to forsake you or to withdraw from you, but I will only go unto the Holy of Holies to inquire of the Mighty One concerning you and concerning Zion, if in some respect I should receive more illumination' (2 Bar. 34). Later he described the final state of the blessed:

> For they shall behold the world which is now invisible to them, And they shall behold the time which is now hidden from them: And time shall no longer age them. For in the heights of that world shall they dwell, And they shall be made like unto the angels, And be made equal to the stars . . .
> For there shall be spread before them the extents of Paradise,

and there shall be shown to them the beauty of the majesty of the living creatures which are beneath the throne. (2 Bar. 51.8—10)

Moses had been shown all secrets when he was in the presence of God:

For he showed him many admonitions together with the principles of the Law and the consummation of the times . . . and likewise the pattern of Zion and its measures, in the pattern of which the sanctuary of the present time was to be made. But then he also showed to him the measures of the fire, also the depths of the abyss, and the weight of the winds and the number of the drops of rain . . . And the height of the air and the greatness of Paradise and the consummation of the ages and the beginning of the day of judgement. (2 Bar. 59.4, 5, 8)

The Babylonian Talmud shows that the angels were believed to bring revelations through the curtain, often of a less momentous nature: Gabriel brought advice about the poll tax (b. *Yoma* 77a), and Satan revealed a secret to Abraham 'Thus have I heard from behind the curtain' (b. *Sanhedrin* 89b). The story was told of a man scolded by his wife who went out and spent the night in a cemetery. He heard two spirits talking to each other:

Said one to her companion: My dear, come and let us wander about the world and let us hear from behind the curtain what suffering is coming upon the world. Said her companion to her: I am not able, because I am buried in matting of reeds. But do you go and whatever you hear, tell me. So the other went and wandered about and returned. Said her companion to her: My dear, what have you heard from behind the curtain? She replied: I heard that whoever sows after the first rainfall will have his crops smitten by hail. (b. *Berakoth* 18b)

The man listening in the cemetery was able to profit from this information! Elsewhere the curtain became simply the name for the first of the seven heavens; *Wilon*, the name of the first heaven, was a name for the curtain derived from the Latin *velum* (b. *Hagigah* 12b).

The veil was the means both of concealing and revealing the divine. It represented the material world and thus it concealed, but it clothed the divine and thus made it visible. 'Coming forth' from the presence of God, one who both reveals and is revealed, is one of the great themes of the Fourth Gospel (John 3.13; 6.38; 8.23). The Ascension of Isaiah expressed the idea more vividly if more crudely: 'The Lord will indeed descend into the world in the last days [he] who is to be called Christ after he has descended and become like you in form and they will think that he is flesh and man' (Asc. Isa. 9.13). The Epistle to the Hebrews spoke of one who was both sent out, 'the apostle', and passed back through the veil, 'the high priest' (Heb. 3.1). All these expressed the basic idea of passing from the invisible to the visible, from the *debir* and what it represented into the *hekal* and this world. The *debir* was the timeless place, the place of myths, the principles upon which the creation was built and by which it was to be understood. By a new actualization of these myths, a new beginning was made and a new creative process was begun. It is this aspect of the veil which underlies Irenaeus' mysterious 'recapitulation', the explanation of the work of Christ which develops the ideas of Eph. 1.9—10: 'For he has made known to us in all wisdom and insight the mystery of his will, according to his purpose which he set forth in Christ as a plan for the fulness of time, to unite all things in him, things in heaven and things on earth.' God restored the divine plan for mankind, said Irenaeus, which had been marred by the fall of Adam. His entire work from the beginning was restored in his Son, who lived as Adam but did not fall as Adam had done. By becoming again the first man, the whole human race was renewed and restored. This is the mythological view of history; all which we experience only in time exists outside time and eternity. Those in eternity grasp all history in a moment ('all the kingdoms of the world in a moment of time', Luke 4.5). 'When he became incarnate and was made man, he recapitulated in himself the long history of man, summing up and giving us salvation in order that we might receive again in Christ Jesus what we had lost in Adam, that is, the image and likeness of God' (*Against Heresies*, III.18.1). By this gathering up, this recapitulation, Christ renewed everything, thus linking recreation and revelation, Eden and the One who walked in Eden.

CHAPTER FOUR

THE THRONE

Beyond the veil there was the holy of holies, the most sacred part of the temple. In Solomon's time it had housed the cherub throne; in the descriptions of the desert tabernacle this became the mercy seat, the place of the presence of the Lord, which was at the very heart of the cult. By New Testament times the holy place had been stripped by enemy action and it was empty. The rituals were practised 'as though' the throne was there. St Paul built upon this when he spoke of Jesus as the new 'mercy seat' (Rom. 3.25). The word translated 'expiation' in the RSV is the same as that translated 'mercy seat' in Lev. 16.14. The poignancy of this is not apparent if the temple setting is lost. St Paul was saying that the heart of the cult had been restored.

The throne of God in the holy of holies, which represented the highest heaven, passed into all Christian imagery of the last judgement. The angels around the throne were the basis of the earliest expressions of the Trinity, and, most crucial of all, the man figure on the throne, originally a memory of the ancient kings, was thought to have prefigured the incarnation, the presence of the Lord with his people in human form. It is the throne and its associations which proved the most fertile source of inspiration for the expression of early Christian thought.

The Presence of the Lord

> Let all mortal flesh keep silence
> And with fear and trembling stand;
> Ponder nothing earthly minded,
> For with blessing in his hand
> Christ our God to earth descendeth,
> Our full homage to demand.
> Liturgy of St James, tr. G. Moultrie

In the holy of holies, in heaven, was the divine throne. The Lord was believed literally to be present with his people; exactly how this was understood is not known, but it was to become a much debated issue as Israel's religion became more sophisticated. How could the Lord, in any sense, *be* in his temple? This question became even more pressing when the temple had been destroyed and the people were in exile in Babylon.

The psalmist expressed the ancient view: 'The Lord is in his holy temple, the Lord's throne is in heaven' (Ps. 11.4). Habakkuk too: 'But the Lord is in his holy temple; let all the earth keep silence before him' (Hab. 2.20). As late as the time of Jeremiah, this belief about the divine presence continued: 'Is the Lord not in Zion? Is her King not in her?' (Jer. 8.19). Always it was as a part of the idea that the temple was both heaven and earth. The throne of the Lord was in heaven, but also in the temple: 'A glorious throne set on high from the beginning is the place of our sanctuary' (Jer. 17.12). The king had been the earthly manifestation of the Lord in his temple; he had been addressed as the Lord's son (Pss. 2.7; 72.1) and he had sat upon the Lord's throne as king: 'Then Solomon sat on the throne of the Lord as king instead of David his father' (1 Chron. 29.23). The memory of these royal rituals persisted long after the cult itself had been transformed; there was often a human figure on the divine throne, and the ancient enthronement ceremony which had re-enacted the triumph of the Lord over his enemies passed into the vision of the last judgement.

Two great events in the history of the temple virtually coincided at the end of the seventh century BC; the reform of the Deuteronomists and the destruction of the temple and monarchy by the Babylonians. Between them they destroyed the ancient cult. The Deuteronomists had not favoured the monarchy, as can be seen from their surviving writings; they said that the wickedness of a king had caused the destruction of Jerusalem (2 Kings 24.3). They were to reformulate Israel's religion in such a way that the monarch was no longer central to the cult. In addition, the exile of so many people to Babylon meant that they were physically separated from the temple which had been the centre of their life. These two circumstances combined to alter radically the perception of the presence of God in the temple. The events of history necessitated an idea of God not located in the one holy place, but rather of God travelling with his people, and the Deuteronomists rejected all the ancient anthropomorphisms of the royal cult. Theirs was to be a God whose voice was heard and obeyed, but who had no visible form. Since the Deuteronomists are thought to have played a major part in transmitting the sacred texts of Israel, it is not surprising that the older anthropomorphism of the cult has largely disappeared. *The consequences of this for our understanding of Christian origins cannot be overestimated.* Many of the older traditions did survive, however, and can be traced in the apocalypses, texts preserved only by Christian hands. It is in these that we find most of the evidence for the divine throne and the man figure upon it.

The ancient traditions were reworked and in some texts the hand of the editor can be seen. The account of the building of the temple in 1 Kings, for example, comes in its present form from a historian influenced by the Deuteronomists. The dedication prayer has been suitably modified as a result. Solomon begins: 'The Lord has set his sun in the heavens, But he has said he would dwell in thick darkness. I have built thee an exalted house, a place for thee to dwell in for ever' (1 Kings 8.12—13); but then contradicts himself: 'But will God indeed dwell on the earth? Behold, heaven and the highest heaven cannot contain thee; how much less this house which I have built!' (1 Kings 8.27). The Deuteronomists had no place for the literal presence of God, nor for the elaborate visions of heaven which were part of the royal cult. Time and again they insisted that there was no form in which God could be seen: 'Then the Lord spoke to you out of the midst of the fire; you heard the sound of the words, but saw no form; there was only a voice . . . Since you saw no form on the day that the Lord spoke to you at Horeb out of the midst of the fire, beware lest you act corruptly by making a graven image for yourselves' (Deut. 4.12, 15). This prohibition of images and anthropomorphism must have been later than the establishment of the cult itself; how else can we account for the cherubim, or the vision of Isaiah in the temple (Isa. 6) when he *saw* the Lord on his throne? This conflict between those who said that it was possible to have a vision of God, and those who denied it, was to continue for centuries.

The Deuteronomists relocated God in heaven only: 'Look down from thy holy habitation, from heaven, and bless thy people Israel' (Deut. 26.15). Instead of the Lord in his temple, they said that his Name was there. Scholars cannot agree exactly what was meant by this term, or when the distinction between the Lord and his Name was first made, but it certainly *was* made. Compare, for example, two verses in Nathan's prophecy, which in its present form has passed through the hands of the Deuteronomists: 'Thus says the Lord: Would you build a house for me to dwell in?'; and immediately afterwards: 'He shall build a house *for my name* and I will establish the throne of his kingdom for ever' (2 Sam. 7.5, 13). Earlier strata of Deuteronomy seem to have equated the presence of the Lord and his Name (e.g. throughout Deut. 12), but the later Name theology was all a part of that great movement which sought to wean Israel from her older ways. (An account of this can be read in T. N. D. Mettinger, *The Dethronement of Sabaoth*.)

Another aspect of this process can be seen in the fate of the various 'tent' traditions. The stories of Israel's time in the desert, although doubtless ancient in origin, did not achieve anything like the written form we now know until some time after the exile, and when they were compiled, those who did it were not simply gentlemen scholars recording old stories. They were telling them in order to teach something, to put across their point of view in the new situation of Israel's rebuilding herself. They were showing how their beliefs were true to the original desert traditions of Israel. Whether they were or not is another question; similar things happen in the Church today whenever anyone wants to bring about change! As a result of this, two tent traditions were combined; one was the tradition of the prophets and the other of the priests, or perhaps it was the traditions of the northern kingdom and those of the south. The former spoke of God visiting his people and then departing, the latter of his dwelling with them all the time.

The ancient tent of prophecy is depicted in the desert stories as pitched outside the camp, e.g. Exod. 33.7—11; Num. 11.16—30; 12.1—16. These are the three most important passages which describe the *tent of meeting*. Anyone who sought a word from the Lord used to go *outside* the camp and into the tent. A pillar of cloud appeared at the door, i.e. *outside* the tent, and from this cloud 'the Lord used to speak to Moses face to face' (Exod. 33.11). When Moses asked to see the glory of the Lord, he was told: 'You cannot see my face for men shall not see me and live' (Exod. 33.20). Moses was hidden in a cleft of rock and he saw only the back of the Lord as he passed (Exod. 33.21—3). A tradition which says that no man can see God, and which implies that the Lord does not dwell with his people but only visits them has strong affinities with the Deuteronomists' position.

The 'other' tent was the *tabernacle*, the dwelling place, where the Lord was always present with his people. The tabernacle, a name which actually means *dwelling place* in Hebrew, was the elaborate miniature temple described in Exod. 25—31; 35.10—39, which housed the ark and the *menorah*. When we are told that the Lord was in the midst of the camp it is assumed that this refers to the dwelling of the Lord, i.e. to the tabernacle (Exod. 25.8; Num. 5.3). The Lord spoke to Moses *inside* the tabernacle from between the cherubim (Exod. 25.22), because this is where the Lord had settled from the moment the tabernacle was built (Exod. 40.34—8). This is exactly the same as was said of the first temple when it was consecrated by Solomon (1 Kings 8.10). In each case a cloud, the glory of the Lord, filled the place and nobody was able to enter for a while. The word *tabernacle* occurs often elsewhere, but is translated differently in the English versions and therefore does not obviously indicate the tabernacle: 'The *place* where thy glory *dwells*' (Ps. 26.8); 'The *dwelling place* of thy name' (Ps. 74.7). Or where the Hebrew has a plural: 'The holy *habitation(s)* of the Most High' (Ps. 46.4); 'Let us go to his *dwelling place*; let us worship at his footstool' (Ps. 132.7); 'My *dwelling place* shall be with them' (Ezek. 37.27). The dwelling place of the Lord was the temple and those who wrote of the Lord's dwelling must have had their hearts in the Jerusalem temple.

A third type of tent can also be detected; in fact it is the most common of all. This one had the combined name *The tabernacle of the tent of meeting*, a name which involves two contradictory ideas. It is thought that this was a combination of the two traditions, the prophetic and the priestly, or the northern and the southern, as a result of the upheavals of the exile and the common need for survival. Perhaps the original tent in the desert had been the place of oracles, the tent of meeting. Perhaps, when the people were in exile and far from the temple, the Lord had to be shown moving with his people, not dwelling in Jerusalem. Ezekiel expressed this in his vision of the chariot throne leaving the city (Ezek. 10) and travelling to Babylon (Ezek. 1). The compilers of the Pentateuch did the same thing in their own way; they fused tent of meeting and tabernacle. The dwelling became a portable dwelling and the tabernacle of the tent of meeting was the result.

None of this can be proved; fashions in scholarship come and go, and the study of the Pentateuch is at the moment in a state of flux. Unravelling the strands at any time is a complicated business, but as they are separated it is sometimes possible to see how the various traditions about the presence of the Lord with his people received different emphases as their circumstances changed. Something similar happens today in the way that the Christmas stories are preached, for example, depending upon the particular congregation and its needs. (These desert stories *were* used for the ongoing life of a religious community, not for scholarly research.) Faced with overwhelming need, the very different theologies of 'dwelling' and 'meeting and departing' were fused.

The Fourth Gospel also speaks of the tabernacle: 'And the Word became flesh and *dwelt* among us, full of grace and truth' (John 1.14); '"Destroy this temple and in three days I will raise it up" . . . But he spoke of the temple of his body' (John 2.19, 21).

The Ark

> Jesus, where'er thy people meet,
> There they behold thy mercy seat.
>
> W. Cowper

Another aspect of this development can be seen in the relationship between the ark and the cherub throne. In some traditions the ark was the footstool of the throne; in others it seems to have been the throne itself. We do not know how these two traditions related to each other. Those associated with the desert tabernacle describe two miniature cherubim at either end of a mercy seat of gold which was placed on the top of the ark (Exod. 25.17−21), whereas those of the temple describe two enormous cherubim in the holy of holies, each ten cubits across, which formed the throne. The cherubim of the tabernacle faced each other and their wings overshadowed the mercy seat (Exod. 25.10), whereas those of the temple stood side by side and faced down into the *hekal* (2 Chron. 3.13). Since the only dimensions given for the ark are that it was two and a half cubits long, and one and a half cubits both broad and high (Exod. 25.10), it would have been dwarfed by the cherubim of the temple throne. Some scholars think that the desert tabernacle stories were written in their present form *after* the destruction of the first temple, to provide a picture of the Lord moving with his people (i.e. into exile), and not confined to the temple in Jerusalem. The cherubim of the ark and the mercy seat as described in Exodus would, on this theory, have been a vestige of the cherub throne and not its forerunner.

The ark, we are told, was made at Sinai, and was used to carry the two tablets of the commandments, a jar of manna (Exod. 16.33) and Aaron's rod which budded into an almond branch (Num. 17.8; cf. Heb. 9.4). In the stories of the early days, the ark, like the cherub throne, represented the actual presence of the Lord: 'Whenever the ark set out, Moses said, "Arise, O Lord and let thy enemies be scattered; and let them that hate thee flee before thee." And when it rested, he said, "Return, O Lord, to the ten thousand thousands of Israel"' (Num. 10.35—6). A story from the Philistine wars shows the role of the ark: '"Why has the Lord put us to rout today before the Philistines? Let us bring the ark of the covenant of the Lord here from Shiloh, that he may come among us and save us from the power of our enemies." So the people sent to Shiloh, and brought from there the ark of the covenant of the Lord of hosts, who is enthroned on the cherubim' (1 Sam. 4.3—4). This same title was given to the Lord of the cherub throne in the temple; in the time of Isaiah, King Hezekiah prayed in the temple: 'O Lord of Hosts, God of Israel, who art enthroned above the cherubim' (Isa. 37.16). Which cherubim, then, formed the original throne; those of the ark or those of the *hekal*? The question cannot be answered with certainty, but it is more likely that the cherubim of the temple were the originals.

According to the Priestly traditions about the time in the desert, Moses heard the voice of the Lord speaking from above the cherubim: 'And when Moses went into the tent of meeting to speak with the Lord, he heard the voice speaking to him from above the mercy seat that was upon the ark of the testimony, from between the two cherubim; and it spoke to him' (Num. 7.89). This account would have been written down long after the events it describes and may well tell us something of how the Lord was believed to speak to his people in the temple in

Jerusalem. Between the cherubim in the temple would have been the throne; whoever sat on that throne would have acted as the spokesman of the Lord. The belief that the Lord spoke from above the cherubim, as we have seen, survived well into the first century AD and was mentioned by Philo of Alexandria. In his case it was the Logos, the second God who spoke from the cherub throne.

The mercy seat of the desert ark was central to the atonement rites described in Leviticus 16. (The word translated 'mercy seat' is *kapporeth* which derives from the Hebrew root *kpr*, 'atone'.) The high priest took the blood and sprinkled it onto the mercy seat. Now if the tabernacle account has vestiges of the first temple's practices, this implies that the atonement ritual would have put the blood onto the throne itself.

The other dominant tradition in the Old Testament, that of the Deuteronomists, had a different view of the presence of the Lord in the temple. Theirs was the view expressed by the later editor of Solomon's prayer: How could the Lord be in the temple? For them the ark was not a throne but just a wooden box in which the commandments were kept (Deut. 10.1–5; cf. 1 Kings 8.9), and the presence in the temple was only the presence of the Name. There was no form in which God could be seen on the cherub throne.

Whatever the truth may have been as to its history and significance, the ark was brought to Jerusalem and placed in the *debir*. It was placed in such a way that the carrying poles of the ark were visible from the *hekal*, i.e. it was not positioned across the base of the cherub throne as we should expect for a footstool. Nevertheless it was described as the footstool. David said: 'I had it in my heart to build a house of rest for the ark of the covenant of the Lord, and for the footstool of our God' (1 Chron. 28.2). The psalmist too, though not mentioning the ark, seems to refer to it: 'Extol the Lord our God, worship at his footstool' (Ps. 99.5). Psalm 132 is more explicit; it recounts the tradition of going out to search for the ark before it was brought to Jerusalem by David:

> Lo we heard of it in Ephrathah,
>   we found it in the fields of Jaar.
> 'Let us go to his dwelling place;
>   let us worship at his footstool!'

Arise, O Lord, and go to thy resting place.
thou and the ark of thy might. (Ps. 132.6—8)

What eventually happened to the ark nobody knows; there is one tradition recorded in the Babylonian Talmud that it was taken to Babylon along with the treasures of the temple (b. *Yoma* 53b), another that Jeremiah hid the ark, the tent and the altar of incense in a cave, to protect them from the Babylonian looters when the city was captured: 'The place shall be unknown until God gathers his people together again and shows his mercy' (2 Macc. 2.7). Another tradition attributed to Jeremiah said that he looked forward to a time without the ark, when the whole of Jerusalem would be the throne of the Lord and Israel and Judah would be united again (Jer. 3.16—17). Another tradition said that it had been hidden in the temple itself:

> R. Nahman said: It was taught that the ark was hidden away in the chamber of the wood shed. R. Nahman also said: Thus we were also taught: It happened to a certain priest who was whiling away his time that he saw a block of pavement that was different from the others. He came and informed his fellows, but before he could complete his account his soul departed. Thus they knew definitely that the ark was hidden there. (b. *Yoma* 54a)

There was yet another tradition that in the age of the Messiah, five things would be restored which had been in the first temple but not in the second; the fire, the ark, the *menorah*, the Spirit and the cherubim (*Numbers Rabbah* XV.10). This tradition is the basis of Rev. 11.15—19. The seventh angel proclaims the kingdom of the Messiah (Rev. 11.15) and the heavenly temple is opened to reveal the ark of the covenant (Rev. 11.19). By New Testament times there was no ark in the temple; Josephus says that the holy of holies was empty (*Wars*, V.219).

The Cherubim

> Keep me. O keep me, King of kings,
> Beneath thine own almighty wings.
>
> T. Ken

The cherubim were monstrous composite figures which appear frequently in the art of the ancient Near East. In the Old

Testament they were depicted on the tabernacle curtains, on the mercy seat and as the bearers of the chariot throne. It is possible that they originally represented the winds in the Hebrew tradition. 2 Sam. 22 (which is the same as Psalm 18) describes vividly how the Lord came from his temple (2 Sam. 22.7) to rescue David from danger (2 Sam. 22.10—11):

> He bowed the heavens, and came down;
>   thick darkness was under his feet.
> He rode on a *cherub, and flew;*
>   he came swiftly upon the *wings of the wind*. (Ps. 18.10—11)

The parallelism of the poetry shows that the cherub and the wings of the wind are synonymous. There is another vivid description of the temple and the chariot in Ps. 104, and again the parallelism suggests that the cherub chariot was the wind.

> Thou art clothed with honour and majesty,
>   who coveredst thyself with light as with a garment,
> who hast stretched out the heavens like a tent,
>   who hast laid the beams of thy chambers on the waters,
> who makest *the clouds thy chariot,*
>   who *ridest on the wings of the wind,*
> who makest the winds thy messengers,
>   fire and flame thy ministers. (Ps. 104.1—4)

The Hebrew word for wind, *ruaḥ*, can also be rendered 'spirit' and the word for messenger *mal'ak* can also mean 'angel'. The gap between the cherub as an angel figure and the cherub as a depiction of the wind therefore did not exist for the writer of this psalm. These were concrete representations of the spirits of wind and fire which surrounded the divine throne. (One could perhaps compare this with the way in which the dove has come to symbolize the spirit in Christian art.)

The presence of the Lord was often associated with storm clouds: 'Behold the Lord is riding on a swift cloud and comes to Egypt' (Isa. 19.1); 'His way is in whirlwind and storm, and the clouds are the dust of his feet' (Nahum 1.3). Job could ask in despair:

> What does God know?
>   Can he judge through the deep darkness?
> Thick clouds enwrap him, so that he does not see,
>   and he walks on the vault of heaven. (Job 22.13—14)

When Ezekiel saw the great throne of the Lord in his vision, he saw first that 'a stormy wind came out of the north, and a great cloud, with brightness round about it, and fire flashing forth continually, and in the midst of the fire, as it were gleaming bronze' (Ezek. 1.4). By his time the two cherubim had become four, representing the four winds supporting the vault of the heaven on which was the sapphire throne of God (Ezek. 1.5, 22). Ezekiel may well have been the last Old Testament writer actually to know the cherub throne in the temple, and his vision must have depicted what he understood the throne to be. (Some think that the cherub throne had already been removed from the *debir* by Manasseh some fifty years before the time of Ezekiel, see Patai, *Man and Temple*. He had introduced many foreign elements into the cult, one of which was 'the graven image of Asherah' (2 Kings 21.7) which he set in the temple itself, possibly in the *debir*.)

Long after the cherubim had gone from the temple their memory remained; they were not obliterated from Israel's vision of the heavenly world. 1 Enoch 18.2 (possibly from the third century BC) tells how Enoch saw the four winds supporting the vault of heaven just as the cherubim had done. More significant is the undateable material in 1 Enoch 40.2−9: 'On the four sides of the Lord of Spirits [Enoch's version of the Lord of Hosts] I saw four presences . . . and I learnt their names.' The living creatures, the cherubim, have become the four archangels: Michael, Raphael, Gabriel, and Phanuel, the messengers of God and the visible manifestation of his presence.

Philo gave a very sophisticated view of the role and meaning of the cherubim, and, although much of it was expressed in terms of Greek philosophy such as his educated readers would have expected, it is not likely that he invented these beliefs about the cherubim. For him the two cherubim also represented aspects of God; he calls them the two Powers of God, and says that they were represented in the Scriptures by the two names for God: *Yahweh* (Lord) and *Elohim* (God). The two names represented respectively the creative and the kingly aspects of God. This is very similar to the idea of the four archangels who manifested aspects of God, especially as Philo also said that Yahweh and Elohim were both names for the Logos, the archangel of the presence of God who becomes visible in the material world.

> The two primary powers of the Existing One, namely that through which he wrought the world, the beneficent, which is called God, and that by which he rules and commands that which he made, that is the punitive, which bears the name of Lord, are, as Moses tells us, separated by God himself standing above and in the midst of them. 'I will speak to thee', it says, 'above the mercy seat in the midst of the two cherubim' . . . he means to show that the primal and highest powers of the Existent, the beneficent and the punitive, are equal having him to divide them. (*Who is the Heir?*, 166)

Elsewhere he says that the Logos of God stands between the cherubim:

> While God is indeed One, his highest and chief Powers are two, even Goodness and Sovereignty . . . And in the midst between the two is a third which unites them, the Logos, for it is through the Logos that God is both ruler and good. Of these two Powers, Sovereignty and Goodness, the cherubim are the symbols, as the fiery sword is the symbol of reason. (*Cherubim*, 27–8)

Here Philo equates the cherubim of the throne with the two who guarded the gate of Eden, another memory of the throne in Eden. The Palestinian Targum is exactly similar: 'And he cast forth the man and made the glory of the Shekinah* to dwell from the beginning to the east of the garden of Eden between the two cherubim' (Targum *Neofiti* to Gen. 3.24).

Elsewhere Philo spoke of the Word as the charioteer of the Powers (*On Flight*, 101), guiding the universe under the direction of God. It is curious that he should have chosen the term chariot if he did not have the chariot throne in mind. Philo also explained the angels who surrounded the throne of God and tried to make them comprehensible to his Greek readers. He called the heavenly host the 'Powers'; they were what the Old Testament had called the 'Glory of God'. Philo showed this clearly when he explained Exod. 33.18, where Moses had asked to see the glory of God. He was told that he could not see the face of God but only his back as he passed by (Exod. 33.23). Philo said that what was 'behind'

---

* *Shekinah* is related to the word for tabernacle and means *the divine presence*. This implies that the Lord himself guarded the gate in Eden.

the Lord was his Powers. Thus his Moses said, 'By thy Glory I understand the Powers that keep guard around Thee' (*Special Laws*, I.45). What Moses could see of God was his *visible manifestation in the creation*. Since the Logos was the chief of these Powers (*Who is the Heir?*, 166) we see yet again the theme of the second God, the visible God, the Glory.

The Palestinian Targum has a similar understanding of this incident in the life of Moses: 'And I will make the troop of angels pass by who stand and minister before me and you will see the Word of the Glory of my Shekinah but it is not possible for you to see the face of the Glory of my Shekinah' (Targum *Neofiti* to Exod. 33.23).

The cherubim on the lid of the ark, or in the darkened *debir* as the chariot throne, were far more than primitive pagan symbols which had somehow crept into the temple. Throughout the whole history of the temple, and indeed long after the throne itself had ceased to exist as the centre of the cult, the cherubim were remembered as symbols of the presence of the Lord. In St John's vision the four-headed cherubim in Ezekiel became four living creatures each of which had one of those animal heads. One was a lion, one an ox, one a man and one an eagle (Rev. 4.7; cf. Ezek. 1.10). Ezekiel's cherubim had four wings (Ezek. 1.11); Isaiah's seraphim and St John's living creatures had six (Isa. 6.2; Rev. 4.8), all full of eyes. It is as the fiery six-winged creatures, full of eyes, that the cherubim have passed into Christian art, but they still retain their ancient role as the four upholders of the vault of heaven. In the atrium of St Mark's Basilica in Venice, for example, there is a small cupola depicting the creation of the world. On the four spandrels are the four living creatures, the four archangels with their six wings, supporting the firmament, the vault of creation. But let us return to the temple of Solomon, and to the great throne.

The Enthronement

> O worship the King all glorious above;
> O gratefully sing his power and his love.
>   R. Grant

Yahweh was in his temple, enthroned upon the cherubim. The Psalms constantly tell of the Lord in his city, and of the security and hope that his presence brought.

> In my distress I called upon the Lord;
> > to my God I cried for help.
> From his temple he heard my voice,
> > and my cry to him reached his ears. (Ps. 18.6)
>
> May he send you help from the sanctuary,
> > And give you support from Zion! (Ps. 20.2)
>
> One thing I have asked of the Lord, that I will seek after;
> That I may dwell in the house of the Lord all the days of my life,
> To behold the beauty of the Lord,
> > And to inquire in his temple.
> For he will hide me in his shelter in the day of trouble;
> He will conceal me under the cover of his tent,
> > He will set me high upon a rock. (Ps. 27. 4—5)
>
> God is in the midst of her, she shall not be moved;
> > God will help her right early . . .
> The Lord of hosts is with us;
> > The God of Jacob is our refuge. (Ps. 46.5, 7)
>
> Terrible is God in his sanctuary, the God of Israel,
> > He gives power and strength to his people. (Ps. 68.35)

These few examples must suffice to show that the easiest way to enter into the world of the ancient temple is to read the Psalms and try to imagine the setting for which they were written. The vivid imagery which is so familiar to us was originally a literal description of the Lord in his temple, enthroned over the great rock, defending his people and his city.

There are several Psalms which seem to describe a great procession when the Lord entered his temple and ascended the throne. Perhaps this was a ritual associated with a celebration of the Lord as King. Again we have to imagine a setting in which words such as these would have been appropriate:

> Lift up your heads, O Gates!
> > and be lifted up, O ancient doors!
> > that the King of glory may come in.
> Who is the King of glory?
> > The Lord strong and mighty,
> > The Lord mighty in battle. (Ps. 24.7—8)

God has gone up with a shout,
   The Lord with the sound of a trumpet. (Ps. 47.5)

Thy solemn processions are seen, O God,
   The processions of my God, my King, into the sanctuary –
The singers in front, the minstrels last,
   Between them maidens playing timbrels. (Ps. 68.24–5)

Many scholars have contributed to the theory that there was just such a ceremony in the autumn, at the time of their New Year. The Lord was enthroned as King, having triumphed over evil and his enemies. The question is: Did someone represent the Lord in these ceremonies? The most likely answer is that it was the king.

Kingship was inseparable from judgement; this is an important key to understanding much of the later use of throne imagery. The links are clearly seen in Pss. 93–99, thought to be a sequence of psalms associated with this ceremony.

Rise up, O judge of the earth . . . (Ps. 94.2)

He will judge the world with righteousness,
   And the peoples with his truth. (Ps. 96.13)

Zion hears and is glad,
   And the daughters of Judah rejoice,
   Because of thy judgements, O God. (Ps. 97.8)

He will judge the world with righteousness,
   And the peoples with equity. (Ps. 98.9)

Mighty King, lover of justice
   Thou hast established equity;
Thou hast executed justice
   And righteousness in Jacob. (Ps. 99.4)

The Lord came to his people as King and Judge. The ceremony is thought to have taken place at the time of the autumn equinox, in other words, at harvest time, which would account for the way in which images of harvest and images of judgement go together in the biblical tradition. Amos was the earliest example, with the basket of summer fruit which he saw as a warning of judgement (Amos 8.1–3). There was also Isaiah's picture of

Yahweh trampling the winepress (Isa. 63.1—6) and, perhaps the most fearful of all, the harvest of the grapes of wickedness which were pressed in the winepress of the wrath of God (Rev. 14.18—20).

The Great Light

> Sun of my soul, thou Saviour dear,
> It is not night if thou be near.
>
> J. Keble

The autumn equinox probably accounts for another image frequently used of the Lord as King.

> Let thy face *shine* on thy servant;
> Save me in thy steadfast love! (Ps. 31.16)

> Out of Zion, the perfection of beauty, God shines forth. (Ps. 50.2)

> May God be gracious unto us and bless us
> And make his face to shine upon us. (Ps. 67.1)

> Thou who art enthroned upon the cherubim, shine forth . . .
> Restore us O God,
> Let thy face shine, that we may be saved. (Ps. 80.1, 3)

The familiar lines of Isaiah are also a part of this picture:

> The people who walked in darkness have seen a great light. (Isa. 9.2)

> Arise, shine; for your light has come,
> And the glory of the Lord has risen upon you.
> For behold, darkness shall cover the earth,
> And thick darkness the peoples;
> But the Lord will arise upon you,
> And his glory will be seen upon you. (Isa. 60.1—2)

The earliest known blessing of the high priests and one of the latest prayers in the Old Testament, that of Daniel written in the second century BC, both use this image of the rising sun:

> The Lord bless you and keep you:
> The Lord make his face to shine upon you, and be gracious
>   to you:

The Lord lift up his countenance upon you and give you peace. (Num. 6.24–6)

O Lord, cause thy face to shine upon thy sanctuary, which is desolate. (Dan. 9.17)

The gate of the temple faced east; at the autumn equinox, it is suggested, the rays of the rising sun would have shone through the gate and illuminated the great golden throne in the *debir*. This symbolized the coming of the Lord to his people.

Perhaps Ezekiel had this in mind when he described the glory of the Lord returning to the temple. His vision occurred at the New Year (Ezek. 40.1): 'And behold, the glory of the God of Israel came from the east; and the sound of his coming was like the sound of many waters; and the earth shone with his glory.... As the glory of the Lord entered the temple by the gate facing east, the Spirit lifted me up, and brought me into the inner court; and behold, the glory of the Lord filled the temple' (Ezek. 43.2, 4, 5). Zechariah also sang of this dawn when the Lord would come to his people: 'the day shall dawn upon us from on high to give light to those who sit in darkness' (Luke 1.78–9). Something must have given rise to all this imagery. Even if we cannot reconstruct the lost world of the ancient temple in exact detail, significant fossils do break the surface in literature that has survived, not only from the period of the first temple, but from the later centuries.

The rising sun may also account for a curious piece of information in the account of King Josiah's reform: 'He removed the horses that the kings of Judah had dedicated to the sun, at the entrance to the house of the Lord ... and he burned the chariots of the sun with fire' (2 Kings 23.11). This account of Josiah's reform was written by people sympathetic to the ideals of the Deuteronomists, the puritanical reformers of Israel's religion. All that they condemned as pagan may not have been pagan at all. It may simply have been a part of the ancient cult which they did not like, just as they did not like the idea of the Lord present in his temple, seated on a golden throne. These temple horses appear elsewhere as the steeds of the Lord's agents. Zechariah's visions in the sixth century, after the return from Babylon and before the second temple had been built, were all based upon the imagery of the first temple. In the first of his visions he saw four horses riding out to patrol the earth

(Zech. 1.8—11). In another vision he saw four horse-drawn chariots sent out to patrol the four corners of the earth (Zech. 6.1—8). Nobody can explain these horses or how they fitted into the beliefs of the time; there must have been some role for them in the drama of the Lord's judgement being sent forth from his temple. These same horses appear six centuries later in St John's vision of the judgement (Rev. 6.1—8). For an early Christian visionary they were still a part of the Lord's judgement!

Visions of the Throne

> Be thou my Vision, O Lord of my heart;
> Naught be all else to me, save that thou art.
>
> Ancient Irish, tr. M. E. Byrne and E. H. Hull

The Lord enthroned in his temple was the subject of several prophetic visions. It is not correct to say that the prophets' visions were based on temple ritual; rather, the temple ritual made visible the world of the heavenly temple, the divine reality. It was *this* which the prophets saw. In other words, temple ritual derived from the world of the prophets' visions, and not vice versa. When we read these accounts in the prophets we see the golden cherubim of the sanctuary come alive, just as they do in the *Songs of the Sabbath Sacrifice*, when the figures on the temple walls become the spirits of the heavenly sanctuary.

> [And the like]ness of living divine beings is engraved in the vestibules where the King enters, figures of luminous spirits . . . [in] the midst of the spirits of splendour, [is] a work of wondrous colours, figures of the living divine beings (4Q 405.14—15) . . . [fi]gures of the shapes of divine beings, engraved round about their [gl]orious brickwork, glorious images of the b[ric]kwork of splendour and majes[ty]. Living divine beings (are) all their construction, and the images of their figures (are) holy angels. (4Q 405.19 ABCD)

The earliest description of a throne vision is the call of Isaiah in the eighth century BC, and yet the temple imagery is recognizably that of the *Songs of the Sabbath Sacrifice*, used by the Qumran community some eight centuries later. Such similarity suggests that the inner meaning of the first temple had

THE THRONE

not been forgotten in the intervening centuries, even though so little has survived from those years which could add detail to the picture. Isaiah described the throne thus:

> In the year that King Uzziah died I saw the Lord sitting upon a throne, high and lifted up; and his train filled the temple. Above him stood the seraphim; each had six wings: with two he covered his face, and with two he covered his feet, and with two he flew. And one called to another and said: 'Holy, holy, is the Lord of hosts; the whole earth is full of his glory.' And the foundations of the thresholds shook at the voice of him who called, and the house was filled with smoke. And I said: 'Woe is me! For I am lost; for I am a man of unclean lips, and I dwell in the midst of a people of unclean lips; for my eyes have seen the King, the Lord of hosts.'
> Then flew one of the seraphim to me having in his hand a burning coal which he had taken with tongs from the altar. And he touched my mouth, and said: 'Behold, this has touched your lips; your guilt is taken away, and your sin forgiven.' And I heard the voice of the Lord saying, 'Whom shall I send, and who will go for us?' Then I said, 'Here am I! Send me.' (Isa. 6.1–8)

Here are all the elements of the throne vision: the throne in the sanctuary where the Lord is King, the surrounding hosts, the smoke of the incense, the sense of impending judgement, and the song of the angels. Every detail is there; even the altar of incense which stood before the throne provides the coal to purify the prophet's lips. After his vision of the glory of the Lord the prophet became a messenger of judgement.

Micaiah's vision is less well known, but it shows how the prophets, with their visions of the Lord, functioned as political advisers. The kings of Israel and Judah were preparing to go to war and they consulted the prophets. Micaiah told of a vision of the Lord on his throne, surrounded by the hosts. He heard the Lord send a lying spirit into the mouth of the other prophets who were the king's advisers, and then he announced to them the doom which the Lord had decreed for them (1 Kings 22.13–23). Amos saw the Lord in the temple, standing beside (or upon) the altar. He too was given a message of judgement (Amos 9.1–4).

The most terrifying of all the throne visions in the Old Testament are those of Ezekiel. He lived during the exile and had seen the destruction of the temple. The people to whom he spoke were far from Jerusalem, and their question would have been: 'If the Lord dwells in the temple, and the temple is destroyed, and we are far away from the temple, are we far away from the presence of the Lord?' Ezekiel answered this question with his vision of the chariot throne of the Lord leaving the temple in Jerusalem just before the Lord's judgement was poured out upon the wickedness of the city. The chariot throne of the Lord had travelled east with his people and appeared to Ezekiel in Babylon, on the banks of the river Chebar (Ezek. 1.1). In his second vision he was transported to see evil practices in the temple (one of which was sun worship! Ezek. 8.16) and he then saw the Lord sending angels of destruction into the city. They came in through the north gate of the temple and stood by the great bronze altar (Ezek. 9.2). The Glory of the God of Israel rose from the cherubim and ordered the judgement to begin (Ezek. 9.3). A sapphire throne appeared above the cherubim (Ezek. 10.1; cf. Exod. 24.10, a very old account of the vision of the Lord on Sinai). One of the angels was told to throw the coals from the altar onto the city. This must have been the altar of incense beneath the throne in the temple, but here a part of the living scene of the judgement. The cherubim were no longer golden statues but living creatures and beside them the prophet saw wheels. Ezekiel never describes the throne as a chariot but 1 Chron. 28.18 shows that that is what it was, and that is how it was remembered: 'It was Ezekiel who saw the vision of glory which God showed him above the chariot of the cherubim' (Ecclus. 49.8). The chariot rose and left through the eastern gate (Ezek. 10.19).

The prophet's vision in Babylon gives more detail of the chariot. It came with a storm cloud (Ezek. 1.4) and the cherubim were like men but they had four faces and four wings (Ezek. 1.5). Over the heads of the cherubim was a crystal firmament (Ezek. 1.22), and above this was the sapphire throne on which was *a human form* (Ezek. 1.26). This is the earliest reference to a human figure on the throne, and it was made by someone who had been *a priest in the first temple* (Ezek. 1.3). It was 'the likeness of the glory of the Lord' (Ezek. 1.28). In the second chariot vision, Ezekiel saw an identical figure, a man of fire and bronze (Ezek. 8.2; cf. 1.27), who lifted him up and brought him in a vision to Jerusalem. The figure was not on a throne, but

THE THRONE

acted as Ezekiel's guide and showed him the evils for which Jerusalem was to be punished. A careful reading of chapter 9 shows that his man of fire and bronze was directing the judgement; he commanded the six executioners who came from the north, and the scribe of judgement, the man in linen, who accompanied them (Ezek. 9.1). The man figure, according to Ezek. 1.28, was the *likeness of the glory of the Lord*, and in the temple vision Ezekiel saw that this glory had gone up from the cherub throne and was standing at the threshold of the temple (Ezek. 9.3). The sequence is: the glory left the throne, he called to the scribe dressed in linen, the Lord said to him . . . All three (the glory, the man figure and the Lord) are the same person. 'Begin', said the man figure who accompanied Ezekiel, 'at *my sanctuary*'. After the coals from the incense altar had been cast on the city, the glory of the Lord went from the threshold and rejoined the cherub throne (Ezek. 10.18) which then left the temple. Ezekiel knew that this was what he had seen in Babylon, by the river Chebar (Ezek. 10.20). This is the most remarkable piece of anthropomorphism in the Old Testament. A fiery man figure occupied the cherub throne and was described as the likeness of the glory of the God of Israel. He left the throne and accompanied the prophet on his visionary journey, he was worshipped in Jerusalem and he brought judgement upon the city.

Later tradition remembered all these things about the man figure. In the Apocalypse of Abraham, an angel was sent to accompany Abraham on his ascent to the heavenly throne. This angel was called Iaoel. Now Iao is recognizable, even in the Old Slavonic in which this Apocalypse has survived, as a Greek form of the divine name. What we have in this Apocalypse is the memory of an angel originally called Yahweh-el. He was the angel who lived in the seventh heaven (Apoc. Abr. 10.8) and had been assigned especially to Abraham and his heirs; 'Behold I am assigned (to be) with you and with the generation which is predestined (to be born) from you' (Apoc. Abr. 10.17). The angel was dressed as a high priest, with the high priest's turban; he carried a gold sceptre and his face was glowing (Apoc. Abr. 11.2—4). Philo called the Logos 'the man after his image' (*On the Confusion of Tongues*, 146), as well as the archangel and the high priest the universe.

Finally, and perhaps most significant of all as evidence for the later abhorrence of anthropomorphism which explains why so little has survived, it was forbidden to read this chapter in Ezekiel describing the throne chariot: 'They may not use the chapter of the chariot as a reading from the prophets' (Mishnah, *Megillah* 4.10). 'The chapter of the chariot (may not be expounded) before one alone, unless he is a sage who understands of his own knowledge' (Mishnah, *Hagigah* 2.1). After his vision of the man on the throne, Ezekiel was commissioned to take a message of judgement to his people. In later visions Ezekiel saw the glory of the Lord returning to the temple at the New Year and entering by the eastern gate (Ezek. 43.1—5).

There are other places in the Old Testament where the prophets allude to this expectation of judgement. Isaiah warned his contemporaries that the Lord would appear in his temple to render recompense to his enemies (Isa. 66.6). Malachi warned: 'The Lord whom you seek will suddenly come to his temple . . . Then I will draw near to you for judgement' (Mal. 3.1, 5). One who had suffered at the hands of the wicked was wearied, 'until I went into the sanctuary of God; then I perceived their end' (Ps. 73.17). From the time of Isaiah right through until the Book of Revelation, there was a continuous tradition of throne visions; a divine figure in human form sat on the throne and brought judgement. We shall now look briefly at some of these.

Visions of the Throne in the Apocalypses

> Immortal, invisible, God only wise,
> In light inaccessible hid from our eyes.
> W. Chalmers Smith

The apocalypses are revelations of the heavenly world. The word literally means 'unveil', and that is exactly what they did. They disclosed what was beyond the veil of the temple, and the dominant theme of the apocalypses is, as we should expect, the divine throne. It is customary to draw a line between prophecy and apocalyptic, and between prophecy and wisdom literature; but these lines are only demarcations of convenience drawn by modern scholars. In reality, the wise men and the prophets did very similar things, and the apocalyptists were only the later version of both. This can best be illustrated by the Book of Daniel, which is classed by modern scholars as an *apocalypse*

THE THRONE 155

(the only one in the Old Testament), but is placed among the *prophets* in our Old Testament (which derives the order of its books from that of the Greek Old Testament, not that of the Hebrew where Daniel is among the 'writings' at the end), but Daniel himself is described as a *wise man* who can interpret dreams (Dan. 1.3; 2.25).

The best known of the throne visions is that of Daniel 7:

> As I looked, thrones were placed, and one that was ancient of days took his seat;
> his raiment was white as snow, and the hair of his head like pure wool;
> his throne was fiery flames, its wheels were burning fire.
> A stream of fire issued and came forth from before him;
> a thousand thousands served him, and ten thousand times ten thousand stood before him;
> the court sat in judgement, and the books were opened . . .
> I saw in the night visions, and behold, with the clouds of heaven there came one like a son of man,
> and he came to the Ancient of Days and was presented before him.
> And to him was given dominion and glory and kingdom,
> that all peoples, nations, and languages should serve him;
> his dominion is an everlasting dominion, which shall not pass away,
> and his kingdom one that shall not be destroyed.
> (Dan. 7.9—10, 13—14)

The context of this vision was the persecution of the Jews by Antiochus Epiphanes. The temple had been desecrated and the daily burnt offering taken away. Antiochus was seen as one of the fallen angelic figures who had dared to come against the Lord and his city. In a later vision Daniel described him as the little horn who had 'magnified itself, even up to the Prince of the host; and the continual burnt offering was taken away from him, and the place of his sanctuary was overthrown' (Dan. 8.11). If the prince of the sanctuary was cast out, as was shown in Ezekiel's oracle against the Prince of Tyre, his people were defeated. The vision of Dan. 7 shows the reverse of this process; the Prince is restored to his heavenly place, and thus, as the interpretation of the vision shows, the restoration of their Prince meant the restoration of the people: 'And the kingdom and the dominion and the greatness of the kingdoms under the whole heaven shall be given to *the people* of the saints of the Most High' (Dan. 7.27).

There have been many attempts by scholars to explain this vision: it is related to Ps. 2 and clearly has the same enthronement setting; it also resembles the ancient Ugaritic account of the god Baal going up before the throne of El, the Canaanite High God. Now this description of Baal and El is about one thousand years older than Dan. 7 and there is no way that it can possibly have been the immediate source of the imagery. But there is another possibility, namely that those who first described the relationship of Israel's king to her God described it in terms of Baal and El. The period of the early monarchy was only a couple of centuries distant from the Ugaritic account of Baal, and all this would mean is that the guardian angel of Israel, who was manifested in the king, was believed to ascend to the presence of God Most High in the same way that Baal ascended to El or the Prince of Tyre ascended to the garden of Eden. Israel's culture was not sealed off from the influence of the surrounding peoples; it would not be surprising if they had expressed their own ideas in similar terms. It *does*, however, mean that the earliest Israelite cult would have had this belief in the second divine figure whom Philo described as the Logos and whom the Christians identified with Jesus even to the extent of finding pre-incarnation appearances of Jesus in the Old Testament. Justin, for example, said

> that it was Jesus who appeared to Moses and Abraham and all the other Patriarchs and conversed with them, ministering to the will of his Father (*Trypho*, 113).

> Then neither Abraham nor Isaac nor Jacob nor any other man ever saw the Father and the ineffable Lord of all things whatever and of Christ himself; but they saw him who according to his will is both his Son and his angel form ministering to his will. (*Trypho*, 127)

Hippolytus, who wrote at the end of the second century, knew that the bronze angel who appeared to Daniel (Dan. 10.5−6) was 'the Lord and not just an unnamed angel': 'He sees the Lord, not yet indeed as perfect man, but with the appearance and form of a man as he says' (*Commentary on Daniel*, IV.36). Irenaeus knew that it had been the Word of God who walked in the garden of Eden: 'And so fair and goodly was the Garden, the Word of God was constantly walking in it; He would walk round and talk with the man, prefiguring what was to come to pass in the future' (*Proof*, 12). He had been one of the three angels who met Abraham (Gen. 18.1−2): 'Two, then, of the three were angels, but one the Son of God . . . the Son, the same who spoke with Abraham, being "the Lord", received power to punish the men of Sodom "from the Lord out of heaven", from the Father who is Lord over all' (*Proof*, 44). These few examples must suffice to show how widely this second divine figure was known both in Judaism and in early Christianity. Daniel's vision had all the components of that older pattern; there were beasts and a hostile sea surrounding the heavenly throne, there was a second divine figure who took human form ('one like a son of man') and travelled on the clouds. The second divine figure was installed as the agent of the judgement.

Contemporary with Daniel, or perhaps a little older, is the earliest material in 1 Enoch.

> And behold I saw the clouds: And they were calling me; and the course of the stars and the lightnings were rushing me and causing me to desire; and in the vision the winds were causing me to fly and rushing me high up in heaven. And I kept coming (into heaven) until I approached a wall which was built of white marble and surrounded by tongues of fire; and it began to frighten me. And I came into the tongues of fire and drew near to a great house which was built of white marble and the inner wall(s) were like mosaics of white marble, the floor of crystal, the ceiling like the path of the stars and lightnings between which (stood) fiery cherubim and their heaven of water; and flaming fire surrounded the wall(s) and its gates were burning with fire. And I entered into the house which was hot like fire and cold like ice, and there was nothing inside it; (so) fear covered me and trembling seized me. And as I shook and trembled I fell upon my face and saw a vision. And behold there was an opening before me (and) a second house which is greater than the former and everything was built with tongues of fire. And in every respect it excelled (the other) . . . in glory and great honour . . . to the extent that it is impossible for me to recount to you concerning

its glory and greatness. As for its floor, it was of fire and above it was lightning and the path of the stars; and as for the ceiling it was flaming fire. And I observed and saw inside it a lofty throne . . . its appearance was like crystal and its wheels like the shining sun; and (I heard) the voice of the cherubim; and from beneath the throne were issuing streams of living fire. It was difficult to look at it. And the Great Glory was sitting upon it . . . as for his gown which was shining more brightly than the sun, it was whiter than any snow. None of the angels was able to come in and see the face of the Excellent and Glorious One, and no one of the flesh can see him. The flaming fire was round about him and a great fire stood before him. (1 Enoch 14.8—22)

First, this was a vision of heaven. Enoch was taken upwards by the clouds and winds, perhaps the cherubim and spirits of the earlier texts. He saw the chariot throne, which means that this must have been a temple vision, and the descriptions must be of what the earthly temple represented. He walked through the walls of marble and fire and came to the outer house, also built of marble. Zechariah had described the Lord as a wall of fire around his city, which may have been an allusion to the same belief, but there was also Isaiah 33, which asked who could dwell with the everlasting fire (Isa. 33.14). The person who could withstand the fire was exactly like the one who would be allowed to stand in the Lord's tent on the holy hill (Ps. 15.1). This person, said Isaiah, would 'dwell in the heights' and 'see the king in his beauty' (Isa. 33.16, 17). The fire must have been a part of the heavenly temple, even as early as the time of Isaiah. The outer house, which in the earthly temple represented Eden, had in the vision a floor of crystals; Ezekiel's heavenly Eden had been the place where the Prince of Tyre walked 'in the midst of the stones of fire' (Ezek. 28.14). Enoch saw there fiery cherubim, just as there were on the walls of the *hekal*, and from that place he saw a second house also built of fire. This was the holy of holies and in it was the chariot throne and the sound of the cherubim. There was the Great Glory in white robes but not described as a man figure. No flesh could look upon him. We then see that Enoch has a priestly role in this vision. He had been sent by the fallen angels to intercede with the Great Holy One, but was told that they should have been interceding for men and not a mortal for them. Instead, Enoch had to take to them a message of judgement. Enoch was then taken on a tour of the heavens, to see the sources of all the natural phenomena and also the final place of punishment for the fallen angels. The implications of this vision are important: Enoch has a priestly role and in this capacity he ascends to the divine presence. When he returns he brings a message from the throne. This must have been the role of the high priest and it is exactly how Philo describes the role of the Word, the second God who was also the true high priest. He interceded with God and brought the divine commands to earth (*Who is the Heir?*, 205; see Chapter 3).

There is a second account of Enoch's ascent to the throne, which is even more remarkable, since it describes how Enoch's spirit ascended to the heavens and saw the sons of God. He was shown all the secrets of heaven by the archangel Michael, who then took him to the highest heaven, 'the heaven of heavens', where he saw the house of crystal and the throne of glory guarded by the seraphim, the cherubim and the *ophannim* ('the wheels' of the chariot who are also alive). The angels went in and out of the house, and Enoch felt himself transformed before the Antecedent of Time (1 Enoch 71.11).

This transformation vision is the conclusion of the Similitudes or Parables of Enoch, a collection of three virtually parallel accounts of a throne vision. These are remarkable for two reasons: first, the Enoch figure only appears in the framework of the visions, as though he had been grafted on to an older text; and second, the three accounts in parallel suggest that they were all variants of an older traditional account. There are, for example, variant names for the central figure; sometimes he is called son of man (e.g. 1 Enoch 48.2) and sometimes the elect one (e.g. 1 Enoch 49.4). He is the anointed one of the Lord of the Spirits (Hosts) (1 Enoch 48.10), and sits on the throne of glory, either as *the elect one* (1 Enoch 51.3; 55.4; 61.8) or as *that son of man*. These are remnants of the old royal tradition, full of temple imagery.

In the first Parable the elect one was 'under the wings of the Lord of the Spirits' (1 Enoch 39.7), i.e. on the throne beneath the wings of the cherubim. Philo's Logos spoke from between the cherubim, as did the Lord in Exodus. Around the throne were 'those who sleep not' singing the song of Isaiah's seraphim: 'Holy, holy, holy, is the Lord of the Spirits: the spirits fill the earth' (1 Enoch 39.12). Here it is not the Lord of Hosts filling the earth with his Glory as in Isa. 6.3, but the same understanding of the Glory as we found in both Philo and the Targum; it was the spirits, the powers of God who surrounded him and were made visible in the world. The four presences, the four archangels, stood around the throne (1 Enoch 40.1–9).

The second Parable promises that the elect one will sit on the throne of Glory as the judge. He will dwell among the elect and in his time the Lord will transform the earth. Here there is the characteristic blending of heaven and earth; the elect one sits on the heavenly throne, and yet lives among the chosen ones to transform the earth (1 Enoch 45.3–6). There follows a detailed description of the same figure, this time called 'that son of man' (1 Enoch 46.2), who was with 'One to whom belongs the time before time. And his head was white like wool.' The second figure was 'another individual whose face was like that of a human being. His countenance was full of grace like that of one amongst the holy angels' (1 Enoch 46.1). He was the revealer of hidden things (1 Enoch 46.3) and his role as the judge is described in terms very like those of the Magnificat: 'This Son of Man whom you have seen . . . shall loosen the reins of the strong, and crush the teeth of sinners; and shall depose the kings from their thrones and kingdoms. For they do not extol and glorify him, and neither do they obey him, the source of their kingship' (1 Enoch 46.4–5). That son of man was named before the creation (1 Enoch 48.3) and kept hidden with the Lord of Spirits (1 Enoch 48.6). He was the anointed one of the Lord of Spirits (1 Enoch 48.10), endowed like the messianic figure in Isa. 11 with the spirit of wisdom (1 Enoch 49.3). He sat on the throne of the Lord of Spirits (1 Enoch 51.3), in a place where there were fountains of wisdom and righteousness (1 Enoch 48.1; 49.1). The mighty of the earth would have to watch as the elect one judged Azazel and all his angels and sent out the angels of judgement (1 Enoch 55.3).

The third Parable has similar themes and details: the elect one sits on the throne as judge (1 Enoch 61.8); he had been hidden by the Most High and revealed only to the chosen (1 Enoch 62.7); he would establish a place for the chosen who would live with him in their 'garments of glory' (1 Enoch 62.14–16). His name was the bond of the great 'oath' which restrained the created order (1 Enoch 69.25–6). The Parable concludes:

[Then] there came to them a great joy. And they blessed, glorified and extolled [the Lord] on account of the fact that the name of that Son of Man was revealed to them. He shall never pass away or perish from the face of the earth. But those who have led the world astray shall be bound in chains; and their ruinous congregation shall be imprisoned; all their deeds shall vanish from before the face of the earth. Henceforth nothing that is corruptible shall be found; for that Son of Man has appeared and has seated himself upon the throne of glory and all evil shall disappear from before his face. (1 Enoch 69.26—9)

The Parables of Enoch present many problems, the two greatest being: When were they written, and by whom? There is no fragment from this section of 1 Enoch amongst the Qumran texts, which means that there is no physical evidence for a pre-Christian date. On the other hand, there are so many themes and details derived from the royal cult in the temple that there can be no question of their being an original composition in the modern sense of those words, no matter when they were written. Whoever wrote them was using the expectations of the second divine figure, the angelic judge and ruler. The setting is the temple, with the cherub throne and the waters of Eden flowing from the throne. If they were pre-Christian in their present form, they depicted the heavenly world which the first Christians would have known; if they are a Christian composition, they show how closely the Christians identified with the older tradition. There is nothing in them which is clearly a Christian innovation; the son of man figure is drawn from the heart of the old temple cult.

One of Jesus' own parables (and note that Enoch's visions were also called parables) describes the heavenly throne. The parable of the sheep and the goats (Matt. 25.31—46) is a throne vision. The Son of man will sit as judge on his glorious throne with all the nations assembled before him. He is the *King* whose *Father* has prepared a kingdom for the blessed (Matt. 25.34). Those judged are sent to the fire prepared for the devil and his angels (Matt. 25.41). The motif of secrecy is also there; the condemned plead that they did not recognize the Lord (Matt. 25.44), and are told that they should have seen the Lord in anyone who needed their help. This is Jesus' own addition to the judgement theme, bringing into the ancient tradition the democratization which had begun with Genesis 1; every man is made in the image of God, and not just the manifested angel figure who had been the earlier 'Adam' in the garden of Eden.

There are many examples of such throne visions in the literature of the intertestamental and early Christian periods. The Testament of Levi is an example, perhaps from the second century BC, but reworked by several hands and now confused in some places. The original version seems to have described three heavens: the first was the place of the great sea (Test. Levi 2.7), the second the place of the heavenly armies prepared for the day of judgement, and 'in the highest of all dwelleth the Great Glory, far above all holiness' (Test. Levi 3.4). This is the threefold pattern of temple court (sea), *hekal* (the garden of the cherubim) and holy of holies. Levi's prayers had been heard and he was to become *a son of the Most High* (i.e. a divine figure; cf. Ps. 82.6), and a servant and a minister of his presence (Test. Levi 4.2). The angel then opened for Levi the gates of heaven and he saw 'the holy temple and upon a throne of Glory the Most High' (Test. Levi 5.1). Levi was installed as a priest until the Lord himself would come and dwell in the midst of his people; this suggests that he was a representative, a substitute for the Lord himself. He was also told to be a warrior and execute vengeance on Shechem; this is the familiar combination of warrior and priest, first found in Deut. 32.43, where the Lord himself avenges the blood of his servants and makes expiation for the land. A second vision seems to be an expansion of this first; Levi is vested as a high priest by the 'seven men in white raiment' (Test. Levi 8.2):

> The first anointed me with holy oil and gave me the staff of judgement.
> The second washed me with pure water and fed me with bread and wine (even) the most holy things, and clad me with a holy and glorious robe.
> The third clothed me with a linen vestment like an ephod.
> The fourth put round me a girdle like unto purple.
> The fifth gave me a branch of rich olive.
> The sixth placed a crown on my head.
> The seventh placed on my head a diadem of priesthood and filled my hands with incense that I might serve as priest to the Lord God.
> (Test. Levi 8.5—10)

The high priest is vested by angels, exactly as happened in the case of Joshua (Zech. 3.1—5). Levi's vision, then, was part of the traditional belief about the high priesthood and not something original to the author of this Testament. The similarity to early Christian baptism customs has led some to suggest that the text has been altered. The bread and wine in particular are thought to be a Christian addition, but this need not necessarily be so. The earliest reference to a priest in Jerusalem is in Gen. 14, where Melchizedek the priest–king brings Abraham bread and wine (Gen. 14.18), and bread and wine were offered with the sacrifices in the temple. We know too little about the priestmaking rituals to state with any confidence that a text has been altered.

The second example is from the Assumption of Moses, a text from the first century AD. It describes the manifestation of the angel of Israel, and, since the whole of the Assumption is an expansion of the last chapters of Deuteronomy, this passage corresponds to Deut. 32.43 and shows how it was understood at this time.

> And then his kingdom shall appear throughout all his creation,
> And then Satan shall be no more,
> And sorrow shall depart with him.
> Then the hands of the angel shall be filled
> Who has been appointed chief,
> And he shall forthwith avenge them of their enemies.
> For the Heavenly One will arise from his royal throne
> And he will go forth from his holy habitation
> With indignation and wrath on account of his sons.
> (Ass. Mos. 10.1—3)

There follows a passage describing terrifying events; the sun and moon darkened, the stars out of order and the sea sucked back into the abyss. Finally, Israel is exalted and taken up to heaven to look down upon its enemies in Gehenna.

This example shows a different use of the throne vision. The Heavenly One is the chief angel, the warrior ('avenge them of their enemies') and priest (his 'hands shall be filled'), who leaves his throne and his holy dwelling in order to save his people. It is usually assumed that the angel was Michael, but since the passage corresponds to one in Deuteronomy about the Lord, it is more likely that this is a vision of the Lord leaving the holy of holies. There are other passages in the Old Testament where this is described, both from the eighth century BC: 'For behold, the

Lord is coming forth out of his place ... and the mountains will melt under him' (Mic. 1.3, 4); and 'For behold, the Lord is coming forth out of his place to punish the inhabitants of the earth for their iniquity' (Isa. 26.21). This vision, then, is of the same type as Ezekiel's when he saw the Lord, described as the angel of fire and bronze, leaving the chariot throne in order to bring punishment upon the city.

A third example is in the Apocalypse of Abraham, where the patriarch ascends and sees first a great fire and then:

> under the fire a throne of fire and the many-eyed ones round about, reciting the song, under the throne four fiery living creatures, singing. (Apoc. Abr. 18.3)

> And while I was standing and watching, I saw behind the living creatures a chariot with fiery wheels. Each wheel was full of eyes round about. And above the wheels was the throne which I had seen. And it was covered with fire and the fire circled it round about, and an indescribable light surrounded the fiery crowd. (Apoc. Abr. 18.12—13)

Some of this text has probably become corrupted in the course of transmission, but what follows is clear enough. Abraham is given a panoramic view of the history of Israel as he looks down from the place of the throne.

The throne is also described in the Life of Adam and Eve and the very similar Apocalypse of Moses. Adam had a vision: 'When we were at prayer there came to me Michael the archangel, the messenger of God. And I saw a chariot like the wind and its wheels were fiery, and I was caught up into the Paradise of righteousness, and I saw the Lord sitting, and his face was flaming fire that could not be endured. And many thousands of angels were on the right and the left of that chariot' (*Life* 25.1—3). The chariot throne in Paradise was surrounded by a sea (*Life* 28.4). Later the archangel Michael called all the angels to Paradise to see the judgement of Adam: 'And when God appeared in Paradise, mounted on the chariot of his cherubim, with the angels proceeding before him and singing hymns of praises, all the plants of Paradise both of your father's lot and mine, broke into flowers. And the throne of God was fixed where the Tree of Life was' (Apoc. Mos. 22.3—4).

The greatest of the biblical apocalypses is that of St John,

THE THRONE 165

which had all the features of those other throne visions. The setting for the whole apocalypse was the heavenly temple: John saw the sevenfold lamp (Rev. 1.12), the altar (Rev. 6.9), the crowd in white robes with their palm branches, the heavenly Feast of Tabernacles which was the time of the enthronement of the ancient kings (Rev. 7.9—12), the golden incense altar before the throne (Rev. 8.3; 8.5; 9.13) and the ark of the covenant (Rev. 11.19). He saw the judgement as the great harvest (Rev. 14.14—16). He heard the heavenly music (Rev. 4.8, 11; 5.9; 11.17; 15.3—4; 19.6—7). He saw the beast rise from the primeval sea (Rev. 13.1). He saw the throne (Rev. 4.1—4), in front of which were the seven torches, the seven spirits of God, Zechariah's 'eyes of the Lord' (Rev. 4.5). Round the throne were the cherubim (Rev. 4.5—8) and in front of it was the sea (Rev. 4.6; 15.2). On the throne was one who appeared like jasper and carnelian (Rev. 4.3), not described as a man figure, though he had a hand (Rev. 5.7) and we are probably to assume a human form. The heavenly judge was revealed (Rev. 5.6—7), and he was the one who had the seven spirits of the Lord, i.e. he was the one represented by the ancient *menorah*. He was also a sacrificed lamb. The anointed one was revealed and his kingdom proclaimed (Rev. 11.15). The judgement began, and the heavenly agents, the four horsemen, went out from the holy place onto the earth (Rev. 6.1—8). As in Ezekiel's vision, the chosen were marked with the name of the Lord (Rev. 14.1). (Ezekiel's scribe marked them with a letter tau, the sign of the sacred name (Ezek. 9.4), which in the ancient Hebrew script was a cross. This was doubtless the origin of the Christian custom of signing with a cross, even though it later became associated with the cross of the crucifixion.) Fire was cast upon the earth from the altar of incense (Rev. 8.5), as in Ezekiel's vision (Ezek. 10.2). The divine warrior rode out from heaven to fight upon the earth (Rev. 19.11—16). His eyes were like fire and he had a secret name, which must have meant the sacred name. He was called the Word of God, the name given to the divine warrior in an almost contemporary text, the Wisdom of Solomon. On the night of the Exodus the angel of death had passed through Egypt and the original Exodus account says that this had been the Lord himself (Exod. 12.12, 29). The writer of the Wisdom of Solomon, however, described the death of the firstborn thus: 'Thy all powerful *Word* leaped from heaven, from the *royal throne*, into the midst of the land that was doomed, a stern warrior carrying the sharp sword of thy authentic command, and stood and filled all things with death, and touched heaven while standing on the earth' (Wisd. 18.15—16). The warrior of Revelation was also named King of Kings and Lord of Lords. He had the sword and rod of judgement (as did the messianic figure of Isa. 11), and he was to tread the winepress of the wrath of God Almighty. Now the one who trod the winepress in Isa. 63 was the Lord himself. As in other throne visions, the seer was commissioned to prophesy (Rev. 10.11), and as in other visions, the seer wrote his words at the command of the angel. In John's case the angel was the angel of Jesus (Rev. 22.16).

The Mystics' Visions of the Throne

> Angel voices ever singing
> Round thy throne of light.
>
> F. Pott

One of the most remarkable descriptions of the heavenly throne is to be found in the *Songs of the Sabbath Sacrifice*, which were found in fragments at Qumran and at Masada. Too little has survived for any extensive or certain translation to be made, but where there are substantial readable portions, the picture which emerges must alter forever what we understand as the background to Revelation or Hebrews. This *must* have been the way that the people of first-century Palestine regarded their temple cult. The heavenly *debir* was envisaged as a place of *elohim* (i.e. gods or angelic beings), spirits of truth and knowledge who were many-coloured and surrounded the throne.

> The cherubim bless the image of the throne chariot above the firmament and they praise the majesty of the luminous firmament beneath his seat of glory. When the wheels advance, angels of holiness come and go. From between his glorious wheels there is as it were a fiery vision of most holy spirits. About them the appearance of rivulets of fire in the likeness of gleaming brass, and a work of . . . radiance in many coloured glory, marvellous pigments, clearly mingled.
> (4Q 405 20.ii 21—2)

At their marvellous stations are spirits, many-coloured like the work of a weaver, splendid engraved figures. In the midst of a glorious appearance of scarlet, colours of the most holy spiritual light, they hold to their station before the King, spirits of pure colours in the midst of an appearance of whiteness. The likeness of the glorious spirit is like a work of art of a weaver. These are the Princes of those marvellously clothed for service, the Princes of the kingdom, the kingdom of the holy ones of the King of holiness in all the heights of the sanctuaries of his glorious kingdom. (4Q 405. 23.ii)

There is nothing in the surviving texts to say who was observing these heavenly places. Other texts, however, describe a mystical ascent to contemplate the chariot throne; indeed the divine throne chariot became the central theme of early and medieval Jewish mysticism, which was known as Merkabah Mysticism (from the Hebrew *merkabah* meaning chariot). Such ascents were thought to be dangerous and to need the special protection of a guiding angel. They also became the centre of great controversy; the figure who appeared in human form on, or off, the divine throne was seen to present a threat to monotheism, and the argument raged over whether or not there were two powers in heaven. It is not easy to date these mystical texts or references to them. The existence of 1 Enoch and the *Songs of the Sabbath Sacrifice* at Qumran show that their roots go back at least to the first century BC in Palestine, and the rabbis associated with the controversies are all Palestinian. (A full account of this can be found in A. F. Segal, *Two Powers in Heaven*.)

The Hebrew Book of Enoch (3 Enoch) was originally called the *Sepher Hekalot*, the Book of the Palaces. It was not the work of a single author but rather the accumulated tradition of a school of mystics. There is no agreement as to the date of the form we now have, although the fifth/sixth century AD has much to commend it. The tradition purports to go back to Rabbi Ishmael, the Palestinian scholar who died in AD 132. He ascended in a mystical trance and passed through six heavens. At the door of the seventh heaven, R. Ishmael prayed for protection from the angels who might throw him down, and the Holy One sent him Metatron to be his protector. He entered and saw the throne. Later he asked Metatron who he was, and discovered that he was the exalted Enoch, transformed into a great angel with seventy names. Metatron described how he had been lifted from the earth as an Elect One and transported in a fiery chariot. He was then installed as a Prince of the Presence:

> After all this, the Holy One, blessed be he, made for me a throne like the throne of glory and spread over it a coverlet of splendour, brilliance, brightness, beauty, loveliness and grace, like the coverlet of the throne of glory, in which all the varied splendour of the luminaries that are in the world is set. He placed it at the door of the seventh palace and sat me down upon it. And the herald went out into every heaven and announced concerning me: I have appointed Metatron my servant as a prince and a ruler over all the denizens of the heights. (3 Enoch 10)

Metatron was then given a robe of honour and a garment of glory; he was crowned with a splendid crown and given the name the Lesser Yahweh. Finally, the Holy One wrote on his crown the sacred letters by which the world had been created. All the heavenly princes trembled at the sight (3 Enoch 12—14).

No matter what the date of this text, it is not hard to see where it had its roots. Metatron was a human being who had been exalted to the highest status in heaven. In this respect, 3 Enoch gives the next stage of the tradition recorded at the end of the Parables of Enoch, where Enoch had been named as the Son of Man. Metatron was enthroned at the gate of heaven, behind a glorious curtain, and installed as the great judge. He was given the name of Yahweh, and the sacred name was put upon his crown. 3 Enoch shows how the royal mythology was remembered even at that late date. A human figure had been elevated to heaven and enthroned as the divine judge; he had been given the name Yahweh and had worn the sacred name on his crown, exactly as did the high priest in the temple. He sat behind the curtain on a throne at the gate of heaven, exactly as Philo's Word had been enthroned between the cherubim at the gate of Eden and the Lord had been enthroned between the cherubim behind the veil in the temple. Metatron, the human figure, the second power in heaven, was at the centre of the two powers controversy.

Elisha b. Abuyah was also known as Aḥer ('the other one') to avoid naming one who had been such a notorious heretic. He lived in the early second century AD and had been a mystic. In one of his visions he had seen Metatron in heaven sitting as the heavenly scribe (just as Enoch had been, Jub. 4.23). Aher had assumed from this sitting position that Metatron was enthroned. The story, as recorded in the Babylonian Talmud, depicts Aher's horror at this idea: 'He saw that permission was granted to Metatron to sit and write the merits of Israel . . . Perhaps, God forfend! there are two powers. Thereupon they led Metatron forth and punished him with sixty fiery lashes, saying unto him: "Why didst thou not rise before him when thou didst see him?"' (b. Hagigah 15a). The story is also told in 3 Enoch 16: 'But when Aher came to behold the vision of the chariot and he set eyes upon me, he was afraid and trembled before me . . . Then he opened his mouth and said: "There are indeed two powers in heaven!".' Aniyel the Prince then came and lashed him and made him stand up, because he had been responsible for giving such evil thoughts to Aher.

The account of Aher's heresy in the Babylonian Talmud is preceded by the widely told story of how four rabbis, Ben Azzai, Ben Zoma, Aher and R. Akiba entered a 'garden'; the first looked and died, the second looked and was struck, the third 'cut the plants' and the fourth, Akiba, 'went up in peace and came down in peace'. This mysterious account shows that the ascent was recognized as a dangerous practice, and even though there is nothing to say what they saw, they saw it in a garden and the sight proved fatal for two of them. What they saw must have been the chariot throne in the garden of Eden.

The two powers controversy was waged over certain passages of Scripture and how they were to be understood. One of these was Exod. 24.1: 'And he said to Moses, "Come up to the Lord".' Why, it was asked by a heretic, did God not say, 'Come up to me'. Were the Lord and God two separate powers in heaven? The official answer given, attributed to R. Idi in the early third century, was that *Lord* here meant *Metatron*, the angel of whom it was said, 'My name is in him' (Exod. 23.21). The fact that there was this controversy shows that there were some at that time who found two divine powers in the Old Testament. The rabbis said that it was an angel who had been manifested there, but the heretics must have said that that angel was the Lord himself (b. *Sanhedrin* 38b).

The crucial text was Dan. 7.9, which says that thrones (plural) were placed in heaven, one for the Ancient of Days and the other, presumably, for the son of man figure when he was given 'dominion and glory and kingdom' (Dan. 7.14). The Babylonian Talmud records a dispute over interpretation between two rabbis who taught in the early part of the second century AD:

> One passage says: His throne was fiery flames (Dan. 7.9) and another says: Until thrones were placed; and One that was ancient of days did sit . . . there is no contradiction; One (throne) for Him and one for David: this is the view of R. Akiba. Said R. Yosi the Galilean to him: Akiba, how long will you treat the divine presence as profane! Rather, one for justice and one for grace. Did he accept (this explanation) from him, or did he not accept it? Come and hear: One for justice and one for grace; this is the view of R. Akiba. (b. *Hagigah* 14a)

R. Akiba must at one time have said that the second throne was for the Davidic Messiah, but as a result of the dispute, he agreed that the two thrones were for two aspects of God, his mercy and his justice. These two aspects of God were eventually offered as the solution to the problem of the 'two powers'; the name *God* in the Old Testament signified the aspect of justice, they said, and *Lord* the aspect of mercy.

The problem of the two thrones in Daniel was made more acute by other texts which seemed to show God in different aspects. Two texts in particular were used in the debate: Exod. 15.3, 'The Lord is a man of war', and Exod. 24.10, where they assumed that it was the Ancient of Days on the throne, as in Dan. 7. The later rabbis argued that this showed the two aspects of God, one like an old man and one like a warrior, not that there were two powers which is what these texts imply. The problem is that *these* texts require an exactly opposite allocation of the two attributes to those of the later rabbis; the Lord as the man of war would exhibit the justice, and the God of Israel on Sinai would exhibit the mercy. These were, in fact, how Philo had allocated the attributes of God one century before the dispute between R. Akiba and R. Yosi; he had said that Yahweh (Lord) signified justice and Elohim (God) signified mercy (Philo, *Who is the Heir?*, 166). Further, in Philo, both these were attributes of the Logos, the manifested God, and not of God Most High.

From this considerable confusion there emerges the fact that in the second century AD there was controversy over the differing ways God was described in the Old Testament, particularly over the manifestations in human form. Interpretations were being redone and positions being redrawn. This was just the period when Justin was arguing with the Jew Trypho in his *Dialogue with Trypho* that the Word had been manifested in the Old Testament in those places which had described the Lord as an angel in human form. This, combined with the tradition about the great angel named Metatron who also bore the divine name (as was the case with the angel of Exod. 23.21ff.), and was a human figure enthroned in heaven, shows that the throne visions were at the very heart of those controversies which separated Judaism from Christianity. One has only to think of early Christian claims such as 'Therefore God has highly exalted him and bestowed on him the name which is above every name, that at the name of Jesus every knee should bow, in heaven and on earth and under the earth' (Phil. 2.9—10); or: 'We have such a high priest, one who is seated at the right hand of the throne of the Majesty in heaven, a minister in the sanctuary and the true tent which is set up not by man but by the Lord' (Heb. 8.1—2), to realize who the 'two powers heretics' must have been.

The Fiery Angels

> My God, how wonderful thou art,
> Thy majesty how bright,
> How beautiful thy mercy-seat,
> In depths of burning light!
> F. W. Faber

The throne was a place of fire. Ezekiel's is the earliest description of the great fire, 'like torches moving to and fro among the living creatures; and the fire was bright, and out of the fire went forth lightning. And the living creatures darted to and fro, like a flash of lightning' (Ezek. 1.13—14). The *fire was composite and the living creatures were a part of the fire*. Above the fire was a human form, also fiery; the upper part was like molten bronze but the lower part was not separated from the fire (Ezek. 1.26—7). When the figure was seen off the throne he was still a man of fire (Ezek. 8.2). The psalmist had implied something similar: 'who makest the winds thy messengers [i.e. angels], fire and flame thy ministers' (Ps. 104.4). *The Songs of the Sabbath Sacrifice* described the angels as fiery creatures:

> From between his glorious wheels there is as it were a fiery vision of most holy spirits. About them, the appearance of rivulets of fire in the likeness of gleaming brass, and the work of ... radiance in many-coloured glory, marvellous pigments, clearly mingled. (4Q 405.20.ii 221−2)

> In the midst of a glorious appearance of scarlet, colours of the most holy spiritual light, they hold their holy station before [the K]ing, spirits of [pure] colours in the midst of an appearance of whiteness. The likeness of the glorious spirit is like a work of art of sparkling fine gold. All their pattern is clearly mingled like the work [of art] of a weaver. (4Q 405.23.ii).

They too were a part of the glory, the coloured flames which mingled into the great fire. On his heavenly journey, Enoch was taken to a place 'where there were (the ones) like the flaming fire. And when they (so) desire, they appear like men' (1 Enoch 17.1). When he contemplated the throne he saw 'the holy sons of God. They were stepping on flames of fire: Their garments were white [and their raiment], And their faces shone like snow' (1 Enoch 71.1). The angels of fire around the throne which were aspects of the Lord were also mentioned in the *Apocryphon of John*, a gnostic text found at Nag Hammadi. Since the teachings of this work were known to Irenaeus, it must have been in use by the end of the second century AD. It described the origin of Yaltebaoth, the son of Wisdom, in whom we recognize the God of the Old Testament, though he is described with the hostility characteristic of the gnostic texts. Wisdom rejected her offspring when she saw him, and cast him from the highest heaven.

> And she surrounded it [her offspring] with a luminous cloud, and she placed a throne in the middle of the cloud so that no one might see it except the holy spirit who is the mother of all living. And she called his name Yaltebaoth. (CG. II.1 10)

> But Yaltebaoth had a multitude of faces ... so that he could bring a face before all of them according to his desire, being in the middle of the seraphs. He shared his fire with them; therefore he became Lord over them. (CG.II.1 12)

The weird distortions of this gnostic text are distortions of a familar picture: the fire which separated into the living beings who became the visible forms of the Lord.

These angels of fire also explain the remarkable descriptions of how the mystics were themselves transformed into the angelic state. When Enoch saw the throne and its fires, 'my whole body mollified, and my spirit transformed' (1 Enoch 71.11). As Isaiah ascended, 'the glory of my face was being transformed as I went up from heaven to heaven' (Asc. Isa. 7.25). Enoch was transformed in the same way into Metatron:

> When the Holy One, blessed be he, took me to serve the throne of glory, the wheels of the chariot and all the needs of the Shekinah, at once my flesh turned to flame, my sinews to blazing fire, my bones to juniper coals, my eyelashes into lightning flashes, my eyeballs to fiery torches, the hairs of my head to hot flames, all my limbs to wings of burning fire and the substance of my body to blazing fire. (3 Enoch 15.1)

From one of the later mystical hymns, a text known as the *Greater Hekalot*, comes this description of the experience of contemplating the robe of God:

> His garment is engraved inside and outside and entirely covered with YHWH YHWH. No eyes are able to behold it, neither the eyes of flesh and blood nor the eyes of his servants. Whoever beholds it, whoever glimpses and sees it, his eyeballs are seized by balls of fire, his eyeballs discharge fiery torches which burn him and consume him. For the very fire that springs out of the man beholding the garment burns him and consumes him.
> (Trans. in *The Penguin Book of Hebrew Verse*, p. 199)

It may be that the very earliest reference to this transformation before the throne of God is in Exod. 34.29—35, which says that Moses had to veil his face after meeting with the Lord. His face was glowing, which suggests that the fiery transformation was a very ancient belief.

The angels of fire around the throne were also the earliest expression of the ideas which became the Christian Trinity. There were two angels on either side of the great throne in early visions; perhaps these were the cherubim whom Philo knew as the two aspects of God. These two angels were variously described, as can be seen by comparing the Ascension of Isaiah, 2 Enoch and the *Shepherd* of Hermas, three approximately contemporary texts from the first century AD. Hermas described a glorious man flanked by six others: 'The Glorious Man is the Son of God and those six are the glorious angels supporting him on the right hand and the left' (*Parables*, 9.xii.8). This is the sevenfold pattern on the *menorah* here used of the angels/spirits of the Lord it had always represented. Elsewhere the glorious man was named as the angel of the Lord (*Parables*, 8.ii.1), Michael (*Parables*, 8.iii.3), and the Lord of all the Tower (*Parables*, 9.vii.1). St John had named both Michael and the Word as the heavenly warrior (Rev. 12.7−9; 19.11−16). In 2 Enoch Michael was the angel who guided Enoch into the presence of God; in the Apocalypse of Abraham the guiding angel was Jaoel (i.e. Yahweh-el) the angel in whom was the name of the Lord.

Similar comparisons show that Gabriel was also the Holy Spirit; 2 Enoch described the angel on the left of the throne: 'And the Lord called to me; and he said to me, "Enoch, sit on the left of me with Gabriel"' (2 Enoch 24.1). Isaiah said that this angel was the angel of the Holy Spirit: 'And I saw the Lord and the second angel, and they were standing, and the second one whom I saw was on the left of my Lord. And I asked the angel who led me and I said to him, "Who is this one?". And he said to me, "Worship him, for this is the angel of the Holy Spirit who has spoken in you and also in the other righteous"' (Asc. Isa. 9.36). Both the Lord and the angel of the Holy Spirit worshipped the Lord who was called the Great Glory. This strange vision is one of the earliest descriptions of the Trinity, as the angels on either side of the throne.

These two angels were also identified with the two living creatures on either side of the throne. Two passages of the Old Testament were used: Isa. 6.2−3 and Hab. 3.2, which in the Greek has the additional line 'in the midst of two living creatures you shall be known'. Origen, who wrote in the first half of the third century, said that both these texts referred to the Son and the Holy Spirit and that he had learned this from a Jewish teacher: 'The Hebrew master used to say that the two seraphim, whom Isaiah describes . . . were to be understood as the only-begotten Son of God and the Holy Spirit. For our part we think that what is said in the Psalm of Habakkuk, *"In the midst of the two living creatures you shall be known"*, is also to be taken as referring to Christ and the Holy Spirit' (Origen, *De principiis*, I.3.4). In his commentary on Romans he also identified the two cherubim on the ark with the Word and the Spirit which both dwelt in Christ, the mercy seat (Rom. 3.25).

All these angels were the fiery ones around the throne, aspects of the presence and powers of God which could be made visible. This accounts for one of the earliest images used to explain the Trinity. Justin was a native of Palestine, born near Shechem about AD 100. In his *Dialogue with the Jew Trypho* he explained the relationship of the Father and the Son:

> God has begotten as a Beginning before all His creatures a kind of Reasonable Power from Himself, which is also called by the Holy Spirit the Glory of the Lord, and sometimes Son, and sometimes Wisdom, and sometimes Angel, and sometimes God, and sometimes Lord and Word . . . as we see in the case of fire another fire comes into being, without that one from which the kindling was made being diminished, but remaining the same, while that which is kindled from it appears as self-existing, without diminishing that from which it was kindled. (*Trypho*, 61)

Justin later explained to Trypho that 'Christ being the Lord, and ever God the Son of God, and appearing by His power in olden time as man and angel, appeared also in the glory of fire, as in the bush, so also in the judgement that was done to Sodom' (*Trypho*, 128). He would not accept any suggestion that God and the Word were identical:

> But [they assert] that this power can never be cut off or separated from the Father, in the same way, as they say, the light of the sun on earth cannot be cut off or separated, though the sun is in heaven. And when the sun sets the light is borne away with it. So the Father, they affirm, makes, when he will, His power to spring forward, and when he will, He draws it back again to himself. They teach that in this way also he made the angels.* (*Trypho*, 128)

---

*This refers to a passage in the Babylonian Talmud expounding Ps. 33.6: 'Every single day the angels that minister to Him are created from the stream of fire, and they utter a song and cease to be . . . From every single utterance that goeth forth from the mouth of the Holy One, blessed be He, is created one angel, for it is said, By the word of the Lord were the heavens made and by the breath of his mouth all their host' (b. *Hagigah* 14a).

There were, and always had been, several ranks of angels, and could we but understand the angelology of this period we should better understand the origin of Christian thinking, especially in such passages as the first chapter of Hebrews, or this debate of Justin and Trypho.

Philo shows that there were Jews of the first century AD who believed that there were two powers in heaven: the Most High (the Father) and the Word (the Son, the Angel of Israel). This is a survival of the oldest temple tradition where the Angel of Israel had been manifested in several forms, just as the *menorah* had had seven lights. The Word, Philo had said, was the chief of the powers, and the two names for God in the Old Testament, Yahweh and Elohim, had indicated two of these powers, two of these aspects. Trypho represented another type of Judaism, the Judaism which had identified God most High and the Lord; he would no longer have accepted the old idea of the sons of God Most High who were the patron deities of the individual nations. For him and those he represented there could only have been one possible illustration, that of the sun and its rays. But Justin and the Christians were heir to the older beliefs and they held that Jesus had been the manifestation of the Lord, the Son of God Most High. For them the only possible illustration was that of the torch kindled from the fire and having a separate existence.

The human figure on the throne is fundamental to our understanding of what was meant by 'Messiah'. Further, the hostility to this throne tradition explains the hostility between the first Christians and the Judaism from which they eventually separated. From the time of the monarchy when contemporary cultures had described their kings as the image of God, Israel's anointed kings had also sat upon the divine throne in the temple as the visible manifestation of the Lord, the patron angel of Israel. Not all the angels had human form; the evil angel in one of the Dead Sea Scrolls, the Testament of Amram (4Q Amram), for example, was a snake-like creature: 'his appearance and his face was like that of an adder'. The evil archon of the Gnostics was a lion figure; in some texts he was described as a composite lion and human figure: 'a ruler first appeared out of the waters, lion-like in appearance and androgynous' (CG. II.5.100); and in others as a serpent-lion: 'a form of a lion-faced serpent. And its eyes were like lightning fires which flash' (CG. II.1.10). The human form is therefore significant. The angel whom the king had represented did not disappear with the demise of the monarchy, but survived in the non-biblical texts as the Great Angel, the high priest and warrior, the heavenly judge installed at the right hand of the Most High.

The great prophet of the exile, the Second Isaiah, had proclaimed that there was only one God and that all the others were nothing. What happened in fact was that the Most High and the patron angel of Israel were fused and appeared in subsequent texts and interpretations as one God with two names. Having lost his name in some circles, the Great Angel was not forgotten. Some gave him no name, some named him Michael, others remembered that he was Yahweh, the Lord. It was these people who kept the distinction between the Most High, whom they called the Father, and the Lord, whom they called the Son. They recorded the birth of one who was the Son of the Most High (Luke 1.32) and who was recognized as the Lord in human form. They interpreted his whole life and death in terms of the ancient messianic angel. From the beginning there was a consistent use of this temple imagery to describe and interpret the life, death, and ascension of Jesus. Those who had tried to suppress the Great Angel found the Christians a threat and the Merkabah Mystics a great problem. There could not be two powers in heaven, they said. But their most ancient traditions, as reflected in the temple cult, had said otherwise.

> 'The person who contemplates the beauty of the image also achieves knowledge of the original model.'
>
> Gregory of Nyssa

CHAPTER FIVE

'BUT ISRAEL HAD NO MYTHOLOGY'

For many years it has been an orthodoxy of scholarship that Israel had no mythology. Mythology, we were told, was not possible in a monotheistic culture. Mythology was tales of divine and semi-divine beings and Israel knew of only One. Mythology was for the lesser breeds without the Law. It smacked of priestcraft and arcane rituals and was something which, quite obviously, any Chosen People would have quickly outgrown. Israel, after all, was different. There have always been voices of dissent, scholars attempting to read behind the psalms and prophets in order to reconstruct the ancient cult. Their works have been read with interest but perhaps a little suspicion. What they wrote has not been ignored, but it has not been internalized and become the way the Old Testament is read. Mythology is one possible *conclusion* for Old Testament study, but still far from being an essential premise. Perhaps this is because it is too imprecise a study, or perhaps it is because the implications of any study of this mythology are rather painful. I can only speak for Christian scholars, but I have been acutely aware of an unwillingness actually to read the Old Testament as it is. There is a great concentration upon essential preliminary studies such as language and archaeology, and peripherals such as sociology and story, but very little by way of theology. This is in no small part due to the pressures of an ecumenical age; we avoid conflict with other Old Testament users by avoiding the discussion of anything that might lead to disagreement. Or, in church as opposed to academic circles, the Old Testament is simply regarded as obsolete and the New Testament is wrenched from its roots in the interests of making it immediately available to all.

The New Testament cannot be understood apart from the Old, and by this I do not mean a detailed study of the desert wanderings or the tribal structures of ancient Israel. These are academic. What gave life to the New Testament and shaped the early Christian liturgies was the mythology of the Old Testament centred on the temple. At some stage the mythology of the temple had lost its centre and begun to disintegrate. This could well have been with the first destruction by the Babylonians and the Deuteronomists, but later writers' frequent use of temple imagery suggests that the mythology was current in some circles well into the period of the second temple. The days came when not one stone of the temple was left standing upon another, and yet even those isolated stones were embellished with fragments of an ancient pattern. Reconstructing the patterns is only the beginning; the greater task will be to reconstruct the whole, to see how the patterns related to each other and to the entire building. In other words, how did these fragments of mythology fit into the earlier cult of Israel? And how early was early? And how much more of Christian origins will they illumine?

Another of the problems which bedevil reconstruction is the unacknowledged hope of discovering the pure original in a form we find palatable. Despite all the work of textual criticism, there remains a hankering after the unsullied source of Israel's religion. Scholars still speak of additions to the text, excisions and so forth, paring down to the older purities. The rational part of us, however, knows that the reverse is true, that the excisions and additions are evidence of a series of changes which eventually produced that recognizable and rational system we wished had been delivered on Sinai. Thus we live with a curious tension; Israel outgrew its earlier mythology, yes, but somehow returned to an even earlier truth. This truth was monotheism, the Mosaic law and the Deuteronomists' view of history as the means by which God spoke to his people. The mythology had been a pagan intrusion, a deviation from pristine purity. Even when the same mythology appeared in Christian texts, there was an overwhelming pressure to assume that it, too, was brought into the faith by Greek converts who had not really left their paganism behind. Thus the essential imagery came to be explained as paganism in texts which were crucial for understanding both Jewish and Christian origins.

The myths of Israel will not have existed as a written compendium of stories like Robert Graves's collection of the Greek myths. Rather, they were a world view, an expression of normality or a statement of the obvious. One lived in relation to them, knowing that they affected life just as much as our knowledge of gravity limits what any sane person will attempt to do. Like any knowledge of the world, these myths grew and developed. There is no point in Israel's history where we can stop the film and say: 'Here is the fullest and clearest expression of the myths. Before this point they were inchoate and after it they declined.' The recovery and understanding of myth can never be an exact discipline; to minds which yearn for precision and hard evidence it will appear so imprecise as to be better excluded. But in matters of theology, the word which replaced mythology, there can be no precision and hard evidence.

The death blow to mythology was dealt by those who made the myths into history. We still have problems with Adam and Eve to this day as a result! By incorporating myth into history on a once-for-all basis, the power of myth was broken. Eden became part of a historical process and the Last Judgement became something for the remote future. History, real history, happened between the two. In sharp contrast, we realise from such mythology as remains that Eden and the Last Judgement were one and the same. First and last were simultaneous. It is only by dwelling on facts such as this that the enormity of our problem of perception becomes apparent. For many in Israel, 'history' did not happen between the two mythological parts, but rather in parallel to them. The myths expressed a consistently valid natural law; Eden and Judgement lay beyond and gave shape to events of everyday life. The divine presence could pass through the curtain of the material world and assume visible form.

Central to the myths was belief in the human manifestation of God. A human figure occupied the divine throne and came to bring judgement. The presence of the figure also brought renewed life and fertility. The human figure was probably once the king who was also the high priest. He was able to enter the holiest place. In later times the high priest carried life-blood to the place of the throne, to the point beyond time and place from which all things could be seen and known; one wonders what was done by the earlier kings who went up to occupy that throne. Behind the letter to the Hebrews there seems to lie a belief that the high priest carried a substitute for his own life-blood. What picture of reality lay behind this ritual? Why was it necessary for the human manifestation of the divine to carry his life-blood into the holy place? What did this joining of heaven and earth achieve? These questions cannot yet be answered but they are vital, for the mythology and symbolism of the ancient temple are the key to understanding much of Christian origins. Modern translations of the New Testament which obscure this imagery are counter-productive. We must recover an understanding of this symbolism, not modernize it to a point where it says nothing, for when the meaning of these symbols is lost, the meaning of Christianity will also be lost.

> Then Jacob awoke from his sleep and said, 'Surely the Lord is in this place; and I did not know it.' And he was afraid, and said, 'How awesome is this place! This is none other than the house of God, and this is the gate of heaven.' (Gen. 28.16−17)

BIBLIOGRAPHY

Primary Sources
JEWISH TEXTS

The Mishnah is the collection of Oral Law made by Rabbi Judah ha-Nasi I in the early third century AD, representing the traditions of the earlier Scribes and Pharisees. It became the basis of the Talmud. There is an English translation by H. Danby (Oxford 1933).
The Tosefta is the 'additions' to the Mishnah. There is an English translation by J. Neusner (New York 1979–81).
The Babylonian Talmud was produced by Babylonian rabbis in the third to fifth centuries and records their interpretations of the Mishnah. Soncino translation, ed. I. Epstein, 35 vols. (London 1948–62). (There is also a shorter version, usually called the Palestinian Talmud.)
Targum Pseudo-Jonathan is one of the Aramaic translations of the Pentateuch in the Palestinian tradition. Tr. in J. W. Etheridge, *The Targums on the Pentateuch* (London 1962–5).
Targum Neofiti is another Aramaic translation of the Pentateuch in the Palestinian tradition. There is an English translation in *Targum Neofiti*, ed. A. Diez Macho (Madrid 1970–8).
The Midrash Rabba is a collection of texts which comment upon Scripture and were derived from the sermons delivered in synagogues rather than from learned deliberations in the academies; i.e. they represent the preaching tradition, making Scripture relevant to the problems of its day. *Genesis Rabbah* probably dates from the sixth century and later, but it incorporates much traditional material which would have been older than this. There is an English translation in *Midrash*

Rabbah, ed. H. Freedman and M. Simon (Soncino translation, London 1939).
The Dead Sea Scrolls in English, tr. G. Vermes (3rd edn, London 1987).
Josephus was a general and historian who lived from about AD 37 until after AD 100. *Works*, tr. R. Marcus and others, 9 vols. (Loeb Classics, London, 1961—5).
Philo was a Jewish philosopher who lived in Alexandria from about 20 BC until after AD 40. *Works*, ed. and tr. F. H. Colson and others, 12 vols. (Loeb Classics, London, 1929—53).
1 Enoch, 2 Enoch, the Assumption of Moses, the Testament of the Twelve Patriarchs, the Apocalypse of Abraham, Jubilees, the Letter of Aristeas, the Life of Adam and Eve and the Apocalypse of Moses can all be found in R. H. Charles, ed., *The Apocrypha and Pseudepigrapha of the Old Testament*, vol. 2 *Pseudepigrapha* (Oxford 1913). All these and more, including 3 Enoch, can also be found in J. H. Charlesworth, ed., *The Old Testament Pseudepigrapha*, vols. 1 and 2 (New York and London 1983, 1985). Unfortunately, there are places where the English of the latter is not good, and reviewers warned about some inaccuracies in the translations. For non-specialists, however, it does make available far more material than other collections.
Some Merkabah Hymns in English can be found in *The Penguin Book of Hebrew Verse*, ed. T. Carmi (Penguin 1981).

CHRISTIAN TEXTS

Justin Martyr, *The Dialogue with Trypho*, tr. and notes by A. L. Williams. London 1930.
The Epistle of Barnabas, in *Early Christian Writings. The Apostolic Fathers*, tr. M. Staniforth. Penguin 1968.
The *Shepherd* of Hermas, and the *Stromata* of Clement of Alexandria in The Ante-Nicene Fathers, vol. II, *The Fathers of the Second Century*, ed. A. Roberts and J. Donaldson. Reprinted Michigan 1979.
Hippolytus, *On Daniel*, in The Anti-Nicene Christian Library, ed. A. Roberts and J. Donaldson (hereafter ANCL) vol. vi, *The Writings of Hippolytus*. Edinburgh 1868.
The fragments of Theodotus, in *The Excerpta ex Theodoto of Clement of Alexandria*, Studies and Documents I, tr. R. P. Casey. London 1934.

Irenaeus, *The Proof of the Apostolic Preaching*, tr. J. Armitage Robinson (London 1920); *Against Heresies* in ANCL vols. v and ix, *The Writings of Irenaeus* (Edinburgh 1868).
Origen, *Homilies on Genesis and Exodus*, tr. R. S. Heine (Washington 1982); *De Principiis* in ANCL vol. x, *The Writings of Origen* (Edinburgh 1869).
Eusebius, *The History of the Church*, tr. G. A. Williamson. Penguin 1965.
The Odes of Solomon, in *The Odes and Psalms of Solomon*, tr. J. Rendel Harris. Cambridge 1909.
Melito of Sardis, *On Pascha*, text and tr., ed. S. G. Hall. Oxford 1979.
The Liturgy of James, in ANCL vol. xxiv, *Early Liturgies and Other Documents*. Edinburgh 1883.
The Book of James, in *The Apocryphal New Testament*, tr. M. R. James. Oxford (1924) 1980.
St Ephrem, *Hymns on Paradise*, tr. S. P. Brock. New York 1990.
The Gospel of Thomas, The Hypostasis of the Archons, the untitled work usually known as On the Origin of the World and the Apocryphon of John can be read in *The Nag Hammadi Library*, ed. J. M. Robinson. Leiden 1977. These gnostic texts are designated both by their name and by their number within the Coptic Gnostic (CG) Library.
Also Pausanias, *Description of Greece*, tr. W. H. S. Jones, 5 vols. Loeb Classics, London 1954—71.

Suggestions for further reading

Barker, M., *The Older Testament*. London 1987.
Cassirer, E., *The Philosophy of Symbolic Forms*, 3 vols., tr. R. Mannheim, vol. 2, *Mythical Thought*. New Haven 1953—7.
Childs, B. S., *Myth and Reality in the Old Testament*. London 1960.
Clements, R. E., *God and Temple*. Oxford 1965.
Clifford, R. J., *The Cosmic Mountain in Canaan and the Old Testament*. Cambridge, Mass., 1972.
Cook, R., *The Tree of Life. Image for the Cosmos*. London and New York 1974.
Cross, F. M., *Canaanite Myth and Hebrew Epic*. Cambridge, Mass., and London 1973.

Daniélou, J., *A History of Early Christian Doctrine before the Council of Nicaea, I: The Theology of Jewish Christianity*. 1958, ET London 1964.
Eaton, J. H., *Kingship and the Psalms*. London 1976.
——, *Festal Drama in Deutero-Isaiah*. London 1979.
Edersheim, A., *The Temple*. London 1874, reprinted Eerdmans 1987.
Emerton, J., 'The Origin of the Son of Man Imagery', in *Journal of Theological Studies*, New Series, vol. ix, Pt. 2, 1958.
Engnell, I., *Studies in Divine Kingship in the Ancient Near East*. Oxford 1967.
Ginzberg, L., *Legends of the Jews*, 7 vols. Philadelphia 1909–38.
Goodenough, E. R., *Jewish Symbols in the Greco-Roman Period*, 11 vols. New York 1953–65.
Gray, J. G., *The Legacy of Canaan*. Supplements to Vetus Testamentum 5. Leiden 1957.
——, *Near Eastern Mythology*. London 1969.
Haran, M., *Temples and Temple Service in Ancient Israel*. Oxford 1978.
Johnson, A. R., *Sacral Kingship in Ancient Israel*. Cardiff 1967.
Keel, O. *The Symbolism of the Biblical World*. London 1978.
Meeks, W. A., 'Moses as God and King', in J. Neusner, ed., *Religions in Antiquity*. Leiden 1970.
Mettinger, T. N. D., *The Dethronement of Sabaoth*. Lund 1982.
Meyers, C., *The Tabernacle Menorah*. Missoula, Mon., 1976.
Morgenstern, J., 'The Mythological Background of Psalm 82', in *Hebrew Union College Annual* 14, 1939.
——, 'The Cultic Setting of the Enthronement Psalms', in *Hebrew Union College Annual* 35, 1964.
Murray, R., *Symbols of Church and Kingdom*. Cambridge 1975.
Patai, R., *Man and Temple in Jewish Myth and Ritual*. London 1947.
Rapoport, S., *Myths and Legends of Ancient Israel*. London 1928.
Rosenau, H., *Vision of the Temple*. London 1979.
Rowland, C., *The Open Heaven*. London 1982.
Safrai, S., and Stern, M., *The Jewish People in the First Century, II*. Amsterdam 1974–6.
Scholem, G., *Jewish Gnosticism, Merkabah Mysticism and the Talmudic Tradition*. New York 1960.
——, *Major Trends in Jewish Mysticism*. New York 1965.

Schürer, E., *The History of the Jewish People*, II. Edinburgh 1979.

Segal, A. F., *Two Powers in Heaven*. Leiden 1978.

Selwyn, E. C., 'The Feast of Tabernacles, Epiphany and Baptism', in *Journal of Theological Studies* xiii, 1912.

Suter, D. W., 'Fallen Angel, Fallen Priest', in *The Hebrew Union College Annual* 50, 1979.

De Vaux, R., *Ancient Israel*. ET London 1965.

Widengren, G., *The King and the Tree of Life in Ancient Near Eastern Religion*. Uppsala 1951.

Wilkinson, J., *Egeria's Travels: newly translated with supporting documents*. London 1971.

Yarden, L., *The Tree of Light*. London 1971.

INDEX OF NAMES AND SUBJECTS

Abraham   17, 19, 28, 78
Adam   19, 67, 68-70, 75, 97, 100, 102, 164
advent   86
Akiba, Rabbi   169-70
altar of burnt offerings   30-2, 36, 84; origin of   17-18
altar of incense   28, 38, 52, 141, 151-3, 165; Lord standing by   117
Angel of the Lord   17, 40, 81, 85, 90, 153, 156, 169, 174, 176-7
angel of the sanctuary   124; leaving   53
angels: baptised for believers   123; bridegrooms of souls   123; of destruction   52, 152; fallen   59, 61, 79, 113, 159, 161; of nations   73; as trees of sanctuary   100
angel of Tyre   71-2, 102, 155
angel of Israel   73, 86, 117, 153, 163, 177
Antiochus Epiphanes   9, 31, 72, 105-7, 155
anthropomorphism   135-6, 154, 167, 170-1, 175-6, 180
Antonia, garrison   23
apocalypses   111, 154-66; meaning of word   127-8; as relics of old traditions   135
archangels   120-1, 128, 143
Ark of the covenant   14, 15, 52, 62, 76, 91, 96, 138-41, 165
Asaph   46
Azazel   41-3

baptism   97, 163
Beersheba   14, 17
Ben Azzai and Ben Zoma, heavenly ascent   169
Bethel   14, 17
bread of the presence   14, 28-9, 129

calendar   24; controversies over   12
calves, golden   14
candlestick, seven branched (*see* menorah)
Chanukkah   31
chariot throne of the Lord   27, 70-3, 98, 101, 121-2, ch. 4 *passim*
cherubim   26-7, 68, 74, 138-45, 152, 158
Copper Scroll   55
Coptic liturgy   89
council in heaven   74
courts of temple   22-4
Covenant, Eternal   78-82
covenant, new   78
creation   63-5
Cyrus   8

Dan   14
David, king   15-20, 73-4, 78
Day of Atonement   9, 18, 33, 41-5, 62, 80, 106, 111
Deuteronomists: as censors   7, 27, 135; and fertility   83; influence on cult   7-8, 134, 140; attitude to temple   21,

28; democratisers of old traditions 74; rejection of anthropomorphism by 135

Eden ch. 2 *passim*, 144
Elisha ben Abuya (Aher) 168-9
Enoch 69-70, 157-60, 167
ephod 14
Epiphany 86
Eternity 59, 103, 111, 127-8
Ethan 46
Exodus, the 66
Ezekiel, visions of 11-12, 23, 87-8

fertility 62, 77, 82-7
firstfruits 40-1

Gabriel 14, 127, 131, 143, 174
Garden of God 68-70
Gilgal 14
Glory of the Lord 97, 100, 105, 137, 145, 149, 152, 158, 160

harlot, temple as 13, 49, 110
harvest festivals 38-9
Hebrews, epistle to 16, 44, 63, 81, 85, 124, 132, 166
Heman 46-7
Herod the Great 10
Hezekiah's reform 5, 39, 45-6, 69
high priest 12, 18, 23, 28, 41, 43-4, 62-3, 77, 97, 111-14, 140; in heaven 114-15, 118, 123, 153, 162; as Incarnation of Logos 115-17; Enoch as 158; Jesus as 101, 105, 124, 128; Levi as 162; vestments of 97, 104, 111-13
holiness, degrees of 25, 62
Holy of Holies 9, 18, 22, 25-6, 41, 100
horses of sun cult 7, 90, 149, 165
human sacrifice 34

Idi, Rabbi 169

incarnation 7, 102, 104-5, 120, 132-3, 152, 168, 180
incense 28, 41, 43, 51, 69, 76, 88, 113; symbolism of 113
Isaac 19
Ishmael, Rabbi 167

Jacob 19
James, martyrdom of 49-50
Jeduthun 46
Jeroboam 21
Jesus: as high priest 101, 105, 124, 128; as prophet of doom 54
Josiah, reform of 6-7, 38-9
Judas Maccabaeus 9
judgement, last 54, 61-2, 70-5, 113, 127-8, 147-54, 159, 180

king, role of 5, 73-5, 134

lamp of temple 14 (*see also* menorah)
lampstands in temple 28, 51, 84
lavatories in temple 23
Law 60
levites 39, 46-7, 84 (*see also* singers)
liturgy, heavenly 44-5, 61, 105
Logos 115-19, 140-5, 153, 156-7, 165, 168, 170, 175; as Shadow 119, 126, 143-4

Manasseh 8, 143
Melchizedek 15, 19, 62-3, 163
menorah 29, 37, 52, 57, 77, 90-5, 137, 141, 165, 173; as almond tree 93; symbol of Jesus 94-5, 165
mercy seat 133, 138, 140
Messiah 57, 62-3, 75, 77, 81, 86, 91-3, 103, 128, 141, 160, 165, 170
Metatron 128, 167-9, 171-3
Michael, archangel 67, 85, 114, 143, 159, 164, 177
Mizpah 14

INDEX 189

Moreh 17
Moses 16, 75, 78, 131, 139, 173
mountain of gods 63–4, 68, 91, 99
Mount of Olives 43, 87
music in temple 45–9
myth, function of 58–66, 68, 132

Nag Hammadi 118
Name of the Lord 79, 117, 120, 122, 136, 140, 168
Nathan 11, 15–16
Noah 19, 78
Nob 14

Paradise 67, 70, 92, 96, 99, 130
parables 59; of Enoch 158–61; of Jesus 161
Passover 38–41
Pentecost 50, 81, 85
Phanuel, archangel 143
Phineas 80
pilgrimage feasts 38–9
pillars of bronze 29, 57
plan of temple 16; heavenly origin of 16, 44, 57
Pompey, attack on temple 9
porch of temple 22
portents of temple destruction 50
powers of God 140–5, 169, 176
priests: as angels 17, 81, 117; blessing of 38; corrupted 80–1; and covenant 80–1; daily life of 36–7; dress of 31; income of 33; as prophets 47; purity of 12; reform of 7
prophets in temple 47
prophecies of end of temple 49–50, 54
psalms, Hallel 39, 48
purity: laws of 23, 69; of priests 12, 62; of temple courts 23–4, 62–3

rain, prayers for 77, 82–6
Raphael, archangel 42, 143
recapitulation, Irenaeus on 132
restoration of temple cult 5, 8
red line around altar 32
Revelation, Book of 24, 48–9, 61, 67, 74, 85, 87, 166
rivers of fire 123; of life 57, 69–70, 86–9, 93
robes of glory (*see* white robes)
rock, foundation 18–20, 22, 43, 146; Dome of 18

sacrifices 8, 23, 32–8, 45; human 34
Samuel 14–15
scapegoat 41–4; Jesus as 44–5
sea of bronze 30, 65–7; representing primeval sea 65–7, 76, 102
sea 65–7, 73, 162
serpent of bronze 6, 69
Shepherd of Hermas 85
Shiloh 14, 21, 35
Siloam 84
singers in temple 46; as prophets 47
Solomon 5, 21, 57, 83
Son of Man 54, 66, 74, 79, 89, 94, 152, 159–61, 168–70
Songs of the Sabbath Sacrifice 44–5, 61, 72, 101, 117, 121, 150, 166
Suffering Servant 36, 94
sun imagery in cult 148–50

tabernacle 10–11, 16, 26, 28, 76–7, 105, 136–8; symbol of incarnation 127
Tabernacles, feast of 63, 80, 82–6, 87; Jesus at 88
talmudic tradition 19, 55, 65, 131, 141, 169
Temple Scroll 11–12, 24, 68
tent of meeting 14, 136–7
Titus, attacks temple 105–7

tower, as symbol of temple and church 11, 85, 128, 130
tree of knowledge 100
tree of life 70-1, 88-95, 99, 103, 164; Jesus as 99
Trinity, angelic imagery of 133, 173-4
trumpets of ram's horn 39, 46-8, 84

Uriel, archangel 12

veil of temple 27, 43, 51-2, 76, ch. 3 *passim*; composition of 106-9; symbolism of 108-10
visions in temple 47, 59, 66-7, 127-31, 150-71

waters of life (*see* rivers of life)
waters, primeval 19-20, 63
water supply of temple 9
white robes 62, 85, 104, 113-14, 125, 158, 162, 165, 172
Wisdom 57, 88-9, 95, 119-21, 172
wood for altar fires 37

Zaphon, Mount 64
Zechariah, father of John the Baptist 29
Zeus, temple dedicated to 9; veil offered to 107

INDEX OF PRIMARY SOURCES

OLD TESTAMENT

Genesis
1.2   88
1.27   120
2.7   88
2.10–14   88
2–3   60
3.19–20   102
3.22   70, 75, 126
3.24   144
9.16   80
12.6–7   17
14.18–20   15, 163
18.1–2   157
22   34
26.24–5   17
28.18   17

Exodus
12.1–10   38
12.12   165
12.13   40
12.29   165
15.3   170
15.17   66
16.33   139
19.6   74
20.24–5   31, 35
23.14–17   39
23.18   35
23.21   169–71
24.1   169
24.10–11   64, 152, 170
25–31   10, 137
25.8   137
25.10   91, 96, 138
25.17–21   91, 138
25.22–3   91, 137
25.31–40   28, 91–94
25.40   16
26.1–33   26
26.31   106
26.33   105
27.20   29
28   112
30.34–8   28
33.7–11   136
33.18   144
33.20   136
33.21–3   137, 144
34.29–35   171
35.10–39   137
36–40   10
36.35   106
37.1   91
37.6   91
37.10   91
37.17–24   28, 91
37.25   91
38.8   28
40.34–8   137

Leviticus
1–7   33–4
2.1   28
3.1   35
3.3–4   39
4.17   36
6.15   28
12.1–5   69
16   41–3, 80, 140
16.4   113
17.14   33
19.19   26
23.11   40
23.40   84
24.5–9   29

Numbers
5.3   137
6.24–6   149
7.89   139
10.35–6   139
11.16–30   136
12.1–16   136
15.27–31   35
17.8   93, 139
24.17   92
25.12   78, 80–1
28.2–8   36
28.9–10   38

Deuteronomy
4.12–15   135
6.4   29
8   8
10.1–5   140
11.13–14   83
12   136
12.5–7   6
12.11   29
14.1–2   74
22.9–11   26
26.15   135
32.1–43   44
32.43   162–3

Joshua
18.1   14
19.51   14
22.29   14

Judges
6.26–8   33
13.15–20   33
17.14   14

1 Samuel
1.21 14
2.12–17 35
3.3 14
3.21 14
4.3–4 139
4.17–22 14
7.9 34
8.1–7 16
8.10–22 15
10.5–6 47
10.17–25 14
11.15 14
13.14 16
15.28 16
15.33 14
21.6 14
21.9 14

2 Samuel
6 15
6.5 46
6.6–7 62
6.17–18 34–5
7 11, 136
7.2 15
21.17 92
22.7–11 142
22.12 108
22.29–32 90
23.1–2 74
24.16 17

1 Kings
5–8 5
5.10–11 19
5.15 20
5.17 21
6–8 106
6.2–10 22
6.15–29 26–7
6.20 22
6.7 21
6.29 69
6.36 22
7.12 22
7.15–22 29
7.23–6 30
7.38 30
7.46 21
7.48–9 28
8.6 27
8.9 140
8.10 137
8.12–13 135
8.27 135
8.35–6 83
8.62–4 30, 35
9.10–11 21
9.25 34
9.27 21
11.26–12.20 21
11.36 92
12.28–9 14
18.23–33 34
22.13–23 151

2 Kings
3.15–16 47
3.27 34
8.19 93
12.16 36
16.10–16 30
16.15 38
18.4–7 6, 69
19.35 6
21.1–9 6, 22, 143
22.8–13 6
23 7
23.11 149
23.22 39
24.3–4 5, 8, 134
25.8–17 5

1 Chronicles
6.31–47 46
9.33 47
16.4–6 47
21.15 17
22.1 17
25.1 47
25.5 47
28.2 140
28.3 16
28.18 27, 152
28.19 16
29.2–9 20
29.23 74, 134

2 Chronicles
2.13 21
2.15–16 20
2.17–18 21
3–4 5
3.5–7 26
3.9 72
3.13 138
3.14 27, 106
4.1–6 30
4.7–19 28
5.11–13 46
8.7–10 21
20.5 22
26.16–21 100. 126
29–30 6, 39
29.27–30 46–7

Ezra
1.7–11 8
2.36–54 8
3.1–6 8, 42
3.8–13 5
4.1–5 8
6.1–12 8
6.4 22
6.16–18 5, 8
7.11–20 8
9.5 38

Nehemiah
10.32–9 8
12.1–26 12

Job
22.13–14 142
36.29 71
41 67

Psalms
2 156
2.6–7 73, 134

INDEX

11.4 134
15.1 158
18.6 146
18.11 108, 142
20.2 146
20.23 45
24 48, 66
24.4 86
24.7-8 146
26.6 45
26.8 137
27.4-5 71, 146
29.10 19, 66
31.16 148
31.20 71
33.7 48
36.7-9 86
46.4 86, 137
46.5-7 146
47.5 147
48 48
48.2 64
61.2-3 129
66.13 45
67.1 148
68 83, 146-7
72.1-3 77, 134
73.17 154
74.7 137
74.13 48
76.2 71
78.60-1 14
80.1-3 148
81 46, 48
82 48, 62, 73, 162
89.9-11 20, 66
89.20 73
89.25-7 20
92 48, 69
93 48, 66
94 48
94.2 147
96.13 147
97.8 147
98.9 147
99.4 147
104.1-4 108, 142
107.22 45
113—18 39, 48
116.17 45
118.25-7 84
132.6-8 137, 141
150 46

Proverbs
3.18 95
8.22-31 88

Isaiah
1.11 35
2.2-4 69
4.2 93
5.1-7 129
6 47, 74, 135, 145, 151, 160, 174
7.14 93
9.2 148
10.13-19 6
11 68, 79, 160, 166
11.1-2 93, 95
14 79
14.12-15 65, 75, 92
14.24-7 6
19.1 142
19.21 35
22.8 71
24.4-6 78-80
24.21-3 80
26.21 164
33.14-21 87, 158
37.16 27, 139
37.35 6
40.1-2 61
40.22 108
41.8 74
42.3-4 94
43.27-8 72
51.3 68
51.9 67
52.7 63
53.10 36
54.10 78
57.7-8 13, 110
60.1-2 148
63.1-6 148, 166
65.17-25 68
66.1 11
66.6 61, 154

Jeremiah
1.1 47
1.11-12 93
3.16-17 141
5.22 66
8.19 134
17.12 134
23.5 93
25.38 71
31.35-6 78
33.15 93
36.10 23
36.32 52

Lamentations
4.11-13 53

Ezekiel
1 137, 152
1.3 47, 73, 152
1.4, 5.22 143, 152
1.9 53
1.10-11 145
1.13-14 171
1.26 152, 171
1.27-8 152-3
8.2 152, 171
8.16 152
9.1-3 113, 152-3
9.4 117
10 137, 152-3, 165
16.59 80
23 110
28 27, 60, 64
28.9 102
28.14 158
28.18 72
37.27 137
40—8 12, 69
40.1 87, 149
40.17 23
40.38-43 23

40.39 36
40.47 23
41.17–19 27, 69
42.13–14 23, 36
42.15–20 23
43.2, 4, 5 87, 148
43.13–17 30
44.29 36
45.18–20 42
46.1–3 23
46.21–4 23
47.1–12 69, 87, 89

Daniel
1.3 155
2.25 155
7 66–7, 155–6, 169–70
8.11–13 36, 72, 155
9.17 149
9.21 38
9.27 31
10.5–6 113, 156
11.29 36
11.31 31
12.11 31

Joel
1.1–17 60

2.13 60
2.23–8 81, 88
3.18 69, 87

Hosea
2.18 80
4.8 36
4.15 14
9.15 14
12.11 14

Amos
3.3 14
3.7 74, 128
4.4 14, 35
5.23 46
7.13 14
8.1–3 147
9.1–4 117, 151
9.11 71

Micah
1.3–4 164
4.1–3 69
6.7 34

Nahum
1.3 142

Habakkuk
2.1–3 129
3.2 174

Haggai
1.1 90
1.9–11 77

Zechariah
1.1 90
1.7–8 90
1.8–11 150
3.1 47, 90
3.1–10 12, 114, 163
3.8 93
4.2 47
4.10 29, 90
4.11–14 90, 92
6.1–8 90, 150
6.12 93
14 87
14.8 69
14.16–17 83

Malachi
2.1–9 12, 81
3.1 117, 154
3.5 154

NEW TESTAMENT

Matthew
2.2 92
25.31–46 161
27.51 124

Mark
13 49, 54
15.38 105, 124

Luke
1.8–10 38
1.11 117
1.32 177
1.78–9 149
4.5, 9 130–2

19.41–6 49
21.5–36 54
23.45 124

John
1.14 138
2.19–21 138
3.13 132
6.38 132
7.14 88
7.37–9 88
8.23 132
15.5 103

Acts
2 81
21.27–40 24

Romans
3.25 133, 175
8.12–21 81
11.16 40

1 Corinthians
15.20 40

Ephesians
1.1–10 132

Philippians
2.6 75
2.9–10 171

Colossians
1.15 75
2.15 44, 63

Hebrews
3.1 132
4.14 105
8–9 44
8.1-2 171
8.5 17
9.4 139
9.15 81
10.19-20 105, 125
12.22-4 85

13.8 128

1 Peter
2.5 129

Revelation
1.12-13 94, 165
4.1-4 111, 114, 165
4.5-8 67, 165
4.7-11 49, 145, 165
5.6-10 49, 165
6.1-8 150, 165
6.9 165
7.3 117
7.9-12 85, 87, 114, 165
8.3-5 165
9.4 165

9.13 165
10.11 166
11.15-19 141, 165
12.7-8 85, 174
13.1 165
14.1 117, 165
14.14-16 40, 165
14.18-20 149
15.2 67, 165
15.3-4 49, 165
17.1-16 13, 49, 110
19.6-7 165
19.11-16 165, 174
19.13 85
21.12-16 25
22.1-2 88, 103
22.16 166

DEUTEROCANONICAL WRITINGS

Wisdom of Solomon
7.27 88
9.8 16
18.15-16 166
18.24 113

Ecclesiasticus
24.10-31 88

1 Maccabees
1.20-4 9, 31, 107
1.54-9 9, 31
4.36 9
4.42-7 32
4.59 9

2 Maccabees
2.7 141
3.25 9
4.13 12
6.1-6 9, 107

PSEUDEPIGRAPHICAL WRITINGS

Letter of Aristeas
83 9
87-8 31
89-91 9
92-5 48
98 117

1 Enoch
6–11 59
10.4-9 42
14.8-22 158
17.1 172
18.2 143

25.3-5 92
39.7 159
39.12 160
40.2-9 143, 160
45.3-6 160
46.1-5 160
48.1 89, 160
48.2-10 159-60
49.1 89, 160
49.3 160
49.4 159
51.3 159-60
55.3-4 159-60

61.8 159-60
62.7, 14-16 160
69.25-9 160
71.1 172
71.11 159, 173
80.2-4 12
87.2 113
87.3-4 128
89.73 129
90.21-2 113
90.28-9 54

2 Enoch
8.3–5 89, 92, 102
22.8–10 114
24.1 174

Ascension of Isaiah
7.25 173
8.14–15 114
9.2, 8–9 114
9.13 132
9.36 174

Apocalypse of Moses
22.3–4 70–1, 164

Assumption of Moses
2.4 129
10.1–3 163
29.5–6 70

Apocalypse of Abraham
10.8, 17 153
11.2–4 153
18.3, 12–13 164
21.1–5 130

Life of Adam and Eve
25.1–3 164
28.4 67, 164

Psalms of Solomon
14.2–3 96

Testaments of the Twelve Patriarchs:
Test. Judah 24.4 93
Test. Levi 2.7; 3.4; 4.2; 5.1; 8.2–10 162
Test. Benjamin 9.4 125

Jubilees
1.14 12
3.9 69
3.27 69
4.23–5 70, 169
4 59
16.24 28
21.12–13 37

2 Baruch
1.1–4 53
4.2–7 68
6.3–8.2 53
20.2–4 54
34 130
51.8–10 130
59.4–8 131

4 Ezra
7.47–8 54
13.5 110

JEWISH WRITINGS

Philo, *Who is the Heir?*
  166 144–5, 170
  197–9 28, 113
  205 94, 116, 159
  215 94

Special Laws
  I.45 145
  I.66 109
  I.84–7, 96–7 112, 114
  I.151 33

Questions on Genesis
  I.10 92
  II.62 115

Questions on Exodus
  II.13 94, 116
  II.73 110
  II.85 109
  II.91, 95 110

On Dreams
  I.215 116
  I.241 94

On Flight
  101 144
  110 116
  118 94, 116

Allegorical Interpretation
  III.96 120

On the Confusion of Tongues
  41 116
  146 153

Life of Moses
  II.114 117
  II.194 110

On Agriculture
  51 94, 116

Cherubim
  27–8 144

Josephus, *Jewish War*
  I 148 9
  V 193–4 24

  V 212–13 109
  V 218 28
  V 219 141
  V 225 32
  VI 228 50
  VI 232–3 50
  VI 252–3 50
  VI 259 50
  VI 299 50
  VI 387–90 50
  VI 420–5 40
  VII 148–50 52
  VII 158–62 52, 107

Antiquities
  III 124–6 109
  III 180 109
  III 181 65
  III 183 109
  III 184 112
  XIV 71–2 9–10
  XV 390–1; 394–6; 421; 425 10

INDEX

Against Apion
  I 198 31
Life
  417–18 55

Mishnah

Pesaḥim
  5.1 38
  5.5–10 39, 48
Shekalim
  6.4 29
  8.4–5 106–7
Yoma
  5.1 106
  5.2 43
  5.6 32
Sukkah
  5.1 84
Megillah
  4.10 154
Hagigah
  2.1 154
Menaḥoth
  11.3 29
Tamid
  1.1 23
  3.1 37
  7.3 48
Middoth
  2.5–6 37, 48
  3.1 32
Kinnim
  1.1 32
Kelim
  1.6–9 25

Babylonian Talmud

Berakoth
  18b 131
Yoma
  52b 106
  53b 141
  54a 19, 141
  77a 131
Sukkah
  51b 65
  53b 19
Hagigah
  12b 131
  14a 170
  15a 169
Baba Bathra
  60b 56
Sanhedrin
  38b 169
  89b 131
Menaḥoth
  28b 91

Tosefta

Kippurim
  2.16 107
Sukkah
  3.15 32, 129
  3.17 85

Targum Neofiti
  Gen. *3.24* 144
  Exod. *33.23* 145
Targum Pseudo-Jonathan
  Lev. *16.21–2* 43

Genesis Rabbah
  XV.6 89
  XXI.8 70
Exodus Rabbah
  XXXVI.16 91
Numbers Rabbah
  XV.9 91
  XV.10 141

3 Enoch
  10–14 168
  15.1 173
  16 169
  45.1 128
  45.6 128

Qumran texts

Commentary on Habbakkuk
  1QpHab VIII 12
The Community Rule
  1QS VIII 97
  1QS XI 97
The Hymns
  1QH III 98
  1Qh IV 98
The Blessings
  1QSb 117
The Copper Scroll
  3Q15 55
Songs of the Sabbath Sacrifice
  4Q 400 117
  4Q 403 72, 117
  4Q 405 150, 166–7, 172
The Testament of Amram
  4QAmram 176
Melchizedek
  11Q Melch 63
The Damascus Rule
  CDIII 13

GNOSTIC WRITINGS

The Apocryphon of John
  CG. II.1.10–12   172, 177
The Gospel of Thomas
  CG. II.2.18, 113   103
The Nature of the Archons
  CG. II.4.93–4   119
  4.95–6   120
On the Origin of the World
  CG. II.5.98–100   121, 176
  5.101   102
  5.105   122
A Valentinian Exposition
  CG. XI.2.25–6   122

CHRISTIAN WRITINGS

Epistle of Barnabas
  7   45
The Shepherd of Hermas
  Parable 3.ii.4   129
  8.ii.1–3   85, 174
  8.iii.3   85, 174
  9.iii.1   129
  9.vii.1   129, 174
  9.xii.1   129
  9.xii.8   85, 129, 174
Justin, *Dialogue with Trypho*
  42   125
  61   175
  113, 127   156
  128   175
Melito, *On Pascha*
  98   124
New Fragments
  II.101–6   125
Hippolytus, *On Daniel*
  I.17   89, 96
  IV.36   156
Clement of Alexandria, *Stromata*
  V.6   95, 111, 125
Excerpts from Theodotus
  22, 26, 27, 35, 38, 42, 64   122–3
Irenaeus, *Against Heresies*
  III.18.1   132
  V.10.1   96
The Proof of the Apostolic Preaching
  9   95
  12   156
  31   126
  44   156
  71   126
The Book of James
  X   127
Origen, *Homily on Exodus*
  IX   127
De Principiis
  I.3.4   175
Eusebius, *History of the Church*
  2.23   49
Ephrem, *Hymns on Paradise*
  1.6–7; 2.11; 3.2–3, 14–15; 4.4; 5.6; 6.8; 12.4   99–101
  3.14   126
Nisibene Hymns
  43   126
Hymns on the Nativity
  11   126
The Odes of Solomon
  11, 20, 25, 36, 38   97–8

OTHER WRITINGS

The Pilgrim of Bordeaux
  18
Pausanias, *Description of Greece*
  V.12.2   107
Procopius, *History of the Wars*
  V.xii.41   55